TESTIMONIALS

Andrew Coplon

"I have always enjoyed my Dad's teachings and it has been an incredible process watching him go from making his first podcast to compiling such a collection of inspiring stories. I am honored to have been asked to take part and hope his teachings can motivate others just as they have me for the past 35 years."

Jim Stovall

"I am proud to be a part of this collaboration. Each message is good, but together they are transformational."

Johnnie Lloyd

"The overarching power in this book will remind each of us how important it is to be authentic with character and integrity. Every word we speak matters, be a person of power by being a person of your word."

Richard Kay

"It has been such a joy to be part of this project. My prayer is that this work will impact many lives to learn and practice simple obedience to God."

Don Price

"I am honored to be included among such a select group of very talented, giving individuals of all ages and walks of life who exhibit personal qualities that serve as shining examples of how to live your life in the proper manner. Their stories have inspired me, and I know they will inspire many others."

Donna Coplon

"It has been a blessing to be part of this wonderful inspiring book. Steve and I have discussed many times how very important it is to keep your word, because that's how you become a trustworthy person. I love the examples in each chapter of how keeping your word makes a difference in one's life. My prayer is that lives change after reading this book."

Dave Richards

"Steve is like few I've ever met in my life; his full-hearted commitment to helping his fellow man, from family, to friends, to distant acquaintances, to those incarcerated and forgotten by society, is a testament to his unshakable faith. I'm truly honored he asked me to share my thoughts for this book."

Reginald Ponton

"I'm very grateful to have participated in this project. Every message that was stated will help to inspire, motivate, encourage, and reorganize people's lives."

Sofia Giannascoli

"When Steve asked me to help him with this project, I didn't entirely know what I was getting myself into. *"From the Lip to the Hip is a Pretty Far Distance,"* are words I have typed and read hundreds of times through all the edits. The impact these words and this book have had on my outlook and my mindset are something I wasn't expecting when I signed on to help. To me, this feels like the beginning of finding ways to use my stories and experiences to help others in whatever ways I am meant to. Thank you, Steve!"

Randey Faulkner

"How could I ever hope to receive a better introduction to Steve Coplon, than from someone so esteemed as Don Green, CEO, of The Napoleon Hill Foundation. That alone speaks volumes regarding Steve's character. I consider it a great privilege to be included with this group of champions. I love Steve's podcasts that are filled with exhilarating and uplifting messages. He is to be applauded by his vision to take one set of podcasts, inspired by his mother – *"From the Lip to the Hip is a Pretty Far Distance"*, and create a work that will undoubtedly enthuse many, for many years to come. Thanks mom and thank you, Steve!"

Lefford Fate

There are times in your life when you just have to say, "Thank You Lord." The day I met Steve Coplon was just such a day. My life has been drastically changed since he came into my life. I have met Don Green, Director of the Napoleon Hill Foundation, authored 3 books, and traveled internationally as a speaker, trainer, and coach. Those were all amazing experiences, but now I have the opportunity to participate in this body of work. I am so very blessed! These stories and lessons will be lights and lamps on your pathway of life. Thank you, Steve, you are my brother and my friend. This book is going to change lives.

FROM THE LIP TO THE HIP IS A PRETTY FAR DISTANCE

DOING WHAT YOU SAY YOU'RE GOING TO DO

LESSONS IN CHARACTER AND INTEGRITY

FROM THE LIP TO THE HIP IS A PRETTY FAR DISTANCE

Doing What You Say You're Going To Do

Lessons In Character And Integrity

STEVE COPLON

Foreword by Don Green, Executive Director
The Napoleon Hill Foundation

Featuring:
Jim Stovall, Donna Coplon, Lefford Fate,
Don Price, Richard Kay, Dave Richards,
Reginald Ponton, Johnnie Lloyd, Randey Faulkner,
Andrew Coplon and Sofia Giannascoli

New Dominion Press ● Norfolk ● Virginia

From the Lip to the Hip is a Pretty Far Distance:
Doing What You Say You're Going to Do
Lessons in Character and Integrity

Published by:

New Dominion Press
New Dominion Media/New Dominion Press
1217 Godfrey Avenue, Norfolk, Virginia 23504-3218

www.NewDominionPress.com

First Printing: December 2020

Cover Design, Graphics Design, and Typography by New Dominion Press
Cover Design and Photographs by Steve Coplon

Publisher's Cataloging-in-Publication Data

Names: Coplon, Steve., 1951- author.

Title: From the lip to the hip is a pretty far distance: doing what you say you're going to do: lessons in character and integrity / Steve Coplon.

Description: Norfolk, VA : New Dominion Press, 2020.

Identifiers: LCCN 2020924435 | ISBN 978-1-7357483-0-6 (paperback.) | ISBN 978-1-7357483-1-3 (eBook.)

Subjects: LCSH: Self-help techniques. | Self-improvement. | Education. | Prisoners--Education. | Trust in God—Christianity. | Biography. | Autobiographies--Memoirs. | BISAC: SELF-HELP / Personal Growth / General. | EDUCATION / Leadership. | BIOGRAPHY & AUTOBIOGRAPHY / General.

First Edition

DEDICATION

I dedicate this book to my mother,

Rose

She taught me how to love.

She was the original "Never met a stranger" and "Give you the shirt off her back" person.

She passed these on to me.

TABLE OF CONTENTS

To listen to the original interviews, scan this QR Code with your camera, or visit:
https://rightthinkingeducation.com/FromtheLiptotheHip/

FOREWORD

 It is an honor and a pleasure to write this foreword for my deeply admired friend, Steve Coplon. Steve has done a tremendous job of compiling the advice of a wide array of successful individuals that I am sure will be beneficial to you. I believe you will truly enjoy and treasure what you read and appreciate Steve for the mission he is doing to make the world a better place in which to live. I also believe you will do as I do and continue to return to certain pages of advice as you are taking your journey to become a better person.

Steve is an expert on education in America's prison system. He has spent years teaching and giving seminars to those incarcerated individuals who are seeking a better life once they are released. Additionally, I think Steve's new book, "From the Lip to the Hip is a Pretty Far Distance", is a great tool that will help change the current prison system in the United States.

Recidivism is when prisoners are released from prison then commit another crime, are arrested, convicted, and then sent back. Statistics show that almost half of those individuals who are released from prison often go back within three years. However, I think Steve's new book will help eliminate some of those recidivism levels. One tool that often helps prisoners achieve a normal life after their release is education. Incarcerated individuals need to know how to live after being released and need skills that will help them adapt to their new life. Steve and the other contributing authors have done a great job of educating readers in "From the Lip to the Hip is a Pretty Far Distance".

I urge you to read this book and use it to educate yourself and others. I also urge you to make a financial contribution to the Right Thinking Foundation, which is the tool Steve uses to complete his prison work.

Knowing Steve personally and being a dear friend of mine, I cannot think of a better person who is following their "definite major purpose". I support Steve in his goal to make this world a better place in which to live.

Don Green

Executive Director
Napoleon Hill Foundation

INTRODUCTION

Have you ever met someone who has never experienced having to deal with a person who told them that they were going to do something, and they never did what they said they were going to do? I doubt that you have, because every single one of us has unfortunately had that happen to them. Even worse, every single one of us has done it to another, whether intentionally or unintentionally. Saying that you are going to do something and never doing it is a universal issue. It is part of human nature.

The purpose of "From the Lip to the Hip is a Pretty Far Distance" is to help each of us become people of our word and strive to minimize, as much as possible, the undesirable behavior of not doing what you say you are going to do. Jesus says in Matthew 5:37, in the Sermon on the Mount, "Let your Yes be Yes, and your No be No."

On Friday morning, February 28, 2020, I was scheduled to do an interview to air the following Monday morning on my weekly radio show, *Right Thinking with Steve Coplon*. It was to be my 159th episode. I was very excited about the interview with Officer L. I had met this fine person two weeks earlier when I went to one of my doctor's offices to pick up a prescription. Officer L was the security guard at the door. As I was exiting the building, I turned around and approached him to introduce myself. I was drawn to him because of his incredibly contagious, warm smile.

Officer L had served in the Navy for six years and upon release he returned to his hometown and became a mid-size drug dealer. He left that all behind and became a police officer on the streets of a major municipality for twenty years. While serving as a police officer, he started a program in the community where he and other officers went undercover into high school classrooms as substitute teachers to help teach teenagers about the importance of not breaking the law. He later became a pastor.

When Officer L learned of the work that I do through Right Thinking Foundation in prisons, he became very excited. He invited me to join with him in his street ministry to change lives. Our conversation lasted over thirty minutes. I was so captivated by his life story that I asked him if he would let me interview him on my radio show. He responded, "Absolutely. I would love to."

He told me his schedule and said that Fridays were his days off. He said that we could do the interview right away. He gave me his cell phone number and email and I told him that I would call to schedule. It took two weeks before he finally answered my calls. He said that he didn't recognize my number, so didn't answer. We scheduled the interview for Friday morning February 28th. I put in my normal five hours of preparation for the show.

At 10:00 am on that day, I sent him the prearranged Zoom invite and waited by my computer. At 10:15, I texted him. At 10:30, I called him and left a message. No response from him. At 11:15, he called me. He told me that he had been called into a meeting and was unable to contact me any sooner. I asked if he still wanted to do the interview, offering to reschedule. He strongly said that he wanted to do the interview and that we could do it at 1:00 pm. That was fine with me, so I waited for him to join me on Zoom at 1:00.

At 1:00, no Officer L. I reached out and he did answer my call at 1:45. This time, he again said that he wanted to do the interview and asked if 5:00 would work for me. He did share what he had to do for the remainder of the afternoon and assured me that he could make 5:00 work. I said that it would, but again offered to reschedule if it would be better for him. I let him know that it would be fine and would not inconvenience me to reschedule but that I had to know because I would have to prepare for a new show. He said he was good to go at 5:00. I requested that he check in with me at 4:30. He said that he would.

He called me at 4:45 to let me know that he was caught up in traffic but that we could start at 5:30. I said thanks for checking in, see you at 5:30.

5:30 came and went. No Officer L. I reached out several times, praying that nothing bad had happened to him. I waited until 8:00. I did not hear from him anymore and it was three weeks later before he answered one of my calls. He gave no apology or explanation.

During the time that I was waiting to do the show, I knew that it might not happen. I needed a fall back in case Officer L was a no show. I had recently been reading again "Think and Grow Rich" by Napoleon Hill. A section of the very last chapter of the book came to my mind. It was ""Fifty-Seven" Famous Alibis By Old Man IF." This particular wisdom by Napoleon Hill focused me on lessons that my mother had taught me as a child. It was at that moment that I decided to finally deliver my message on the importance of doing what you say you are going to do.

Several years ago, Don Green, Executive Director of the Napoleon Hill Foundation, obtained permission for me to use in my prison seminars an excerpt from "How to Own Your Own Mind" by Napoleon Hill. The excerpt was called "The Major Benefits of Organized Thinking." When I knew that there was a strong possibility that I needed to record a different show for Monday, I decided to ask Don if he could get me approval to use "Fifty-Seven" Famous Alibis By Old Man IF" on the show. Within a few hours, Don delivered the approval.

I recorded Episode 159 "From the Lip to the Hip is a Pretty Far Distance" as the first show in a series exploring why people don't do what they say they are going to do. I invited as my guests for each show, people whom I greatly respect and admire to share their wisdom and insights on the subject. They are a very diverse group, offering many very different perspectives on the theme of the book.

The interviews that were done with my eleven guests were so powerful that I decided to use the transcripts from the shows for what ultimately became this book that you are about to read. Three and a half years ago, when I first launched *Right Thinking with Steve Coplon*, Don sent me a copy of "Napoleon Hill is on the Air." It is a book that contains transcripts from a series of radio broadcasts that Napoleon Hill did in Jackson, Mississippi in 1953. The editor of that book states that "It allows you, the reader, to experience almost verbatim what Napoleon shared directly with his listeners." I have followed in Napoleon Hill's footsteps as I have kept the edited transcripts of my shows as close to the actual broadcasts as possible.

Through the process of converting the transcripts to the chapters of "From the Lip to the Hip is a Pretty Far Distance," I have learned a tremendous amount about the difference between conversational dialogue and the written word. I wish to thank Randey and Cindyrae Faulkner for volunteering to edit the transcripts line by line as a gift of love because they wanted this book to be made available to each of you, the readers. I could not have completed this book without the incredible assistance of Sofia Giannascoli. She has been a God sent. I would like to thank my wife, Donna, for being with me every step along the way, as she gave me the love and support that I needed to write this book as well as provided countless hours of proofing and editing. To each of my guests, thank you for sharing your wisdom and caring so much about other people.

Special thanks to Don Green, for all that he has done for me as my friend and mentor. He sets the example every day of how to give of yourself to make the world a better place. This book would not have become a reality if not for Napoleon Hill, whose teachings and wisdom have influenced me more than anyone else in my life.

What started out as a compilation quickly became a collaboration. I have personally been transformed by the conversations that I had with my guests who became contributing authors. Each of them are individuals of the highest character and integrity. It has been my honor and privilege to share them with you.

It is my heartfelt hope and prayer that "From the Lip to the Hip is a Pretty Far Distance" will transform your life as it has mine and help everyone who reads it to a better life.

God Bless You,

Steve Coplon

CHAPTER ONE
From The Lip To The Hip Is A Pretty Far Distance
Right Thinking With Steve Coplon - Episode 159

Steve Coplon: Good morning. Welcome to *Right Thinking with Steve Coplon.* I'm your host, Steve Coplon. Thank you for tuning in. Let's have a great day!

Steve Coplon: Good morning, everybody. Glad to be with you. Today's show is going to be a little different. I'm just going to talk about something that is part of human nature. It affects each one of us, and it has something that can be very, very irritating, for lack of a better word.

Steve Coplon: *Right Thinking with Steve Coplon* is very pleased to announce that this week's show is called ***"From the Lip to the Hip is a Pretty Far Distance."*** Tune in and hear Steve talk about the importance of doing what you say you are going to do. Successful people are those who accept responsibility for their lives. That's what today's show is all about.

Steve Coplon: Every one of us has been really disappointed by having someone tell us they are going to do something, and then they don't ever do what they said they were going to.

Every one of us has been greatly inconvenienced because we were depending and relying on what someone said they were going to do. Unfortunately, there are a lot of people in the world who don't do what they say they're going to do. As I began by saying, this is part of human nature, sometimes people say things that they never do.

Steve Coplon: What I want to do today, is reflect. I want to talk about two areas of concern.

First, I'd like to offer some straight advice by directly addressing those who say they are going to do something and never do it. They may not even realize that they are inconveniencing people, disappointing, and upsetting people.

Second, I also want to point out, the affect it has on the people they have made these promises to. Suppose you are the person depending on someone to perform a certain task, as promised, and they don't ever do it. I would like to advise you on how to move forward with your life, so that you do not suffer from this inconvenience.

Steve Coplon: What it all comes down to is this. People who never do what they say they're going to do, generally are not going to be very successful. Likewise, people who are dependent upon this type of person, many times are not going to be successful either. It's usually due to the fact that they are too passive about life.

5

Steve Coplon: *Right Thinking with Steve Coplon* is for people who are going through hardship and for those who want to support them. Many of us create our own hardship by not acting the way that we should. That's what we are going to study today. We are going to take a serious look at excuses and alibis, versus the responsible action of following thru with what we say.

Steve Coplon: If you are a person who does what you say you are going to do, and is dependable and honors your commitments, you are going to do well. When you take responsibility by not making excuses, you have set yourself on the right path. My sincere hope is that I will be able to share some thoughts with you today, that will help you reach more success in your life.

Steve Coplon: Now let's go back to today's title, *"From the Lip to the Hip is a Pretty Far Distance."* This is a specific example, of how I'm relating to something that my mother taught me when I was a kid. In sales, you're always getting your hopes up. You've made a presentation and you're going to make a sale. Someone said they were going to buy something from you, and in the end, they don't. This can be quite disappointing.

Steve Coplon: Right Thinking has a lot to do with how we handle our money, and how we earn an income. Let me get specific for a second here regarding money. Our lives generally depend on money, to pay our bills, keep our credit straight, and feed our families. A lot of us have a livelihood that requires sales where we sell something to someone, or we provide a service, which requires an exchange of money. My mother taught me by saying, "Stevie, a lot of times people don't do what they say they're going to do, you can't always depend on them. You can't always wait around." This is exactly what the show is about today.

Steve Coplon: The term *"From the Lip to the Hip is a Pretty Far Distance,"* is what my mother taught me. Let's look at it again from a sales point of view. Let's say someone has made a commitment and agreed to make a purchase from you. My mother said it this way; When someone agrees to make a purchase from you, then it crosses their lips, they must then reach down to their hip, to get their wallet, to get the money, to finish this transaction. Sometimes this can be a pretty far distance. So, if they agree and they do not reach for their wallet to pay as they said they would, then it might not have been true to begin with.

Steve Coplon: Another thing that she always said was "Talk is cheap." I learned early out that you can't always believe what people say. You can't always depend on people. This lesson was a great advantage because I learned that I might not always be able to do something when I needed other people to help me, so it taught me to be somewhat more independent.

Steve Coplon: I've done a lot of shows on character and taking responsibility. I did a whole series of shows going back to around Episode 87. It was a four-part series titled *Responsibility – Taking Control of Your Life*. It was primarily geared toward character, and obviously a huge part of character and integrity, is to do what you say you're going to do, and to honor your commitment. In all the courses that I teach on finance and credit, credit is really all about honoring your commitment, and doing what you say you're going to do.

Steve Coplon: Another show that my wife, Donna, and I recorded together, was Episode 53, *"The Functional Family."* The subject was on respect. If you tell someone you're going to do something and you don't do it, that's kind of disrespectful in my mind. In reality, I think it's just outright disrespectful, to be honest with you.

Steve Coplon: The reason I chose this topic for today's show, is that I've had a lot of people in the last month or two, say they were going to do something and then it just never happened. It appears to be more and more prevalent, in our culture, to tell somebody they're going to do something with no intention of ever doing it, just to get them off your back. I don't agree with that.

Steve Coplon: Let me ask you these questions. Have you been telling people that you're going to do something, knowing that you're not really going to do it? I think that's lying. Are you waiting for someone to do something that you fully expect them to do, and they never do it? Do you feel that maybe they lied to you?

Steve Coplon: Well, I think I've pretty much established the topic of today's show.

Steve Coplon: I've got a lot of Scripture today that relates to the point of our subject. Let's begin with:

Matthew 5:33-37

And don't say anything you don't mean. This counsel is embedded deep in our traditions. You only make things worse when you lay down a smoke screen of pious talk, saying, 'I'll pray for you,' and never doing it, or saying, 'God be with you,' and not meaning it. You don't make your words true by embellishing them with religious lace. In making your speech sound more religious, it becomes less true. Just say yes and no. When you manipulate words to get your own way, you go wrong.

Steve Coplon: One of the best books on human nature, that I've ever come across, is *Napoleon Hill's* book, **"Outwitting the Devil."** I highly recommend it. It's basically a conversation that Napoleon Hill had with the Devil. Some people don't believe it to be an actual conversation, but you can make up your own mind after you've read the book.

Steve Coplon: I believe the biggest single lesson in Hill's book, which is also my advice to all of you, is to take control of your life. Do not depend on those who are making promises that they never intend to keep. When Napoleon Hill interviewed the Devil, he boastfully told him, the reason he can control 98% of all of mankind who have ever walked on the face of the earth, is because he can control their minds. They do not think for themselves. What a major statement, that 98% of people don't think for themselves. If we accept this statement to be somewhat true, as I do, then our goal should be to strive for the ability to think for ourselves.

Steve Coplon: I came across a book by *Earl Nightingale* that I read years ago, titled "**The Strangest Secret**," it contains wonderful quotes by some remarkable people. This first quote by Marcus Aurelius, a Roman emperor, says that the secret to success or failure is that we become what we think about.

Marcus Aurelius

"A man's life is what his thoughts make of it."

Steve Coplon: Here's a very, very important quote by *William James,* an American philosopher and psychologist.

William James

If you only care enough for a result, you will almost certainly attain it. If you wish to be rich, you will be rich. If you wish to be learned, you will be learned. If you wish to be good, you will be good. Only you must then really wish these things, and wish them exclusively, and not wish at the same time 100 other incompatible things just as strongly.

Steve Coplon: He is suggesting that you focus on what you are thinking about, because if you are too distracted, it's easy to lose focus. I am going to impress upon you the power of your own thinking, and controlling your own mind, and how it relates to being around people who are not truthful to you. People who don't do what they say they're going to do generally are going to make excuses. Some will even believe their excuses. They are lying to themselves and they're lying to you. We are going to talk about that a great deal in a moment.

Steve Coplon: For those of you who believe in controlling your mind and having thoughts that will help you become successful, here is a beautiful piece of Scripture:

Matthew 7:7-8

Ask, and it shall be given you; seek, and you shall find; knock, and it shall be opened unto you; for everyone that asketh receiveth; and he that seeketh findeth; and to him that knocketh, it shall be opened.

Steve Coplon: I think that's a proactive approach to going after life and getting the most out of it, and not just being passive and waiting for others. I have been very blessed with a beautiful relationship with **The Napoleon Hill Foundation**. I first came across the book *"Think and Grow Rich"*, when I was in my early 20s. Bill, *"The Plant Man"*, gave me a copy around 1973-1974, ever since then, I've been immersed in *"Think and Grow Rich"* and I have tried to pass on the many principles that I've learned from it. It is a major part of my teachings.

Steve Coplon: Don Green, the executive director of **The Napoleon Hill Foundation**, is a man I truly love. He is a great man. Yesterday was his birthday. I would like to wish him a Happy Birthday. Don, I hope your birthday was wonderful!

Steve Coplon: In 2018 Don gave me permission through The Napoleon Hill Foundation, to use a page out of a book called, *"How to Own Your Own Mind"*, by Napoleon Hill. It is a page that is titled, *"The Major Benefits of Organized Thinking"*. I would like to read the language that he instructed me to include whenever I use it, *"Special thanks to The Napoleon Hill Foundation for granting permission for the use of the excerpt from 'How to Own Your Own Mind', by Napoleon Hill, an official publication of The Napoleon Hill Foundation. You can find Napoleon Hill at: www.naphill.org."*

Steve Coplon: This is taken from a conversation between Napoleon Hill and Andrew Carnegie, and it goes like this:

Napoleon Hill

"Mr. Carnegie, will you briefly describe the major benefits of organized thinking from the viewpoint of the man who wishes to make the best use of his time and ability?"

Andrew Carnegie

The benefits are so numerous that it is difficult to decide where to begin or where to stop, but these are some of the more obvious advantages of this habit.

A. *Organized thinking enables one to become the master of his own mind. This he accomplishes by training his faculty of will to control his emotions, turning them on and off as occasion may require.*

B. *Organized thinking forces one to work with definiteness of purpose, thereby enabling him to set up a habit that prohibits procrastination.*

C. *It develops the habit of working with definite plans instead of blundering ahead by the hit-or-miss method.*

D. *It enables one to stimulate the subconscious mind to greater action and more ready response, in the attainment of desired ends. Instead of allowing the subconscious mind to respond to the tramp thoughts and destructive influences of one's environment.*

E. *It develops self-reliance.*

F. *It gives one the benefit of the knowledge, experience, and education of others through the medium of the master mind alliance, which is an important medium used by all able thinkers.*

G. *It enables one to convert his efforts into greater material resources and larger income. Since an organized mind can produce more than one that is not organized.*

H. *It develops the habit of accurate analysis, through which one may find the solution to his problems instead of worrying over them.*

I. *It aids in maintaining sound health because mind power that is organized and directed toward the attainment of desirable ends has no time to be wasted in connection with self-pity or imaginary ailments. Idle minds tend to develop ailing bodies.*

J. *Last but by no means least, organized thinking leads to peace of mind and that form of permanent happiness which is known only to the man who keeps his mind fully occupied. No one can either be happy or successful without a planned program for the use of his time. Planned programs are based on organized thinking.*

Steve Coplon: *Andrew Carnegie continues,*

Andrew Carnegie

As I have stated before, the brain is something like a rich garden spot in that it will voluntarily grow a fine crop of weeds if it is not organized and kept busy growing a more desirable crop. The weeds are represented by the stray thoughts that take possession of the unorganized, idle mind as the result of one's daily environment. Study this list of benefits carefully, and you will reach the conclusion that any one of them offers sufficient reward to justify all the effort one puts into organizing his thinking habits. The sum total of all of these benefits represents the difference between success and failure. Success is always the result of an ordered life. An ordered life comes through organized thinking and carefully controlled habits.

Steve Coplon:	I use *"The Major Benefits of Organized Thinking"* in today's conversation, as I speak directly to those who say they're going to do things that they don't do, and to those who are dependent upon the people who make those promises. As I said early in the show, these two types, are examples of people who probably are not going to be successful. Their character is not so good, or they are too dependent, or they are not self-reliant.
Steve Coplon:	I want to stay in the positive for a minute. My life is one of acceptance, not giving up, not quitting. I try to help others through example, to persevere, to carry on, to always seek knowledge, learn more, strive for wisdom. I have been given a calling. I am a person who is there for other people. I am here for every one of you listening to this show. I rely on *The Bible*. It is my main source. I have often said that the three most important books in my life are *The Bible*, *"Think and Grow Rich"*, and *"Outwitting the Devil"*.
Steve Coplon:	I want to talk about my program **Right Thinking Foundation**. which gives me access to so many people and it helps them to take control of their thinking. It is a financial literacy foundation, and as I've said over and over again, it's not really about money. It is only 25% about money. It is about persevering, not quitting, not giving up, surrounding yourself with the right people, and making good decisions. I can teach anybody about their money and budgeting. However, if they do not know their purpose, they are going to waste their money and spend it unwisely, on the wrong things. And where do you get your purpose? You get it from the Word of the Lord. What I am doing with my life, that I have been called to do, is help people find their purpose and lead them to the Lord.
Steve Coplon:	While I was reading the *book "The Strangest Secret"*, by *Earl Nightingale*, (which I highly recommend) I came to a place in the book that I just loved. It was a piece from Napoleon Hill's book, *"Think and Grow Rich"*. It was so powerful that I went back to it. It is in the last chapter of *"Think and Grow Rich."* The title of that chapter is *"How to Outwit the Six Ghosts of Fear."* The piece from the chapter was *called "Fifty-Seven Famous Alibis by Old Man IF."* I wanted to use it on the show because it is so powerful.
Steve Coplon:	I knew that I couldn't read it and use it on the show without asking permission of **The Napoleon Hill Foundation,** due to copyright laws. I called Don Green and left him a message, he happened to be in a board meeting. He called me back shortly after checking his messages, so I requested permission and I gave him a written request to use the *"Fifty-Seven Famous Alibis by Old Man IF."* He then had to send it to legal and within a couple hours, legal said, "Yeah, Steve, you can use it."
Steve Coplon:	I believe the reason that they gave me permission is because they know I am trying to help the world become a better place, which also happens to be their mission statement. I am trying to expose people to the great writings of Napoleon Hill. *"Think and Grow Rich"* was written in 1937 and is a phenomenal book. I want to say thank you again to **The Napoleon Hill Foundation**. Again, I'm going to read the special language they instructed me to include when using these *"Fifty-Seven Famous Alibis by Old Man IF."* *"Special thanks to The Napoleon Hill Foundation for granting permission for the use of the below excerpt from Think and Grow Rich by Napoleon Hill, an official publication of The Napoleon Hill Foundation. You can find them at www.naphill.org."*
Steve Coplon:	I want you to be thinking as if you are one of the people Napoleon Hill refers to, who use these types of alibis. A lot of people think the word alibi is synonymous with excuses. Back in 1937, I believe Napoleon Hill was using it as excuses. Alibi is a legal word for "I wasn't

there. I can prove that I wasn't there when something happened."

Steve Coplon: The definition of excuse from the dictionary is,

ex·cuse (*verb*)

"An attempt to lessen the blame, attaching to a fault or an offense; seeking to defend or justify."

Steve Coplon: Alibi is more of a claim or piece of evidence that one was elsewhere when an act, typically a criminal one, is alleged to have taken place. For the purpose of what I'm going to read, these are all excuses starting with the word "IF". If you are using any of these excuses, and I bet you are, then now is the time to stop using them. I say I bet you are, because unfortunately, I too have recently used some of these excuses myself.

Steve Coplon: Now, it is my pleasure and my honor, and with great appreciation to the **Napoleon Hill Foundation**, I'm going to read Napoleon Hill's:

"Fifty-Seven Famous Alibis by Old Man IF"

Fifty-Seven Famous Alibis by Old Man IF. People who do not succeed have one distinguishing trait in common. They all know the reason for failure and have what they believe to be airtight alibis to explain away their own lack of achievement. Some of these alibis are clever, and a few of them are justifiable by the facts. But alibis cannot be used for money. The world wants to know only one thing - HAVE YOU ACHIEVED SUCCESS? A character analyst compiled a list of the most commonly used alibis. As you read the list, examine yourself carefully, and determine how many of these alibis, if any, are your own property. Remember, too, the philosophy presented in this book, makes every one of these alibis obsolete.

IF I didn't have a wife and family...

IF I had enough "pull"...

IF I had money...

IF I had a good education...

IF I could get a job...

IF I had good health...

IF I only had time...

IF times were better...

IF other people understood me...

IF conditions around me were only different...

IF I could only live my life over again...

IF I did not hear what they would say...

IF I had been given a chance...

IF I had a chance...

IF nothing happens to stop me...

IF I were only younger...

IF I could only do what I want...

IF I had been born rich...

IF I could meet the right people...

IF I had the talent that some people have...

IF I dared assert myself...

IF I only had embraced past opportunities...

IF people didn't get on my nerves...

IF I didn't have to keep house and look after the children...

IF I could save some money...

IF the boss only appreciated me…

IF I only had someone to help me...

IF my family understood me...

IF I lived in a big city...

IF I could just get started...

IF I were only free...

IF I had the personality of some people…

IF I were not so fat...

IF my talents were known...

IF I could just get a break...

IF I could only get out of debt...

IF I hadn't failed...

IF I only knew how...

IF everybody didn't oppose me...

IF I didn't have so many worries...

IF I could marry the right person...

IF people weren't so dumb...

IF my family were not so extravagant...

IF I were sure of myself...

IF luck were not against me...

IF I had not been born under the wrong star...

IF it were not true that what is to be will be...

IF I did not have to work so hard...

IF I hadn't lost my money...

IF I had lived in a different neighborhood...

IF I didn't have a past...

IF I only had a business of my own...

IF other people would only listen to me...

IF, ***and this is the greatest of them all***

I had the courage to see myself as I really am, I would find out what is wrong with me *and correct it. Then I might have a chance to profit by my mistakes and learn something from the experience of others, for I know that there is something WRONG with me or I would now be where I WOULD HAVE BEEN IF I had spent more time analyzing my weaknesses and less time building alibis to cover them.*

Building alibis with which to explain away failure is a national pastime. The habit is as old as the human race and is fatal to success. Why do people cling to their pet alibis? The answer is obvious. They defend their alibis because they create them. A man's alibi is the child of his own imagination. It is human nature to defend one's own brainchild.

Building alibis is a deeply rooted habit. Habits are difficult to break, especially when they provide justification for something we do. Plato had this truth in mind when he said, "The first and best victory is to conquer self. To be conquered by self is, of all things, the most shameful and vile."

Another philosopher had the same thought in mind when he said, "It was a great surprise to me when I discovered that most of the ugliness I saw in others was but a reflection of my own nature."

'It has always been a mystery to me,' said Elbert Hubbard, 'why people spend so much time deliberately fooling themselves by creating alibis to cover their weaknesses. If used differently, this same time would be sufficient to cure the weakness. Then no alibis would be needed.'

In parting, I remind you that "life is a checkerboard, and the player opposite you is time. If you hesitate before moving or neglect to move promptly, your men will be wiped off the board by time. You're playing against a partner who will not tolerate indecision."

Steve Coplon: Well, I think that sums up everything we're trying to say here. He finishes up the chapter by saying this.

Napoleon Hill

The master key is intangible, but it is powerful. It is the privilege of creating in your own mind a burning desire for a definite form of riches. There is no penalty for the use of the key, but there is a price you must pay if you do not use it. The price is failure. There is a reward of stupendous proportions if you put the key to use. It is the satisfaction that comes to all who conquer self and force life to pay whatever is asked. The reward is worthy of your effort. Will you make the start and be convinced?

Steve Coplon: *"Think and Grow Rich"* contains some of the greatest wisdom found anywhere. It teaches about human nature and gives you tools to be able to move your life forward and become successful.

Steve Coplon: Here is another positive thought from *Napoleon Hill*. This is from **Thought for the Day**. It is a free service brought to you by **The Napoleon Hill Foundation** at www.naphill.org.

Napoleon Hill

Offer results, not alibis. There are many people who, perhaps with the best of intentions, make promises they somehow never get around to keeping. These folks have usually developed a number of perfectly plausible explanations for not meeting their commitments. They have become experts at explaining away their failures. Successful people, though, are those who accept responsibility for their lives. They know that talk is cheap. Actions are all that really matter. The world is waiting for men and women who seek the opportunity to render real service, the kind of service that lightens the burdens of their neighbors, the kind of service that 95% of people do not render because they do not understand it. When you provide a truly useful service enthusiastically and in a spirit of genuine helpfulness, success will automatically follow. The world seeks out such individuals and rewards them accordingly.

Steve Coplon: The reason I chose to talk about excuses on today's show is because I really care about people who are struggling. Many are people who can't understand why they are not doing better with their lives. I have found that people make excuses. Napoleon Hill expressed throughout his 57 famous alibis, to act and stop making excuses. Now, go back and read them again.

Steve Coplon: Sometimes people really believe that they have not had a fair shake in life. A lot of people say, "Life's not fair." Well, I'm here to tell you, that is probably true. Things happen to all of us. Right when everything is going great, all of a sudden there's an accident, or an illness or some type of adversity. We must keep moving forward. We have to take control of our lives.

Steve Coplon: I'm very, very blessed to be affiliated with **The Napoleon Hill Foundation. I am honored** that they trust me to use some of Napoleon Hill's writings to try to reach people. They want everyone to have a better life.

Steve Coplon: I'd like to read nine or ten pieces of Scripture that I have researched on the subject of telling the truth. It is basically coming from an action list on *actions speak louder than words*. I found this website, openbible.info, and I searched for the phrase, "telling the truth." Here is what I gathered for you.

Proverbs 10:19

"When words are many, transgression is not lacking, but whoever restrains his lips is prudent."

1st John 3:18

"Little children, let us not love in word or talk, but in deed and in truth."

James 2:17

"So also faith by itself, if it does not have works, is dead."

James 1:22

"But be doers of the Word, and not hearers only, deceiving yourselves."

James 3:13

"Who is wise and understanding among you? By his good conduct let him show his works in the meekness of wisdom."

Matthew 5:16

"In the same way, let your light shine before others, so that they may see your good works and give glory to your Father who is in heaven."

Matthew 21:28-32

What do you think? A man had two sons. He went to the first and said, 'Son, go and work in the vineyard today.' He answers, 'I will not,' but afterward he changed his mind and went. He went to the other son and said the same. He answered, 'I go, sir,' but he did not go. Which of the two did the will of his father? They said, 'The first.' Jesus said to them, 'Truly, I say to you, the tax collectors and the prostitutes go into the kingdom of God before you, for John came to you in the way of righteousness and you did not believe him, but the tax collectors and the prostitutes believed him. Even when you saw it, you did not afterward change your minds and believe him.' They professed to know God, but they deny him by their works. They are detestable, disobedient, unfit for any good work.

1st Peter 2:21

"For to this you have been called, because Christ also suffered for you, leaving you an example, so that you might follow in his steps."

James 1:22-25

But be doers of the Word, and not hearers only, deceiving yourselves. For if anyone is a hearer of the word and not a doer, he is like a man who looks intently at his natural face in a mirror. For he looks at himself and goes away and at once forgets what he was like. But the one who looks into the perfect law, the law of liberty, and perseveres, being no hearer who forgets, but a doer who acts, he will be blessed in his doing.

James 2:14-18

What good is it, my brothers, if someone says he has faith but does not have works? Can that faith save him? If a brother or sister is poorly clothed and lacking in daily food, and one of you says to them, 'Go in peace. Be warmed and filled,' without giving them the things needed for the body, what good is that? So also faith by itself, if it does not have works, is dead. But someone will say, 'You have faith, and I have works.' Show me your faith apart from your works, and I will show you my faith by my works.

Steve Coplon: I love each one of you and I want you to do the things you say you are going to do. Do not say things that you do not intend to do. Do not offer excuses. Become a person who develops character and integrity. Be a person who does what you say you are going to do. That is a real wonderful thing in life.

Steve Coplon: I would like you to think about this right now. You know people who do what they say they are going to do, and you respect them. We all need to visualize ourselves becoming that type of a person.

Steve Coplon: I am going to end the show with this. Again, today I chose to talk about life in general, and those of us who are always disappointed by people who do not do the things they say they are going to do. Napoleon Hill and I are telling you to, "Get yourself a plan. Find your burning desire and start moving toward it. Move forward. You don't have to depend on others all the time, however, you will need to work with others." Napoleon Hill teaches about the Mastermind Principle. This is another subject of equal importance, as it teaches us that we must work with others in harmony if we are to succeed.

Steve Coplon: For those of you who have been a victim and disappointed throughout life because others don't do the things they say they're going to do, pick yourself up and start doing things for yourself. Invite others to join with you. If you are a person who's made excuses your entire life and claim that life is not fair, and you don't do things you say you're going to do, you need to change. It takes practice to change, so don't delay, start today.

Steve Coplon: Here's my last Scripture today,

Proverbs 3:6

"Listen for God's voice in everything you do, everywhere you go; He is the one who will keep you on track."

Steve Coplon: Thank you for listening. I hope it's been helpful. Reach out to me at rightthink.org. Please contact me if there is anything I can do for you. I would like to conclude by saying, I love each and every one of you. God Bless you and have a great week.

Steve Coplon: I appreciate your time in listening to *Right Thinking with Steve Coplon*. I look forward to being with you again next week. Remember: **Don't Quit, Plan Ahead, It Will Get Better.** God Bless you and have a great week!

To listen to the original interview, scan this QR Code with your camera, or visit:
https://rightthinkingeducation.com/FromtheLiptotheHip/Chpater-1/

CHAPTER TWO
You Got That Right Steve! with guest Lefford Fate
Right Thinking With Steve Coplon - Episode 160

Steve Coplon: Good morning. Welcome to *Right Thinking with Steve Coplon.* I'm your host, Steve Coplon, and thank you for tuning in. Let's have a great day!

Steve Coplon: Here's the announcement for today's show Episode 160:

Right Thinking with Steve Coplon is very pleased to announce that this week's show is called, *"You Got That Right, Steve!"* with guest Lefford Fate. Tune in and hear Lefford share his thoughts with Steve about being a person who does what he says he is going to do. Lefford has mentored and led thousands to a life of greater success. After listening to this show, you will be on your way to greater success.

Steve Coplon: Lefford thanks for agreeing to be on the show today to talk about Episode 159, *"From the Lip to the Hip is a Pretty Far Distance."* You are the first guest to be interviewed for the series that I am doing on this subject.

Lefford, you're a Napoleon Hill certified coach, you're a mentor, you're a person who talks all the time about the importance of believing in yourself, knowing your own truth, being honest with yourself, believing in the people who got you where you are. You are a role model.

Before I get you started. I am going to read what I used in last week's show, from the *"Fifty-Seven Famous Alibis by Old Man IF"*, taken from *"Think and Grow Rich."* It is the 57th If:

Napoleon Hill

IF, ***and this is the greatest of them all***

I had the courage to see myself as I really am, I would find out what is wrong with me and correct it. *Then I might have a chance to profit by my mistakes and learn something from the experience of others, for I know that there is something WRONG with me or I would now be where I WOULD HAVE BEEN IF I had spent more time analyzing my weaknesses and less time building alibis to cover them.*

Steve Coplon: Truer words were never spoken. What do you think Lefford?

Lefford Fate: I actually think that's pretty powerful. There's another book, ***"Start With Why: How Great Leaders Inspire Everyone to Take Action"*** by Simon Sinek that I really like. He says start with why. So, we'll start with *why* here today. Why, would a person say one thing and do something else? Why don't people feel really good about themselves? Why do they have these 57 excuses about what they don't do? As you said at the very end, "If I had the courage." I think a lot of that comes from those Six Ghosts of Fear, and that one is the fear of fear itself. There are a lot of people that'll say yes because they're pressured into saying yes. They don't have the courage to say no. In the days of mass media, pressure sales, other people having agendas, if you don't know what you want, if you don't know what your definite major purpose is, people can talk you into anything.

Lefford Fate: If you don't have the courage to say no, you will say yes, while all the time trying to figure out a way to get out of that commitment. I've seen that in my life, I've seen that in other people's lives. It's frustrating for the people they're dealing with. I know some of the questions to the thoughts that you had Steve, was why in the world would you say yes to me and then you don't follow-up? Are you just trying to get me off your back? I think a lot of it is for that reason. I don't think people just wake up in the morning and say, "You know what? I'm going to lie to somebody." Now, a few people might because that's what liars do.

Lefford Fate: I think more often than not, people have intentions of doing stuff, however, I don't think they have the fortitude. I don't think they have the definiteness of purpose. I don't think they know what they really want, therefore, they just take the path of least resistance. I think Napoleon Hill said, "All rivers and many men are crooked because of following the law of least resistance."

Steve Coplon: I accept everything that you just said. I want to clarify something.

Lefford Fate: Good, let's talk to it, I love it.

Steve Coplon: Okay, I agree with everything you said. But I need to clarify something that I have said. Just because I talk about people who are not following up with what they say, I still love them, I know that they need love, they need friendship, they need things. Sometimes they are just selfish, sometimes they are withdrawn. One thing that I've said all along, a lot of times people end up in some bad places and have that wall around them where they don't trust anybody at all because of a bad childhood. They were beaten, abused, abandoned, neglected, whatever you want to call it. So, what I'm here to tell you is, I don't judge people. I realize that I might sound like a real hardliner laying out people who don't do what they say they're going to do. As I pointed out in the last show, they shouldn't use these naysayers as an excuse for not moving forward. For example, "Well, I thought Lefford was going to do this, and I waited. And then I lost my own opportunity."

Steve Coplon: More self-reliance is what's necessary. I want to make a statement, because I said a whole lot in the last couple of sentences. Just because someone doesn't do what they say they're going to do, does not mean I'm not here for them. In fact, I want to find out where the problem lies. It's like you said, most of the time they have their reasons. It's a defense mechanism. Like the law of least resistance. That was well said, Lefford, well spoken.

Lefford Fate: The law of least resistance that I quoted, isn't mine. It's Napoleon Hill's. I wish I could own it, but I don't. But yeah, I think a lot of people take the path of least resistance. Again, I go back to the definiteness of purpose, you must know what you want. I recommend this for everyone. If you're busy and you cannot do something, say you cannot do it. Say it. If you find yourself in a situation where you say you're going to do something, and you can't follow up on that, tell the person as soon as possible. Don't leave people out there waiting and trying to find you. I remember something so clearly, that happened probably 43-44 years ago, I remember it like it was yesterday. I've told you that we grew up poor. Well, we had this cousin who said he was going to buy bikes for Christmas, for me and my two youngest sisters. We didn't ask for this, it was just one of those things that he said he was going to do.

Lefford Fate: My parents could not afford new bikes for all of us, that wasn't going to happen. But our cousin made this grand statement that he was going to get us these bikes and we were going to get them on Christmas. And you know, we waited for those bikes, we waited for those bikes, and we waited for those bikes. We didn't get them before Christmas, we didn't get them on Christmas, we didn't get them the week after. But you know, two or three weeks later, when we saw him again, we were expecting those bikes to show up. What happens when you have an expectation and that expectation is not fulfilled? Young people especially, can learn not to trust. That's exactly what you were talking about before. The thought pattern develops . . . *I'm not going to depend on anybody else because I cannot depend on people.* I have kind of lived with that thought pattern. You've heard this many times, Steve. "If it is to be, it's up to me".

Steve Coplon: Yes, I have.

Lefford Fate: This is where I went with that for a while, because I was let down on a number of cases. If it is to be, it's up to me. Because I can't trust anybody, because they're not trustworthy. You see the difference between taking something that is powerful and correct, and adding that little bit onto the back of it that turns that whole thing around. It had to be up to me because I couldn't trust anybody. And when you get that mindset, no matter whose fault it is, that's a destructive mindset. If you don't trust other people, you put trust in yourself, and then ultimately you can lose trust in God. And that's not healthy or successful at all. So, there's a lot to it. There's something I want to throw out there and we can talk about this a little bit later.

Lefford Fate: I think that if we're going to take 100% responsibility for our lives, even if we're waiting on somebody, we have to do what you did, Steve. When you had that guy stand you up for an interview that led to this series, you gave yourself a backup plan. You realized that he might not show, you put together another show, just in case. You called Don and got permission to use the *"Fifty-Seven Famous Alibis by Old Man IF"*.

Lefford Fate We have to have a backup plan. Because sometimes people will disappoint you by not being able to fulfill what they said they would do. It's not their fault that your job doesn't get done, or that I don't get my job done if I'm waiting on them. This is some tough stuff that I'm glad we're talking about. Because a lot of people struggle with this.

Lefford, this scripture relates to what you're saying:

Galatians 6:4-5

"Each one should test their own actions. Then they can take pride in themselves alone without comparing themselves to someone else. For each one should carry their own load".

Steve Coplon: We do not need to be completely independent. Look at Napoleon Hill's the Master Mind principle. We can't do without others. We both know, it's a pleasure to be the dumbest guy in the room. When you're surrounded by other people who are lifting you up, you're going to benefit from it.

Matthew 5:37

"Just say yes and no. When you manipulate words to get your own way, you go wrong".

Steve Coplon: What we're talking about is absolutely true. But I tell you, Lefford, there are reasons why people don't know how to say no. You know that, you were just speaking to it.

Steve Coplon: My wife, always tells me, "Hey, Steve, you can get just about anyone to say okay to what you ask them to do, because you've got that kind of enthusiasm." But a lot of times, they do not end up following up with me. When that happens, she often says, "They didn't tell you, because they didn't know how to tell you no." I understand that.

Steve Coplon Lefford, I want to share something personal that your bike story brings to mind. I was born Jewish. When I was 13 in 1964, I was Bar Mitzvah-ed. There is a tradition that when a Jewish boy gets Bar Mitzvah-ed, he gets to ask his parents for a big gift to celebrate the milestone event in his life.

Steve Coplon: Well, the TV that I had in my room, was an old black and white model. Hey, this is completely off subject but thinking about that TV makes me remember the 1966 NCAA Basketball Championship game between Texas Western and Kentucky. You probably remember the game. Texas Western upset Kentucky with Louie Dampier and all those guys who were the best team in the country. The reason that game comes to mind is that my TV had an 11 inch screen that had shrunk down to where it had less than one inch of visibility. I could barely see what was happening. I changed every tube in that TV for years. The good old days.

Steve Coplon Anyway, back to my Bar Mitzvah story. So, my Dad asked me before my Bar Mitzvah what I wanted as my Bar Mitzvah gift? And I said, "Can I get a TV for my room? Just a little TV for my room." He said, "That's a reasonable gift, okay." He instructed me to research what I wanted, then price shop at a minimum of three stores. I was 13 years old and very excited about getting a new TV. I took the assignment very seriously. I checked out TVs at four different stores, found the TV that I wanted and had prices.

Steve Coplon: When my dad would come to Norfolk from D.C. to celebrate a Jewish holiday, I would be expecting that he would buy me the TV. But each time he would give me the same excuse, "Can't spend money on a Jewish holiday." I would respond, "Well, you told me that you would do it when you came to town this time." About a year after my Bar Mitzvah, my dad still had not gotten me the TV. Then he wrote me a letter and said, "I can't get it for you because I can't afford to buy my own socks."

Steve Coplon It was rough for me. It was a major disappointment and caused a huge breach in our relationship because he never honored his commitment to me. So, that's kind of a true confession. I finally got over it. It took us years and years to repair our relationship. Not just because of that one incident, but it certainly played a big part. It made me independent. I always thought after that, that my dad had an ulterior motive. He wanted to show me that if you can't even depend on your own father, you better learn to take care of yourself. Well, that is how I was raised.

Steve Coplon	I love my dad. He died last year at 95 years old. But the point is, me and my dad were really, really close the last 20 years of his life. We became close friends. When I was diagnosed with my terminal illness, Multiple Myeloma, he called me every day for six months. Thanks for letting me share that, Lefford, you brought it out of me, about my dad. I guess I still have the stuff that makes me independent because it was put into me hard like that, do you know what I mean?
Lefford Fate:	Yeah, well sorry, bro. Well, I'll tell you something. There was a quote that I love, and it's basically saying, "You may be done with your past, but your past may not be done with you."
Steve Coplon:	Heard that before.
Lefford Fate:	And I think a lot of us are like that, Steve. Because it's one of those things where, if you are hurt, this will hurt you. I was listening to Episode 159, and I was like, "Oh, Steve, don't like people to tell him one thing and do something else. He don't like that." And so now what I see, it's almost like what Wayne Dyer said, "When you change the way you look at things, the things you look at change." It's like that is the thing. If somebody does that to you, that is a hook for you. And so, I can see where that's an issue. But I've got to be honest. We were talking a little bit earlier about dependent and independent. Dependent is flawed, independent is flawed, true interdependence is where we need to get to.
Steve Coplon:	Thank you.
Lefford Fate:	Because, at some point in our lives, we're going to be dependent on someone. Randy Harvey, gave a speech, he says, "Sometimes we're the catcher, sometimes we're the caught." There are times when I'm very dependent on someone else to do something for me. I am. As a baby, as a young person, before I graduated high school, I was dependent on my parents. I was dependent on our nation to defend us. As I got older, I became more independent. There are some things that I can legitimately do on my own. But the reality is, in my opinion, again, this is my humble opinion, if Lefford can be humble, is that the beauty of relationships is that; on the things that you can be dependent on, be dependent. The things that you could be independent on, be independent. But interdependence means that we are better, the sum of the parts is higher than individual parts, everything together.
Lefford Fate:	So, our interdependence is based on being able to trust, when somebody says something, it happens. Let your yays be your yays, and your nays be your nays. And we could do more together because we're dependent on each other to make us better. We're interdependent because if you're doing it right and I'm doing it right, we could be greater. But at the end of the day sometimes we've got to be able to buckle up and hold the line on our line, so we could protect our mate's back. If any of that makes sense.
Steve Coplon:	Yes, all of it did, Lefford. There's a lot of stuff here. First of all, you're a military guy. And you know what it is to have somebody's back. And you circulated something on social media a week or two ago that was just beautiful. I'll tell you one thing, Lefford, I have my close friends and people I know I can count on. I know I can count on them. Lefford, you say you're going to do something, and you do it. I want to add one thing in this show right now. If any of you don't get anything else out of this today, I at least want to show you what a good relationship looks like. I called Lefford to ask him if he would honor me by listening to last week's show, and then we could have a conversation about it. I was certain that there's a lot

of information that everyone can gain from listening to Lefford have a conversation with me. It's always a beautiful thing. Lefford was right up front with me. He told me, "Yeah, I can do it, but I'm not sure I can do it this week, I'm preparing for a speaking engagement next week, I think it's going to be in Indianapolis." That would be fine. I know it is a big event.

Steve Coplon: And he said, "Especially since that's the theme of your show, I don't want to say I can do something and not be there to do it." And I said, "No, no, Lefford. It doesn't have to be this week." We have to be interdependent on each other. We have to communicate. If Lefford knows that I don't have to have it this week, but he doesn't let me know that he won't be able to do it this week until it's too late, he's greatly inconvenienced me. I can get through it when people inconvenience me. He mentioned earlier about having a backup plan. You can't knock me down without having me crawl back onto my feet and stand up and take another punch, and then maybe get up the second time.

Lefford Fate: Up or getting up baby, up or getting up.

Steve Coplon: Yeah, yeah. But here's the thing. I was prepared to do a different show without Lefford. We would then do the show whenever Lefford was available. Having Lefford on the show would require about two or three hours of preparation to handle my side of the conversation. If I didn't have him on the show, it would take four or five hours to get my show ready.

Steve Coplon: I think I saved an extra couple of hours because Lefford is here with me right now. It's the way Lefford handled it. I knew he would let me know, and he did let me know, and now here we are. So, my piece of advice to every one of you out there is, it's okay to say no, but be courteous, say it with plenty of time so that the other person is not inconvenienced, period.

Lefford Fate: Whew, you said a mouthful.

Steve Coplon: Thank you.

Lefford Fate: I felt like Ric Flair there for a second. But the reality, Steve, it is both independence and dependence. Let people know. It's okay to say no.

Steve Coplon: It is.

Lefford Fate: You know, hey, if you can or you can't, we're good. But if you tell me, "I'm depending on you, let me know". And again, this sounds like a lot, right? But honestly, this is what true interdependence is. "Hey, Steve, I need you to do this for me, can you?" "I think so." "Okay, let me know if you can or can't." But, still have a backup plan. That's being responsible, *response-able*, so you don't get caught-up out there. That helps everybody! And again, here's the reason I know this. Some of the biggest fights and arguments, that I've had with my wife, is when I told her I was going to do something, and then I shifted, because something else came up that was hugely important. I used to think, "She'll understand because this is a matter of life or death, this is very serious, somebody really needs me." I took it for granted that she should understand.

Lefford Fate: What happens is, if you continue to do that, you're saying that something is always more important than your significant other. And it took her a couple of times to help me understand what I was doing. Legitimately I made a decision, someone needed me because they were seriously struggling. And they were crying, they were sick, they lost a child, or they lost a parent. And she said, "All you have to do is call me. All you have to do is let me know. I'll understand if you just let me know. But if you don't tell me, then you don't care as much about me as you care for the other person, or for yourself." And I didn't want to hear that. What I said was, "Oh, you're just selfish, you don't understand. If it happened to you, you'd do it." But I had to develop an awareness that shows it is respect for the other person, and respect for yourself.

Lefford Fate: Steve, whether I say it or don't say it, if I repeatedly go to the well, and sometimes there's water and other times there's not, there's going to be a time when part of my mind says, "I cannot trust that there will be water." Nobody has to say anything. But there will come a time where I can't trust. And whenever that happens, it's not my fault. Because I cannot make myself trust somebody. So, that's the danger about this whole thing. Yays or nays, yays are yays, nays are nays. Because even subconsciously if a person gets to the point where they can't trust you, they're done, it's over.

Steve Coplon When you don't honor your commitment, you might think you're fooling the world, just pulling the wool over everyone's eyes. Then at some point in time you become known as a person who another person cannot rely on and cannot count on. Basically, they can't trust you. And when you lose trust with someone, that is very, very difficult to rebuild. And there are many, many relationships that don't get past it.

Steve Coplon: I don't want to get into people's marriages, but hey, really think about what you are saying, when it relates to your marriage. Because you can lose trust with your spouse, and that's a tough situation. It causes a lot of problems and it affects the kids; it affects everyone around. Just focus on living a good honest life, that's what we're trying to pass onto you here.

Lefford Fate: I'm going to astound you with something. I'm going to throw something out there that is more insidious than losing the trust of your friends and your spouse, your significant other. It is *losing trust with yourself.*

Steve Coplon: Wow!

Lefford Fate: And this is the deal. If you cannot trust that you will do what you want to do, and what's right for you, you will start second guessing yourself. I mean, even in my favorite book, it states, 'What I would do, I do not, what I would not do, I do. How retched am I?" I mean, you think about it. If you do not do what you intend to do continuously, you second guess yourself. That's where low self-esteem comes from. That I cannot trust me. I say I'm going to get up and go do it, if I don't do it, there comes a time when I said, I don't know if I can. So, it's quite insidious and it's dangerous. I think that's one of the major problems, why we have low self-esteem. A lot of people don't do what they can do, because they have let themselves down so many times, that they don't bet on themselves anymore.

Steve Coplon: It leads into being ashamed, living a life of shame and loss of confidence and everything else. After a while you just don't like yourself. Right now, I would like to give my wife a compliment and say thank you Donna. Earlier, when I was preparing, I was thinking about what I hope to bring about with Lefford on this show today? I'm planning to have a series of shows where I bring in several people with different perspectives, who will be able to speak to the matter of the subject. And I asked Donna, "So, what do you think? Lefford's into so many beautiful things, and he's got so much wisdom and topics that he can talk about." Donna said, "Well, you know, when I think about Lefford, he speaks a great deal about believing in yourself." She said, "Knowing your own truth, Lefford speaks to that, people have to know their own truth. Being honest with themselves." She had it right. Those are the things that you are speaking about, Lefford.

Steve Coplon: You have to believe in the people who believe in you. And what that means, and the way Donna wanted me to bring it out from you today is, if you've got someone who is going to be mentoring you, someone you look up to, you've got to trust that they're being honest with you. Because when they tell you, "Lefford, I see something good in you that you don't see in yourself yet, but I know it's in there. We're going to help you bring that out, Lefford. You know, these negative thoughts you have about yourself, you need to let them go, Lefford. Because that might be who you think you are, but that's not who I know you to be." Your sergeant, who was your mentor when you first joined the Air Force, said those things to you. What was the sergeant's name?

Lefford Fate: Sergeant John Gunther.

Steve Coplon: Oh, John Gunther, yeah. I'm sorry I didn't have his name committed to memory, but I remember the advice John Gunther gave you and what he did for you. I remember you were ready to quit. You gave up on yourself, and he picked you up by the back of your neck, and shook you enough to where you started to understand a little bit different about who Lefford Fate is, didn't he?

Lefford Fate: Exactly. And like I said, he didn't necessarily say it nicely either. Sometimes you need the carrot, sometimes you need the stick. I gave a talk on this Sgt. Gunther a couple of weeks ago, and I basically said this, "He didn't see the knucklehead, he saw me. He didn't see my behavior, he saw me." And as Goethe said, "If you see the man as he could be, versus the way he is, you will help him become who he should be." Because sometimes it's hard to see the picture when you're in the frame. Sometimes you can't know that something happened. Sometimes we lose sight. I don't think God ever loses us. I think we lose God. Listen to the reason I say this: He's always got us, always.

Steve Coplon: Always.

Lefford Fate: And sometimes we lose focus of that, we're just all over the place. So sometimes a person outside of us can see our greatness, where we can't see it ourselves. It's just hard to see. Sometimes you have to have faith in other people's faith in you. This is a rather profound statement Steve, so I'd like to repeat it. Sometimes you have to have faith in other people's faith in you. Sometimes you have to do that. And that's why I think it's very important to surround yourself with people who got you. You're the average of the five people you spend most time with. So, who are you hanging out with? If you are part of a team… I have a group of people I work with; I call them my pack. When I was in Korea, we had this thing called Wolf Pack. It was just a part of the thing. It wasn't just cops, it was cops and maintenance military, it was all these people.

Lefford Fate: Because when one wolf gets the kill, the whole pack eats. If one wolf is injured, the whole pack comes to the fight, right? So, if you surround yourself with people who always got you, then you're good. But, the one wolf that gets the kill, sneaks off and eats it alone, can't be trusted. And the rest of the pack will turn their back on him.

Steve Coplon: Wow. Okay, you just threw a whole bunch at me. First of all, regarding what you said about sometimes others see something in you that you can't see. I know a couple who've been married for about 50 years give or take. Junior high school, boyfriend, girlfriend, never dated anyone else, got married right out of high school. Went through the early years of marriage, had some severe problems. The greatest piece of wisdom that I think I've ever heard in marriage was from the wife. She was talking about it one night. I'm not going to give any of the circumstances, because I don't want to say who these people are. Bottom line is this. When there were some bad times going on, and her husband wasn't doing right, she said, "I had to pray. And I asked the Lord to show me what to do." And she said, "And what the Lord showed me was, I need to see this man for who he's going to be as he grows closer to God. And that's the man I'm married to. And my relationship is to be with him as he gets to be the man that he's going to be." She stuck it out through thick and thin, and their marriage turned out to be a beautiful long-lasting marriage.

Steve Coplon: But you're right about the one wolf who can't be trusted. I recently saw the movie, from the *Jack London* book, **"The Call of the Wild"**. Wonderful movie. *Jack London* also wrote **"White Fang"**. I read them in second and third grade. They're the best there is, very wholesome stories. In the **"The Call of the Wild"**, they were up in Alaska and the lead dog on the sleigh did all the wrong things. He ate the food by himself, took it from the other dogs. The pack of dogs that were pulling the sleigh, they didn't want to be with him anymore. When the lead dog turned on Buck, the dog hero of the book and movie, the other dogs turned on him to protect Buck. Then Buck became the leader of the pack because he loved everybody. He gave them his food. He protected them. By the end of the movie, he goes back to his true nature. He goes back to the wild. That is where the title comes from: **"The Call of the Wild"**. That's the storyline.

Steve Coplon: Hey, Lefford, let me completely change the direction for a second if I can.

Lefford Fate: Let's do it.

Steve Coplon: Okay. Well, Lefford, there's one thing that I'd like to bring out in this conversation with you as it relates to helping people become more successful. You know, the whole idea behind all of my shows and my foundation is to be there for people who are going through hardship, and those who want to be there to help them overcome their hardship. So, hopefully, a lot of people listening to this show, might pick up a pointer or two. Maybe they've got it completely right, even better than we have. We're always ready to learn. But, we're not here just for those who are going through hardship. We're here for those who are praying for others who want to be able to help other people as well. Well, here's the point. A lot of people aren't successful in their life because of their bad character traits. When they're not honest, they make a lot of excuses.

Steve Coplon: They do a lot of grousing and complaining, and it's always someone else's fault. When I visit prisons, I do this little exercise where I ask the question, "What are the five things that cause the most stress in your life?" I tell the returning citizens that I want a spontaneous answer, to write their answer down quickly. They don't have to really write the answer down, but just think of the five things quickly. I've been asking that question for years.

What I want to have them understand, is that money problems cause stress. And if we can reduce stress from money problems, we'll be better focused. Money is something we have some control over at least. When we get better at understanding and dealing with money, it will reduce stress in our lives. Then when life's unexpected things happen that we have no control over, such as illness, job lay-off, divorce, car accident, bad economy, or whatever; then we can face them with a clearer mind because we don't have as much stress from money problems hitting us. We can keep something that should be no more than a temporary setback from turning into a major failure that we can't overcome.

Steve Coplon: So, when I asked the question of the men out in Powder River Correctional Facility in Baker City, Oregon on a visit a few years ago, they started raising their hands right away. I really love these guys. They've gotten to know me pretty well and they are very comfortable with me. These are their answers: Stop signs, ex-wives, police officers, you get the gist. They were making some of the best excuses for not taking responsibility you can imagine. Not sure if they were being serious or joking. We had a beautiful time together.

Steve Coplon Lefford, a lot of people don't like people who are trying to help them become successful monetarily. A lot of people have an aversion to having financial success, as one of their goals. For some reason, they think it's not godly. They think that it's too materialistic. They may be thinking that a person with financial goals is only thinking about themselves. Well, *"Think and Grow Rich"* isn't just about money, but it does have a lot to do with money.

Steve Coplon: Sustainability is the word that I want to throw at you. You know, it's like, if you're on an airplane and they drop those oxygen masks, put yours on before you try to help the person next to you or your own child. Because if you're fumbling because of lack of oxygen, and you're trying to put a mask on your child, both of you are going to have a hard time. But it's very, very important to be financially stable. Life is just a lot easier when you're financially stable. So, I would like to just gear this for a moment or two toward your Napoleon Hill background, wisdom, training, teachings, knowledge. Can you go into that now?

Steve Coplon: Would you give some positive reasons to focus on money without seeming that it is for selfish reasons? Without catching that dread disease of not enough. Can you speak to the fact of why being financially stable and being a person of your word will help you be more successful?

Lefford Fate: Well, you threw two things out there. One, if you're a person of your word, you can be trusted. And when you can be trusted, over a few things, you will be made ruler over many things.

Steve Coplon: Amen.

Lefford Fate: One of our requirements is to be good stewards of resources. I think, and you remember this going through the *"Design Your Empowered Year"* program. I think God makes things two ways, perfectly and abundantly. And there's enough everywhere. This whole, not enough thinking is a scarcity mindset, and that's not of God. Listen, I grew up with poverty, with a poverty mindset. I grew up with the whole poverty thing and because of the lack of understanding, I thought if I wanted money, if I wanted good things, then I was an idolater. I was idolizing something. But that's not true. The richest man in history was given his riches because he first asked for wisdom, and then he was given wisdom. And then he was given riches.

Lefford Fate: Some people forget that. They try to make it a negative thing. It is not that. You can have abundance and glorify God, you just have to make sure you don't glorify the stuff first. I think money is freedom. I don't think it's something to be idolized. I just think it is freedom. You cannot pour from an empty cup. Steve, you can't give what you don't have. So, if you have what it takes to be good and successful, and you keep yourself fed, then you could do more stuff for more people.

Steve Coplon: That's a beautiful way to say it. I recorded a show with Rob Brown on investing, two parts to it. And the first show was called *"Investing: The Path to Less Stress, More Income and Greater Personal Freedom"*. Exactly what you said. So, it all ties together. I think that might be all we really need to do on the subject of money. I'm just trying to point out that successful people, those who can be trusted, they do what they say they're going to do, they have strong character and integrity because they honor their commitment. They honor their word.

This is a life mission for me, Lefford. One reason why I'm so happy these days is because I finally found a way to put it out there and let it grow in all kinds of different directions. Everything that I do is tied into what we're talking about. I want to read something to end the show with.

Lefford Fate: Well, before you end the show though, can I do this? You are always about helping people. I think it's important to help people come to an understanding of the benefits of following through with what they said they would do. I think it's paramount for people to understand the importance of letting others know if they cannot carry through with their commitment. Not only let them know, let them know as soon as possible. I think that's probably one of the best gifts you can give, Steve, and this is why. As I said earlier, I don't think people wake up thinking that they want to screw people over, excuse my English. I think they fall into that drift; they're drifting. If we can help people figure out what they really want out of life, and to be able to know what their North Star is, then they can answer specifically with a yes or a no to a commitment. Then they can actually practice it.

Lefford Fate: It's not enough to just think about it, Steve. It's necessary to actually have people practice it. When you say you're going to do something, do whatever you can to keep your word. And then if you're going to have to not keep your word, like my wife said, "Call me and tell me, and I can forgive you." When you can trust yourself and believe that you're going to do what you're going to do, then you'll be better off. But I'd almost say, tell somebody that, so they'll challenge you to help you. I'm big into giving people tools and techniques. When people can be helped to see what they should do so that they trust themselves more, I think it's going to make a powerful impact, my friend.

Steve Coplon: I appreciate you going through the journey with me. I'm going to read something. I have about 30 pages of notes here. I only have two notes that are new for this show. One is from Galatians and the other one is a Napoleon Hill quote about starting now where you're at. And if you would give us that quote, I would appreciate that. You know, I know you have that handy because it's probably in your memory.

Lefford Fate: Was that... wait, which quote are you looking for?

Steve Coplon: You know, the best time to start is now, and start where you stand.

Lefford Fate: Oh yeah.

Steve Coplon: Go ahead, just give us the paraphrase or the exact quote, whichever you prefer.

Lefford Fate:	Okay, the paraphrase, and I'll give it to you as another analogy. The two best times to plant a shade tree: the first one was 25 years ago, and the next best time is right now.
Steve Coplon:	Lefford, I'm going to give you a high five, and I'm going to give you the first, I love you man on today's show. Listeners, Lefford is a world class speaker. He has his TEDtalk, I don't know how many people now have viewed. The last count was 600,000 give or take, probably growing. Lefford's a toastmaster international, top competitor, South Carolina, finalist. Lefford knows how to tell a story. He knows how to bring it to life. He knows how to animate it. Today's show was with no preparation. Totally spontaneous. This was just a candid conversation. And I love having them with Lefford. He's my go-to guy. Lefford, that was absolutely beautiful with the shade tree.
Steve Coplon:	So, here's what we're saying. If you're a person who we helped to identify some of your character traits, and you're not so glad to look in the mirror because you realize that maybe you haven't really been honest with yourself, and you've been making too many excuses, remember Steve's your friend. Lefford is here for you also. Reach out to me at RightThink. org. I'll put you directly in touch with Lefford. If you send me some information, I'll forward it on to Lefford and he'll be there for you. We're here for you. So, break some of your bad habits. It takes a while to break a habit. It took a while to form a bad habit, and it's going to take a while to break one. But you have to start with that shade tree that you didn't plant back then.
Steve Coplon:	We're saying it's never too late. It's never too late. Forgive yourself. We can go into hours on that theme. It's about forgiveness, forgive yourself, forgive others. You know you've been wrong. That's what Napoleon Hill said in the 57th Famous Alibi, " *I know that there is something WRONG with me or I would now be where I WOULD HAVE BEEN*" And if you accept that, you can correct it. There's plenty of people out there who can help you. There's plenty of good books starting with the Bible itself. Anything else you'd like to bring up before we stop?
Lefford Fate:	Let's get on a show and talk about habits soon.
Steve Coplon:	Sounds great. Let's schedule it.
Lefford Fate:	I wrote this at the very beginning when we started talking, "The worst excuse in the world is a good excuse." If it's a terrible excuse, you put it out there. When you use excuses such as, "I'm tired, I'm old, I'm sick, I'm black, I'm tall, I'm fat, I'm rich, I'm poor," if you say this is who I am, and it's true, then you have an excuse for all kinds of negative stuff. The worst excuse is a good excuse. Don't let it hold you back. Say, "Even though I have a good excuse, I want to be better."
Steve Coplon:	Yeah, excuses are what you think are reasons. Stop with the excuses and start working toward self-improvement. Get mentors, read good books. In Lefford's book, **"Pathway to a Positive Mental Attitude"** in Chapter 12, *Teamwork, Interview with Lefford Fate*, here's what he says about himself. "I believe there is a 'why' for everyone. That each of us was created with the potential to achieve greatness, to make a difference in the world, to add value to others. And as a result, experience a full and rewarding life. For over 30 years my purpose was to defend our nation. And now that purpose is helping people discover their life's purpose and grow to their full potential."

Lefford, you're a beautiful person. Thank you for being on the show. A lot of people's lives have been enriched today by you being here. I pray that everyone listening to this show is blessed the same way I am, by having a true friend that you can love who loves you, like I have Lefford, and Lefford has me. God Bless you, and I can't wait to get back with you and talk about habits.

Lefford Fate: God Bless my friend.

Steve Coplon: Thank you, Lefford.

Steve Coplon: Thanks for listening to *Right Thinking with Steve Coplon*. I look forward to being with you again next week. Remember: ***Don't Quit, Plan Ahead, It Will Get Better.*** God Bless you and have a great week!

To listen to the original interview, scan this QR Code with your camera, or visit:
https://rightthinkingeducation.com/FromtheLiptotheHip/Chapter-2/

CHAPTER THREE

Start Doing It Right Now! with guest Richard Kay
Right Thinking With Steve Coplon - Episode 161

Steve Coplon:	Good morning. Welcome to *Right Thinking with Steve Coplon.* I'm your host, Steve Coplon. Thank you for tuning in. Let's have a great day.
Steve Coplon:	Good morning, glad to be with you. Well, today is a very special show for me. You've heard that for the umpteenth time, I know. I have one of my favorite people as my guest today, Richard Kay. Now, Richard was on the show a year and a half, maybe two years ago on Episode 37 and it was called *"Incarceration: Its Affect on Families."* And that was such a powerful show.
Steve Coplon:	Richard is one of my best friends. I want to say this real straight forward before I bring him on. He is one of the most discerning people I know, and whenever I have anything serious to discuss, I know I can go to Richard and he'll give me the right perspective. That's kind of what today's show's going to start off with, let me just give you the title of today's show.
Steve Coplon:	*"Start Doing It Right Now."* Episode 161, *Right Thinking with Steve Coplon* is very pleased to announce that this week's show is called *"Start Doing It Right Now"* with guest, Richard Kay. Tune in and hear Steve and Richard talk about obedience from a godly perspective. The habit of being obedient is so important because of its impact on your life and those around you. This show will help you change your life. It's the third in my series on *"From the Lip to the Hip is a Pretty Far Distance,"* and I've asked Richard to be on the show to give a godly perspective.
Steve Coplon:	This whole series on *"From the Lip to the Hip is a Pretty Far Distance,"* is all about people who don't do what they say they're going to do. I had Lefford Fate on last week, it was a fabulous show, titled, *"You Got That Right Steve!"* That was kind of a little humor for me and Lefford. I've got a confession to make here and Richard is the right guy for me to confess to. I don't always get it right; I never have, but I'm trying. Richard, I want to bring you on now and I want to thank you for agreeing to do this very important show. I'm trying to get past the humor, but Richard what we're going to talk about today is really important. We are talking about things that people can do to make their lives better; that's my central theme. With that said, Richard, thanks for being on the show. How are you doing today?

Richard Kay: I am doing great, Steve. Thank you for having me. Once again, we're able to try to impart some of what you've been bringing to your audience and it's just a pleasure to be able to take part in it.

Steve Coplon: Well, Richard, I've been able to broadcast for three years now, because of you. I guess you remember clearly, because you haven't been able to get rid of me! You had me as a guest on your international radio show and at the end of that show, I'll never forget it. You said, "Steve, you ought to have your own show, I'm going to help you get your own show." So, I want to thank you one more time, publicly, for getting me started in radio. We're on the 161st episode right now. You found out about a man named Jeff Heiser. You researched and found him, made the call, and introduced us. Then Jeff invited me to Talk Network Radio as a guest, and here we are.

Steve Coplon: Now Richard, what I said in the introduction about you is true. You and your wife, Ellie, are two beautiful people, I respect you so greatly. Today's subject is people doing what they say they're going to do. I really do want to get your take on it. I asked you to listen to Episode 159 on, *"From the Lip to the Hip is a Pretty Far Distance",* and I know that you did. Thank you for doing that. Did you get anything out of that show, Richard? Did I say anything that was right?

Richard Kay: A tremendous amount of value came from that episode. Being able to see how people sometimes will make a particular type of commitment, either because they don't intend to follow through or they just don't know how to say no. I think in many cases it could be the latter. But there was a lot in what you stated, especially in the area where people will use many different types of excuses to justify not following through or not doing what they have committed to.

Steve Coplon: Richard last year you and I both were contributing authors in a book titled *"GOD in Business: Faith is the Deciding Factor."* Your chapter, was titled *"The Misunderstood Call."* I want to read a couple of sentences from the middle of your chapter. "Then the Lord's voice was clear and audible. He called me by name, and this is what He said, 'Richard, you've given me everything in your life, but the right to run your business. Now I want you to go back into business, commit the business to Me, I will run the business and that will be your ministry." I would say that was a turning point in your life.

Richard Kay: Very definitely. I had been in business for quite some time, but it was always with my own direction, my own personal gain, but I kept hungering more and more for the things of God. I wanted to be able to be so much closer and to work closer with Him. At that time, I felt I was to leave business and go into training for the clergy. After many months of searching and trying to find an entry point into seminaries and Bible colleges, which ordinarily I think I would have probably had acceptance, the Lord continued to close those doors. Then finally, what you read in that chapter came about. I heard His voice and He told me to go back into business and commit the business to Him. He would run the business and that would be my ministry.

Richard Kay: It proved to be the direction that He was calling me to. I think the reason that the chapter was titled, *"The Misunderstood Call,"* is I believe that there are probably many people who are in that same category. They have looked at their business from a very secular view. They have looked at say, church attendance or their religious life in a totally different view. And it's not that at all. It certainly is the composite of both. I do not believe that there is a secular difference in a ministry. I think that we are the same whether it is on Sunday, in front of a congregation and a pulpit, or it's on Monday in front of a boardroom conducting an ethical business. I believe that it's the same individual and it's the same obedience that is being demonstrated.

Richard Kay: And that to me, is the reason why understanding the call in your life is important. Just like in your case, a person with your particular acumen, a person who has all of the financial background and accounting, in the sense of being able to help people in those areas. You take that to a population where in many ways, it's so foreign to them, and yet you show them the love and compassion that the Lord has for them, and how it has changed your direction in life. It's not so much about business, it's about what God has placed in your heart for you to be able to impart the information and its application to the population. I commend you for that because I'm sure that was quite a change in your life. You were perhaps following a different direction and then you realized this is really your ministry.

Richard Kay: This is your obedience to God. Wherever He leads, the doors He opens and the places He takes you, you are finding more and more that He is blessing that obedience. And to me, that is probably the essence of what we are doing, in obedience to what God says for us to do. In your case, it can be reaching in many facets, a population that is forgotten. In others, it could be helping the poor. It could be multifaceted things, but they don't have to be separated from religious life and secular life. It's all one life and it's a life that we want to be able to live in obedience to the Lord Jesus.

Steve Coplon: Thank you Richard, that was absolutely beautiful. We had a preliminary conversation earlier about the direction the show would cover. I'm doing this series and I expect to have ten or eleven friends, talk about the basic theme that I started with. It's very universal, it's a life theme for me. It's about honoring your commitment, doing what you say you're going to do. That's the basis, we're going to have Don Price, a businessman, banker be a guest. That's also the basis for credit. Honoring what you say you are going to do, honoring your good name. But with you Richard, you honed in on obedience after listening to the show *"From the Lip to the Hip is a Pretty Far Distance,"* and people doing what they say they're going to do.

Steve Coplon: The main takeaway you said you got from the episode was related to obedience and being close to the Lord and doing what's right. That's why I gave it the title, *"Start Doing It Right Now!"* But Richard, the theme can also go in this direction; not everybody does what they say they are going to do for a lot of reasons. Lefford brought out last week, some of what you echoed today. A lot of times people say they are going to do something because they don't know how to say no. That is a very valid excuse, but I started with all the different excuses people make to not do something they say they're going to do.

Steve Coplon: It's not just in regard to their interaction with other people. It's also in regard to what their own goals are that they put off, and they don't ever do what they say they're going to do, for themselves. Then, after a period of time they have a very low self-esteem because they look in the mirror and realize, "I'm not what I want to be, I can't even trust myself because I say I'm going to do this and then I don't do it. I get distracted." Now, I've laid that out pretty carefully. You had said that it's very important for people in their relationship with the Lord to be obedient because it affects themselves and their interaction with other people. Can you talk more about how obedience to the Lord, and success in life go hand in glove?

Richard Kay: I think the primary lesson we learn in obedience is, in many cases we have been taught to sacrifice something in our life. And I'm not saying that it can't be applied, but obedience is really worth more than sacrifice. God is not interested in what we perhaps can give Him. He does not need anything that we have to provide Him. It's the other way around. He is blessing us and providing everything we need. But, acknowledging his direction and doing what He says, is the learning process of obedience. I used an example when we were talking earlier in that, there's a cliché, if you will, that slow obedience is really no obedience. And how does that impact our own life and the lives of others?

Scripture Says

"To know to do good and not do it to that person, that's a sin."

Richard Kay: Why would that be a sin? We know that we need to do something that would be right, if we avoid doing it, it is almost the equivalent of disobeying or doing something wrong. In God's view, I believe that He looks at the heart and He takes us, as we are. He expects us to acknowledge His direction and do what He says. I mentioned to you sometime back that my prayer life is not as verbose, as maybe some people would think. It's not so much that I'm looking at other people's approval of the way I pray. To me that is the least important. The essence of my prayer life is I want to surrender to God. I want to be willing to do what He says and to be obedient. It's like if I know that I'm supposed to do something and yet I avoid doing it, or I put it off for perhaps a period of time, am I truly being obedient?

Richard Kay: And, I become more and more aware, especially in a situation such as prayer. I'll give you just a simple example. One aspect of it, is you meet someone who has a particular need. And the general form of trying to address their need is to say, "I'll pray for you." Now I'm not saying that it isn't a genuine statement, but I'm saying that in many cases that is not satisfactory for the need. There may be other things that are required besides, just praying. But praying can open the door to our obedience to the other responses. So rather than saying to the individual, "I'll pray for you." It's a much easier thing for some to say, "Can I pray for you now?" And in that particular way you bring that person and their need into the present. You're addressing it, as it is important to them. Now there may be other things that need to be accomplished, other resources that need to be sought, but the first step is to let them know you care, and you care enough to pray for them right now.

Richard Kay: So that's a part of obedience in its application where you're confronted with a particular circumstance and you need to be able to address it at that moment. There have been many times that I've had people inform me of a health situation or a condition, or something that was going on in their life and they were accustomed to other people responding almost in a sense of, "Gee, I'm sorry for you, I'll pray for you." When that same type of situation presented itself to me, I learned then and am still learning, that the time for prayer was right then and there. It was the opportunity to have a connection with that individual in a way that God moves, because they understand you're doing something that is not necessarily convenient and it's also not necessarily what they would expect. However, it is addressing their need, and that part is just applying a timeframe for obedience.

Richard Kay: So, when is the best time to pray for the needs of others? As soon as we find out that there is a need. Then there's always the continual seeking of God's wisdom in what He wants to accomplish in that situation. So, the beginning step is to pray right then. The second part is to hear what God says about administering to that need, in whatever manner necessary. So, I think that is one illustration we could use. I have another that demonstrates slow obedience, or as we say, no obedience. And I can do this simply on my own experience. It happened rather recently, and I was in route to, believe it or not, a prayer breakfast and there were going to be many, many people there. It was a church gathering and there was a group of men at that particular breakfast. I was driving down the street on the way to the church, and I drove past a homeless man who had a sign saying he was hungry and homeless.

Richard Kay: Now, of course he was on the opposite side of the street. It would have been an inconvenience for me to have stopped to be in contact with him. But, the justification for it was, I'm going in the other direction and he's on the opposite side of the street. As I'm continuing in the same direction, I sensed the Lord saying to me, "Stop and go back to this homeless man." And I didn't do it. I continued driving. The word came much more intensified, "Stop and go back." So, within the next few moments, I stopped, I turned around, I drove the car back in the other direction, I parked in the parking lot adjacent to where he was. I left my vehicle and I walked over to him and I asked him, I said, "Are you hungry?" And he said, "Yes." And I said, "Well, come and go with me and we'll get you fed."

Richard Kay: And quickly he picked up the little bucket he was sitting on, and he put it in the back of my vehicle, and he got inside, and we drove to the prayer breakfast. I introduced him to all the people that were there, probably a hundred plus people, and it was interesting. Had I not stopped; I may not have had the opportunity to reach out to this particular homeless individual. But it showed me something. It showed me that I could have gone on ahead and continued with my plan to go to the prayer breakfast. But that would have been disobedient to what the Lord wanted. He wanted that man to be shown compassion and acceptance.

Richard Kay: Here he was, this stranger. When he came into that particular group, no one knew he was homeless, and no one knew he had other needs. But, here he was, and we could show him care and compassion. That has progressed so that we can see, as I mentioned earlier, there was a time to address the need and then God could reveal more of what He wanted to do. But the question is, what if I hadn't gone back? I would have been disobedient. God was merciful in stopping me and telling me to go back. But I could have continued on. I could have arrived at the prayer breakfast, participated in the entire function, but I would have been very guilty and very disobedient. I would have had to ask the Lord for forgiveness, because going back to the situation we talked about earlier, knowing to do good and not doing it, to that person, it is sin.

Richard Kay: I knew that I had to do something. I didn't know what it was, but I had to reach out to this individual, and show him the love and compassion of God. And thankfully, God was gracious and merciful and allowed me to experience that. But there had been times that I have actually passed someone in a similar situation and have gone well past that distance and then felt convicted of it, turned around and they weren't there anymore. I missed that opportunity. I don't want to be in a process of missing opportunities to be obedient to God.

Steve Coplon: Wow, Richard, that is beautiful. I want to ask you, when he was getting in the car, did he know you were a pastor? Or that you were taking him to a prayer breakfast? You took him there, with 100 people, and when he got there, what was his reaction? Did he stay the whole time?

Richard Kay: Yes, he did because I actually was his ride back. But I think more importantly he was able to participate with the other men and there was no difference. I mean, they may have had homes or apartments to live in and he didn't. But he was still a man, he had the same needs that we all have. And the greatest need was to know that he was accepted, to know that God had not just set him aside regardless of what his life circumstance might've been. He needed to know that God truly cared for him. And I think that to a great degree, that was achieved. Nobody was so concerned that he was homeless.

Richard Kay: It was shared at our particular table and a man who works with homeless people, extended his help to him. That brings about yet another part of the topic. And that's the response of the people we extend ourselves to, in obedience to God. They don't always respond in the way that we think they should, and sometimes it's disappointing, but we still have to be obedient.

Steve Coplon: Richard, when you were relating that story, you brought me back in my mind just now. I've never been "homeless, homeless" to where I didn't have a place I could go, but I have been blessed in my life with friends allowing me to stay with them from time to time. When I lived in Richmond, I went to VCU, I dropped out of Old Dominion University back in 1971, I think it was, and I had a couple of friends who let me stay with them for three weeks. The second time I stayed at my mother's house for about three months when I dropped out of college.

Steve Coplon: I actually had a bed, but I came back and camped out at my mom's. I've been taken in a lot of times by a lot of people and shown the love that you're talking about. I will never forget it, I think it's demonstrating to the listeners why I said what I said about you being so close to me and Donna, and that you're such a discerning godly man. That is why I've asked you to participate on this show today. There was one example during my Richmond years, when my mother once told me, "Stevie, I got four kids and you're the only one who put all these gray hairs on my head. The others didn't put a single one of these gray hairs on me. They're all from you."

Steve Coplon: And I said, "Oh, you honor me mom. Thank you." No, I'm just joking there, but the point is, I was working as the accountant/bookkeeper while I was in college for a father/son owned drapery company. A small manufacturing workshop, they called it a sweatshop. They were interior decorators and they had 12 people working who would make draperies, slipcovers, and other things. They got into tremendous trouble, with the Internal Revenue Service. The Internal Revenue Service came in and chained their doors shut. I'm only saying this because I do financial consulting and I just want people to know a little bit about my background. I'm not a straightforward conventional financial consultant. You and I both care about people and have done a lot to help them. So, they padlocked their door with a chain, and basically put them out of business, unless they paid a sizeable amount of money on back payroll taxes.

Steve Coplon:	Well, they had some very wealthy relatives whom they had borrowed money from once before, and they said, "Well, we'll just go borrow money from them again." They said, I'll never forget this, it was the John Marshall Hotel in Richmond, Virginia. We had this meeting and these relatives were irate. They said, "You've come to us again. You didn't pay back the first time. You're in the same position and you're squandering the money. You're not dependable. You didn't do what you said you were going to do." The son was not living right, he got involved in drugs and other things and the company was in trouble. The 72-year-old father had suicide notes on his chair that I would see when I would arrive in the morning.
Steve Coplon:	So, we are in this hotel room and they needed about $55,000 to settle up with the Internal Revenue Service and back in 1974, that's a lot of money. (It still is.) Anyway, the relatives were irate that they were even asking for another bail out, because they had taken money the first time and not done right with it. And what they said was, "If Steve will agree to be your manager and handle this money and your affairs, we'll loan you the money." They asked me because they trusted me, "Will you sign a contract to do that?" What I ended up saying was, "I'm not going to sign a contract, but I will take the assignment." And I dropped out of college because I needed to work full time for them. I was six weeks from graduating college, but I probably wasn't going to pass anyway.
Steve Coplon:	The point is, I decided that my life vocation is to be able to help people through financial management and affairs like that. When I dropped out, I made the choice that I can put off my education for a while because I've got a real-life circumstance here that needs me. If I had not agreed to it, they would have been out of business. I did it for those 12 people who worked for the company, not just for the two owners. And so that was the direction of my life, Richard. I dropped out of college, I was out for a whole year before I went back. My mother was pretty upset that I dropped out, but she complimented me when I told her the whole story. I turned this company around, and they got everything straight and they moved forward successfully.
Steve Coplon:	I think that sometimes people think they want to be a certain kind of person, but when they have the opportunity, they don't see it. And so, I don't know if that's a decent example for what you just talked about, but I knew that these people needed me; I did what was necessary and I did turn it around. Life doesn't have to be on the same path or timeframe that everybody else takes. But what I do want to tell you is, sometimes people will put their own desires, wants, and needs ahead of other people, and they miss an opportunity that would have been far, far better. That's the third thing that I got out of what you said a minute ago.
Steve Coplon:	A lot of people ask the question, why do people not do what they say they are going to do? Why do people make a commitment and not follow through with it? I think one of the key reasons is that they're quite selfish and they're afraid that if they take the time to do that, it's taking away from something else that they might rather do for themselves. Does that make sense to you, Richard?
Richard Kay:	I believe that obedience is something we learn and I'm not sure everybody's motive is purely selfish. I guess in some ways yes, but it is not wrong to consider your needs in many cases ahead of the needs of others. But it is far better to realize that your needs are met so that you can help meet the needs of others. There is a learning process. One of the things that you

said when you dropped out of school and served in the capacity of helping this company actually function and become solvent again. They expected you would sign a contract, that you would commit to them. But in reality, you were probably exercising simple obedience to what God had presented to you. You set aside your own plan for being able to finish school, and you helped these people.

Richard Kay: I'm sure that they appreciated it, but more so, you probably learned something in that process. Being that you were obedient to what God set before you at that time, and He took care of the rest. When you were able to finish the work with that particular company, you were able to return to school and finish your plan of education. God had prepared a way, but the lesson that you learned and the lesson that we learn going through obedience is, we become a different person. We actually are becoming more like Him. And what you said earlier about being selfish, people not wanting to do what they say because they're selfish and they don't want their plans to be changed for the plans of others, that could be in some ways a part of that.

Richard Kay: I think it is more important that we learn, from a positive view, that God is really merciful. He's really willing to teach us if we're willing to listen and obey. And He is more willing for us to learn that in many cases. So, He gives us countless opportunities to find out. This is what is expected. This is what it means to love Me. Because He says, "If you love me, you're going to keep My commands." And I think the simplest command is we love God with all of our heart, all our soul and all of our mind. But He says that there's a second commandment, which is actually tied to that and it is that we're to love our neighbor as our self.

Richard Kay: If God puts such emphasis on how we are to show love one to another, then obedience is looking for the ways He opens avenues for us to demonstrate that kind of love. It's not so much what we say, it's what we live before the people that see us. They learn more from what we do, than from just what we say.

Steve Coplon: Richard, I just love the conversation. When you talked earlier about praying now and not putting it off, I can't tell the listeners the number of times that you and I have communicated or talked in a personal way about what's going on in our lives, and you have said, "Steve, can we pray now?" or "let's pray." I mean, it's just that natural. There hasn't been one time in the three and a half, four years we've been friends, that your prayer hasn't given me a certain kind of hope. It brought me closer to the Lord, is what I'm trying to say. It's cleared me to where all of a sudden, everything was put into perspective and I had a clear focus on what was going on.

Steve Coplon: And you know, when it comes right down to it, I think this explains what we're talking about, when people don't do what they say they're going to do and how it hurts themselves, or it hurts others that they've inconvenienced. Some are just sad because they might want to do what they promised, but they just can't get up to doing it because they're afraid to. They have inertia, or whatever the reason may be that stops them.

Steve Coplon: I'm not at all saying that everybody who doesn't do what they say they're going to do is a bad person. What I am saying, is that if a person has a life pattern, and does not have the habit that you're speaking to, of following through or being obedient, then they are probably going to have a rough time.

We're tying obedience to the Lord and trusting the Lord into doing right by what you say you're going to do. If a person doesn't follow through and others know them as someone who habitually doesn't tell the truth, and if their personality is that they talk a lot but don't do what they say they're going to do, they're not going to get very far or be successful in life. Because they're not going to have trust.

Steve Coplon: Now, one of my daily scriptures for myself is:

Proverbs 3:5-6.

"Trust in the Lord with all your heart and lean not on your own understanding. In all your ways acknowledge Him and He will make your paths straight."

Steve Coplon: Maybe some people listening to this spend a lot of time on the streets, because that might be where they call home. Your street credit is not going to be very good if everybody knows you as someone who never does what you say you're going to do. You cannot go, far in life, just within yourself. Whether or not it's for selfish reasons, just to get what you want but not care about others. So that's part of it. My mother gave me the reality of life that, "Stevie, you can't depend on everybody. Not everybody does what they say they're going to do."

Steve Coplon: Okay. Talk is cheap. But another way to look at it is, talk can also be conversation. Conversation is one of the greatest things that we can ever have and it's absolutely free. I've always enjoyed a good conversation, I'm a people person, everybody knows that. I've got 161 episodes where we talk for close to an hour. We can do it all day long. I love conversation with people, I love getting to know people, I love being there for people. That's who I am. But the point is, I believe that if we ever have the opportunity to do something for someone else, by all means we should try our very best to fit that in.

Steve Coplon: One of my laws of my life is, whenever anybody seeks me out for conversation, counsel, or to spend time with me, I try to do it. Because I think that's the most important thing in life for me, is to be there for others. Richard, you are always there for me. But the concept of trust is what I'm talking about. If people get to where they are not trustworthy, they're going to have a hard time going through life. They're going to find out that their life today is not going to be much different than five years from now. In 10 years, maybe worse. You are not going to get far in life if you're not a person who can be trusted.

Steve Coplon: Would you try to simplify this point of view? I mean, what you have said is absolutely beautiful. I think people will get a great deal out of this conversation. It's what I knew it was going to be, Richard. It's from a godly perspective. Would you try to relate obedience to God and developing that habit to having success and good experiences in life?

Richard Kay: Well, I think that a lot of what is defined as success in a worldview is not necessarily the same as success in a godly view. And the tendency is to measure success by material gain, and I'm not saying that material wealth is wrong. I'm simply saying if we measure our success by that instrument alone, we probably miss some of the greatest lessons that are taught when we don't have that material gain. When we draw closer to God it's very much the method of being able to decide, do we have a need? In this particular timeframe, the world is very shaky. It's very unsure about what is going to take place next.

Richard Kay: We have what's recently been called a pandemic, a pestilence, a disease, a virus that has impacted and affected lives throughout the whole world. And there's a tremendous amount of uncertainty. But we're going to suffer those things in this life. This is a fallen world. It's a world that has in so many ways rejected a relationship with the God that created it.

Richard Kay: So, as we come into that relationship, we begin to understand that it is not just the material wealth that we have, or what we contain that matters in God's perspective.

Scripture Says,

"Godliness with contentment is great gain."

Richard Kay: And I believe that that is crucial as we come into an obedient relationship with the Lord. Our issue is not so much what we have to give up or what we may not attain because it's not man's measurement that we are actually being evaluated by. God's measurement, God's evaluation is much better. He's not interested in only what we can achieve.

Richard Kay: In fact, He's not only interested in what we think we can achieve for Him, He's more interested in what He can achieve through us. And there is a difference. For a long time in business, I wanted to do great things for God, which could have meant achieving goals that were set before me. But I wanted to do that for God. That was me saying that I wanted to do something that I felt was pleasing God. But He made me realize that He was not as interested in what I can do for Him. He was more interested in what I would surrender of myself and allow Him to do through me. And I think that's the same essence of what He is instructing your listeners to do. As well as, what He's done in your life. He's more interested in how He can touch others through you than He is in what you can do to make others see Him.

Richard Kay: And that's a very close correlation, but I do believe that as we draw closer and closer to Him, He helps us to actually live in that manner. We become what He created us to be. The image of Him. We become more and more like Him. And He is the quintessential description of obedience. Here, He is all mighty God and He sets aside his divinity and becomes a man so that He can live and learn what it is that men have to go through because they have sin. And He does it without sin, in perfect obedience, and then something unbelievable takes place, He dies.

Richard Kay: All the sin of the world is placed on Him. He's obedient unto death so that He can be the pattern of the way that we are to live. A life that is completely surrendered to Him. I mentioned to someone very recently, that it is more important that I am obedient to Him, than it is that I achieve all the world's goals. Because if I'm obedient to Him, I have His peace. He provides all my needs and more. He gives me the ability to be used for Him. What a wonderful life to let God use us individually to touch the lives of others? To me that is learned obedience, surrendering our own agenda, our own plan so that God can accomplish His through us.

Steve Coplon: Wow! I'm not speechless, I'm just humbled because I asked the question and you gave it an answer and I thank you for that.

Scripture Says,

"I am the Way, the Truth and the Life."

Steve Coplon: I want to close the show with that. What we have been talking about today is being truthful. When a person says they are going to do something, doing what they say they are going to do, it's all about being a truthful person. You brought it all together. You brought obedience to the truth. I will end the show with this: Jesus is the Way, the Truth, and the Life. Richard, I want to thank you for sharing and talking today on what we talked about. I love you; I appreciate you. Is there anything you would like to say before we get off the air?

Richard Kay: The only thing I can say is thank you that you are devoting the time to address these very important life issues with your listeners. And you know, Steve, if you will, this is your pulpit. This is the place where you can be heard. But more importantly, this is a place where God can be able to be heard through you. And I appreciate being able to be a part of your life in the direction that the Lord has taken you. I had said this to you many times before, but I hope that it bears the same message. I had mentioned to you when we first got together, and you shared some of the needs that you had and things that you were going through. And if you remember I said, "Steve, I'm going to be available to you."

Richard Kay: As much as I possibly could, regardless of where you or I may have been, we have tried to maintain that type of contact. And I hope that I have been true to that commitment of being available. Even more so, the availability is also giving me the opportunity to speak into or to be utilized in the way that the Lord is taking you, and I consider that a great privilege. So, I thank you for the opportunity to be able to demonstrate obedience in our relationship.

Steve Coplon: Richard, I think we have accomplished what we set out to do today. I am just elated, overjoyed from the way we have covered this topic today. The Lord's been present. The Holy Spirit spoke today. I pray that everyone listening to this show will be so blessed to have a friend like I have in Richard Kay. God Bless you Richard. Everybody have a wonderful week and I will see you next week.

Steve Coplon: Thanks for listening to *Right Thinking with Steve Coplon*. I look forward to being with you again next week. Remember: ***Don't Quit, Plan Ahead, It Will Get Better.*** God Bless you and have a great week!

To listen to the original interview, scan this QR Code with your camera, or visit:

https://rightthinkingeducation.com/FromtheLiptotheHip/Chapter-3/

CHAPTER FOUR

In Order To Achieve You Must Believe In Yourself with guest Reginald Ponton
Right Thinking With Steve Coplon - Episode 162

Steve Coplon: Good morning. Welcome to *Right Thinking with Steve Coplon*. I'm your host, Steve Coplon. Thank you for tuning in. Let's have a great day!

Steve Coplon: Good morning. Glad to be with you. This is going to be a really special show. I've got a wonderful guest, a friend of mine who I've worked with in the past. Today's show is Episode 162 and it's called *"In Order to Achieve, You Must Believe in Yourself."* Right Thinking with Steve Coplon is very pleased to announce that this week's show is called *"In Order to Achieve, You Must Believe in Yourself,"* with guest Reginald Ponton. Tune in and hear Steve and Reginald, a former cognitive counselor for the Virginia Department of Corrections, share valuable insights on how incarcerated individuals can best move forward toward a better life as productive, contributing members of society.

Steve Coplon: I want to thank Reginald for participating. I'm going to tell you a whole lot more about how I met Reginald and what he does. Let me bring him on now. Reginald, are you with us?

Reginald Ponton: Yes sir, thank you for having me on the show, Steve.

Steve Coplon: Reginald, it is an honor. You're a wonderful person and you have a tremendous amount of wisdom that needs to be shared. I've been waiting to do a show with a person who has been working inside correctional facilities. Someone who knows exactly what goes on, how it works, what the goals are, and what the programs are. You are the absolute best person I could have invited to be on the show. You were at Brunswick Women's Work Center for a number of years, as the head of the cognitive community in the workforce development area. You honored me by allowing for me to come in and work with your women for a couple of years. I probably went into your prison at least 80 or 90 times, maybe more. Of all the people I have ever worked with inside prisons, I've enjoyed you more than anyone. We went to a Washington Nationals game once and had a good time on a day off, didn't we?

Reginald Ponton: Yes sir, we sure did.

Steve Coplon: Reginald, I have learned so much from you and you were such a wonderful person to work with. What I loved the most about working with you inside the prison was, how much you loved everyone who was incarcerated there. You cared so much about each one of those ladies as an individual person. I just loved how you brought me in, to work with the women who you were in charge of there; to try to help them prepare for their release. How long ago did we work together in the reentry program?

Reginald Ponton: Steve, I think that was a good little while ago. It was about 10 years ago when I came to Brunswick. It was 2010 and I stayed there 'til about 2014 so between those four years, that's when we were working together.

Steve Coplon: It would have been in 2012 then because that is when I started coming into prisons. So, we worked together in 2012, 2013 and 2014. Let me read something. I am not sure everybody caught why I am so excited to have you on the show. We've got a chance today with you, Reginald, to talk about what's being done inside the prisons for people who are incarcerated. The approach is to try to help them come out of prison, return to society, and never go back. The goal is to bring them out and help them become productive, contributing members of society. The politically correct word is to call them returning citizens.

Steve Coplon: Let me read something I pulled off of the Virginia Department of Corrections website today. *"The Virginia Department of Corrections is a model correctional agency and a proven innovative leader in the profession. Virginia is a safer place to live and work because the department provides appropriate custody, supervision, and programs for offenders through its exemplary services. The employees of the department are the cornerstone of the agency. They share a common purpose and a commitment to the highest professional standards in excellence in public service. The department, through its unwavering commitment to its employees, is a satisfying and rewarding place to work and grow professionally."*

Steve Coplon: Well, Reginald, Virginia has always been the leader in lowering recidivism. The national average of recidivism hovers around 70%. We're talking about those people who are incarcerated, they get out, and they can't make it on the outside. They end up committing a crime, get convicted and go back into prison. Virginia's been in the low 20% range for quite a long time now. For a while, I know they were the number one lowest recidivism in the country. And as that little blurb I just read states, it is because they have the highest quality employees. Reginald, you're at the very tip-top of who they're talking about. I worked with you for a couple straight years there, and I can tell you that not only were you respected by the department, I saw that you were also respected by the women there. It was a women's prison. You've worked in other prisons, but I had the pleasure to work with and be trained by you in a women's prison. It was your respect for the women that impressed me the most. What was it like being in there?

Reginald Ponton: It was a challenge, but it was a reward and an opportunity for me. A lot of times they say working with the female population can be rather challenging. But, I kind of feel like that's not correct, because I feel with the women population, they more easily buy into the process. And when they buy into the process, you're able to get them to understand and learn about what the DOC can offer them. They also learn what the DOC can do to help them in their rehabilitation, so that they can successfully transition back into society.

Our goals were about, rehabilitation. We were trying to equip ourselves with the tools that we felt a returning citizen would need to have that smooth transition back into society. I enjoyed working with the female population.

Reginald Ponton: Matter of fact, I learned a lot from them, whether or not they learned anything from me. That's something that we have to step back and look at, because many feel we can't learn from people who are incarcerated. But, we truly can, because they're going through a process in life that not everyone can walk through. You discover how some of them actually went through tough obstacles in life, and yet they still have the ability to come in and want to take that opportunity or take that chance to change themselves. I was enlightened by that. Sometimes we throw in the towel and give up very easily. But some of those individuals in there, have strong hearts, minds, and souls and want to make a difference. I enjoy working with them because the good Lord has helped me get to where I'm at, and it's about helping people.

Reginald Ponton: In that business, if you don't have the mindset of helping people, then you are not going to be very effective in what you do.

Steve Coplon: That's well said, and you are correct about being enlightened. I've told many people, I have very few regrets in life. One regret is that more people couldn't share the experiences I've had from working in prisons. Since I started, I've received so much training from you, and I am grateful that you have taught me so much about the prison population. I actually developed programs based on your suggestions on how to fine tune my program and add helpful modules. Some of the most wonderful people I've ever met in my life were people incarcerated in prison. A lot of people do not understand that there's some really good people there, who happened to make mistakes in their life, and they paid quite a price for it.

Steve Coplon: I want to refer back to something before we go too much further. This show we're doing, and the reason I invited you to be on, is because I started a series back on Episode 159. The title *"From the Lip to the Hip is a Pretty Far Distance,"* was a phrase that my mother taught me. It basically meant that people don't always do what they say they're going to do. So, it gave me this idea to do a series. I invite people to be on the show who I greatly respect, who have real wisdom. I would ask them to listen to that one episode, #159, and then tell me if they got anything from it? Did anything I say make sense? And then we would just take the conversation from there. It's kind of a universal thing, for some people not to do what they say they're going to do, for any number of reasons. Then they leave the people who are depending on them with just an excuse as to why they couldn't do what they said.

Steve Coplon: So, I sought you out and I asked you, if you would honor me and be on this show, you accepted, and I thank you. Today's theme is to focus on people not doing what they say they're going to do. Did you get a chance to listen to that show?

Reginald Ponton: I listened to Episode 159 and it was very inspiring. It was very inspiring to me, because when you talk about from the lip to the hip, and you're talking about people doing what they're supposed to do, that goes a long way because whether you know it or not, it's almost like if there are people trusting in you, are you trustworthy? Because if you say you're going to do something, then you need to be accountable to that. But the thing that really caught my attention was when you gave the examples about making the excuses. It really kind of honed in on me. I know at times in life, some of those excuses that you named in the show, were a reflection back on me because I have made some of those excuses myself. What people need to realize is something I always say, "In order to achieve, you must believe in yourself," and it's so true. Whether we know it or not, we can accomplish pretty much anything in life if we put our mind to it.

Reginald Ponton: That episode really caught my attention... and I just want to look at how I travel through life. I went through a lot of challenges, but because I made a commitment to myself and said I'm going to do something, and when I did it, everything fell in place. People need to understand that you must be honest with yourself when you make statements about things you want to have happen in your life. That is the beginning point, where your thoughts are going to help you grow in life and help you deal with struggles. If you aren't honest with yourself, then you might not get to your dream job or dream trip, or whatever it may be that you want to accomplish in life. I think that's what was very important to me when I listened to, *"From the Lip to the Hip is a Pretty Far Distance,"* and basically doing what you said you're going to do.

Steve Coplon: When you called me and we had a pre-conversation about how this interview was going to go, you said some beautiful things to me, and I greatly appreciate that. One thing you said was, "I really liked the way that you took *Napoleon Hill's, "Fifty-Seven Famous Alibis By Old Man IF"* and laid out most of the excuses people give. In fact, it all comes from Scripture and being a Godly man." It meant so much to me when you said that, being the Godly man that you are. I want to read one of the quotes I read in that show, and this was from a book that I recommended called *"The Strangest Secret"*, by *Earl Nightingale*, one of the greatest motivational speakers ever. He quoted from the Bible:

Matthew 7:7-8

Ask and it shall be given you. Seek and you shall find. Knock and it shall be opened unto you. For everyone that asketh, receiveth, and he that seeketh, findeth. And to him that knocketh, it shall be opened.

Steve Coplon: This scripture relates to exactly what you said just now, "When you make up your mind to believe, nothing is impossible." Let's talk about this statement some more. You said, "If you're going to achieve anything, you better believe in yourself." I hope when people listen to this show it will help them find a new direction. I think there is some disconnect in the world. We know that you've got to believe to achieve. We're going to talk about that later on.

Here is the very last scripture from Episode 159,

Proverbs 3:6

"Listen for God's voice in everything you do. Everywhere you go. He's the one that will keep you on track."

Steve Coplon: Well, here's the disconnect. I think it's splitting hairs or something for people to say that believing in yourself is wrong. This is where religion gets mixed up in my mind. I'm going to share a psalm with you, it goes hand in hand with what you said. I just don't like that some people might say, "No, no, no. You can't listen to a guy like Reginald or Steve when they say how important it is to believe in yourself." Reginald, one thing we know from working with people is that, we can't make them do anything. They have to make up their own mind, and until they make up their own mind, we're not going to be able to help them. Here's the psalm:

Psalm 18:32-34

It is God who equipped me with strength and made my way blameless. He made my feet like the feet of deer and set me secure on the hike. He trains my hands for war so that my arms can bend a bow of bronze.

Steve Coplon: What I'm saying is, I think anyone who disagrees with this statement, "You need to believe to achieve", is a little mixed up and needs to reconsider. Reginald, I'd like you to speak to it, but here's what I think we are saying,

Steve Coplon: Of course, you have got to turn to the Lord to get your direction and to know everything that you're supposed to be, to surrender to him, and to honor him. But once we make that commitment and are there for him, we still have a lot of work to do. He gives us gifts, and we have to use those gifts. We can't just sit back on a couch and pray and expect our life to turn around simply because we pray to God. That's what the book of James is all about. Faith without works is dead. But let me just turn that whole mouthful over to you for a minute. Because I totally agree with what you said. It's up to each one of us to turn to the Lord to get our strength, but then we have to apply it. And that is a Napoleon Hill concept called "Applied Faith."

Steve Coplon: You've got to put it into action. We have got to use those gifts. What do you think about that?

Reginald Ponton: You know, I totally agree with you on that, Steve, and I'm going to give you some statistics I learned since working in corrections. People may not understand how a lot of returning citizens come back into society and end up being very successful. 98% of those individuals had chosen to turn their life over to Christ. When that information was shared with me, I thought it was amazing. When I talk about "In order to achieve, you've got to believe," a lot of people may struggle with believing what Christ can do for us. One thing I tell people is, life is like an investment. What you put into it is what you're going to get out of it. So, if you look at building that relationship with God as an investment and take the initiative to give yourself to Him; what you put in and give to Him, what He gives you in return, is just amazing.

Reginald Ponton: I know a lot of times some people struggle with this, and everyone has their own opinion, on how they interpret it. At some point in life, someone may have an incident that opens their eyes and makes them see things differently. Then, they may make a change. That's one of the main things we must realize when we're walking in society right now.

Reginald Ponton: When I think about our society, I think about how I want to be remembered. Think about that in totality. Begin to examine and assess that; Do you want to be remembered as a person who made an impact somewhere? I learned that the times when I did not have a strong relationship with God, is when things didn't really click like they were supposed to.

Reginald Ponton: It's amazing that He can put you in certain situations where you can be able to help others. The most important and great thing that has happened in my life is when I started working in corrections. If you think about it Steve, if I hadn't worked in corrections, we would not know each other. The most beautiful thing I loved about it, is when I began to network with so many different types of people outside of the Department of Corrections. I learned how they had such good hearts and also wanted to help people.

Reginald Ponton: Sometimes we can get distracted or get sidetracked from things, however, it's all about the heart. Like I told you, I'm going to speak from the heart. In my heart, I believe that I'm here for a reason. I'm here to do something that God wants me to do. One thing I feel like He did was put me in a place to try to help people. I don't want to be selfish with the help that I give. I want to be unselfish with it. Whatever new knowledge that I've learned, I can pass on to someone to help them better themselves as well as others. Likewise, others can pass on virtues to help me better myself. I think that's the most beautiful thing, Steve. That's one of the reasons why I can say I enjoy working with you. That's how you were when you came in and spoke with the population, from your heart.

Reginald Ponton: You came in and you shared what you wanted to do, you had a mission and a vision. Today, you have actually accomplished those things that you started and wanted to do, because you really wanted to be an asset to the department. You have a lot of resources that you can share with the population. I think the DOC did a great valuable service for those women by giving you the opportunity to come in and speak from your heart. That's something I loved about corrections. When I started in 2004, there weren't a lot of resources coming through the doors and being provided to the population.

Reginald Ponton: When I first came to DOC, I think the recidivism rate was probably around 27, maybe 28%. Once the department began to make some positive changes and offer more resources, the recidivism rate improved. They began to focus on evidence-based practice and what necessary resources and programs they needed to implement. When they found out about the cognitive community program, they did research on it and then implemented a pilot program. When they saw the success of it, they continued the program as part of the curriculum.

Reginald Ponton: It's an excellent program. I think any department of corrections could incorporate this within their system and train their people properly, which would benefit the staff and population a lot. Presenting this type of program to the population, such as learning how to write a resume, or going through mock interviews, are very valuable learning tools. They have individuals such as yourself coming in to talk about financial planning and budgeting. They brought in Probation and Parole Officers to explain what to expect and what was going to be expected of them. They brought in a host of resources from the department of social services and child enforcement. These individuals, shared with the population, and answered their questions. They educated them on how to deal with things when they walked out. I think that was so important because, one thing I realized about the population, that most people don't understand is, a lot of them are very scared. They feared walking outside those gates, because when they walked outside the gates, there would be so much pressure put upon them. They ask themselves how can I come out of here and be responsible? How can I stand on my own two feet and be able to take care of myself?

Reginald Ponton: I think DOC looked at that and said, "Hey, look. What can we do best for this population?" You read the DOC's mission earlier in this program. They are really standing by the mission statement and doing what they say they are going to do. They're trying to provide them as much opportunity as they can for a smooth transition and hopefully to become successful. Another great aspect I also loved about DOC is when those returning citizens went out in society and became successful, the Department of Corrections allowed them to come back in and share their testimonies.

Reginald Ponton: When you look at rehabilitation, by seeing and hearing what others have been able to accomplish upon release, I feel it brings a certain level of confidence to the inmates. If they can do it, so can I attitude. I feel like that's the best evidence-based practice you can ever have. You're showing how these individuals went through this program and learned the skill sets they needed to incorporate within themselves to return to society and become successful. Once they re-entered society and became successful, they then could come back and share with the population by saying, "Hey, these tools really work." They share how in the beginning they didn't believe in it, and then came to be a believer. That's where it goes back to, "In order to achieve, you've got to believe."

Reginald Ponton: Once those people started to believe in it, they walked into society and began to achieve those things they wanted to accomplish in life. They started to reach their goals. The most wonderful thing that made me feel so great about the job I was doing, was that I could see the results. When you see that you've made a difference in someone's life by helping them get to the next level, it feels even better when they come back to share their success story. There isn't a better feeling than learning that you helped provide someone with this gift. Then hopefully, they can pass it along to someone else.

Reginald Ponton: God teaches us how to be more about giving, I think if a lot of us would really think about what we do, we would realize we could do more. I went to a graveside service and the pastor said, "Life is an opportunity, an opportunity to do good, and you know, we get this opportunity the one time and we need to make the best of it." I feel if we really begin to learn and educate ourselves more, we could all help more people. I love those scriptures that you just shared. They are very powerful and they're on point. I look at your slogan, *"From the Lip to the Hip, is a Pretty Far Distance,"* and doing what you say you're going to do and my topic about, *"In Order to Achieve, You Must Believe in Yourself"*. I think once you begin to build this relationship with God, those things are not challenging for you to accomplish. It makes you able to walk through life and be okay with doing those things consistently.

Steve Coplon: Reginald, you are everything I already said you were. For the last few minutes there, people got a chance to hear you speak from the heart. And again, the reason that the state of Virginia is doing so well with rehabilitating people and sending them back out into the world, is because they are providing counselors like you who care so much. Not everyone is like you, I know that. Your program has helped those women greatly. I remember one day I gave a presentation, you had 55 women there. There was a member of your staff who said some powerful things to me. She said, "Steve, your program is wonderful. What you're doing to help them with their finances, their understanding of money, and how to get rid of their wastefulness in their canteen spending, it's wonderful. Your program is absolutely wonderful with what you're doing to help them, because they all definitely need that. It's going to help them in their lives."

Steve Coplon: She said, "You know what the very best thing about your program is?" And I said, "Well, no, tell me what it is." She said, "That you're a man who comes into this facility and you treat all of these women like equals. You talk to them; you don't talk down to them. Almost no one in here has ever been treated that way in their life by a man". I'll tell you what Reginald, that made me almost cry. I understood how important that was to them.

Steve Coplon: The women treated me very good in there, I came in and we just had a great time, I love teaching them. What I learned is the biggest difference about the women in your prison from the men, was that most of those women never-ever wanted to go back to the hellhole they were in. They adapted that attitude from the way you and the other counselors worked with them. Being put into prison was the most awful thing imaginable in their life. Almost everybody in there had a good attitude, I think they got from you. Most understood themselves enough to know they didn't ever need to see the inside of those walls again.

Steve Coplon: If they can learn what changes they need to make, and if they can make them, then they can go back out in life and be successful in anything. Their life can be dramatically different so that they never have to come back again. They were great students because, I believe they were very eager to learn everything they possibly could from me. I had very, very few students in there who were not really engaged in trying to learn what I had to teach. The majority of them understood the reason you brought me in and the fact that it was going to be good for them.

Steve Coplon: I would like to read my program description and goal that is in my workbooks; "The program is based on the premise that if a person is under financial stress, he or she will make bad decisions. A person who has been incarcerated and is making bad decisions has a very high chance that he or she will recidivate. The program teaches an overall awareness of how money works in a person's life and provides tools that will assist them as they learn to think and plan ahead, making right decisions, reducing the amount of stress in their lives, and not reverting back to the old ways of thinking that resulted in their incarceration. The goal of the program is to teach participants responsibility and to help each one to a better chance of success in life."

Steve Coplon: I think the reason you let me in was because my program dovetailed so well with what the Virginia Department of Corrections was trying to achieve.

Reginald Ponton: I agree with you on that, Steve, and just to add, based on what you read there, that's not just for incarcerated individuals. That's for individuals just living in everyday life.

Steve Coplon: I'm going to give you a big hallelujah before you go any further, Hallelujah! Because that is the whole point of this show. It's not just for this one population. It's for all of us.

Reginald Ponton: And it is, and it's so true, and the reason why I say this is because I'm looking at myself. We all go through trials and tribulations. I know there've been times where I felt that type of financial stress, and it did sometimes lead me to make wrong decisions. We all make mistakes. If we didn't make mistakes, how can we learn? How can we grow? That's where the word experience comes in. A lot of times we look at the mistakes people have made and try to kind of downgrade their experiences. That's the point I really wanted to connect with those individuals on, by saying, "You know what, just because I'm standing in front of you and facilitating this program, doesn't mean that I'm better than you." One thing I always share with my population is that I can go out, make the wrong decision, and end up in the same position that you're in.

Reginald Ponton: That's why we have to make sure that we equip ourselves with the things we need to avoid making bad decisions. That's why if you're a person who's dealing with drugs and you've got a drug addiction, it may be important to get with a NA group. This is so, that when you're dealing with a potentially harmful situation, you have someone you can reach out to, call, or talk to. That someone can help guide you through the process. If you're dealing with alcohol, you go to AA. Perhaps you're dealing with some type of mental health issue, you should try to get yourself a session with a counselor or just have someone to talk to who you can confide in.

Reginald Ponton: That is so important for everyone. But to speak directly to the people who are returning back to society from incarceration, it is even more challenging for them. First of all, they're going to be judged when they walk out. They've got to stand tall and stand strong. If they're not built to weather those type of things or go through that type of storm; it can cause them to end up right back into what they knew before. Because think about it, we can easily go back to what we know because we're good at it. When we face challenges but want to do things differently, that keeps us uncomfortable. And when we're uncomfortable, guess what that's doing for us, that's making us grow to be even better than what we are.

Reginald Ponton: So, I tell people, accept the challenge. What that challenge is going to do, is make you find out something about yourself that you might not have ever known, and guess what? Once you cross that hurdle, when the next hurdle comes, you have built up your adrenaline and your confidence to a level that you can say, "You know what? I can get across this hurdle because I got across the last one." We have to encourage them each and every day to incorporate that within themselves. One thing I always ask my clients, my population, is, "Tell me the good about you." And it's amazing that a lot of them would not respond very quickly.

Reginald Ponton: I told them, I said, "Look, see, if you are sitting there and cannot say anything good about yourself, then that's something you need to work on, because you have good in you. You've just been told so much about the bad, or you think you're bad, and that's why it's hard for you to try and bring the good out." The thing I try to share with them is how they can build relationships. Some of them build relationships as far as taking care of each other while they're incarcerated. That is something I really love about working in corrections. I knew every day when I walked in, it would not be the same. I knew it could be somewhat of a challenge, but I knew I had a purpose and a reason to be there. And I loved that purpose and reason for being there because I know those individuals needed someone they could look up to. I love the point you made Steve, regarding what the staff said about you coming in and respecting them.

Reginald Ponton: That was something with the female population they have to understand and grasp. One of the downfalls of going back in society is getting into an unhealthy relationship. We had to educate them about trying to be in a healthy relationship, by showing them what a healthy relationship looked like. The first thing we try to share with them is by saying this; "First of all you've got to take care of yourself before you begin to take care of someone else."

Reginald Ponton: Another big downfall with them is having or not having a relationship with their child. People did not really understand that women struggle with that process and it was a challenge for them. It was something that they wanted to have back in place, but they just didn't know how to work it out. The DOC set up a program out west, where they work with DSS (Department of Social Services). They would participate in video conferencing. Here the mother could speak and talk with her child before she got out. These are some of the programs that the DOC has incorporated and brought in and put in place. Because these women participated and became a part of it, it gave them hope, like "You know what? I didn't know I could do this, but now I know I can. Now I can begin to do what I need to do to build this relationship with my child, I can even get started before I get outside the gates."

Reginald Ponton: That was so wonderful, and it built the women's confidence and courage to where now they feel like they can go back and be the parent they need to be for their child. The DOC has done an awesome job as far as providing the necessary resources that the returning citizen needs. I feel that any person who's incarcerated in the state of Virginia, has enough resources not just inside, but outside in probation districts as well. It's out there with all the other state agencies. Working in that program, I played like a liaison. I went out and talked with employers. I found out what the challenges and barriers of hiring someone with a criminal record were and got their understanding of those issues.

Reginald Ponton: These are the things that the DOC would start to go out into the community to gain input on. One major hurdle is that the population always felt like nobody would hire them, due to the fact that they had been incarcerated. So, we went out and spoke to some potential employers. We took their positive input and shared it with the women. We told them that if they would work and study these specific areas, then they would have a much greater opportunity to be employed." I think it's just wonderful when you can give these individuals this type of information. When we tell them, we heard it from their potential employers, who said they're willing to give them an opportunity if they would work on these specific areas, then it cannot get any better than this.

Reginald Ponton: What I really loved about the DOC is how they implemented and increased their reentry program to the level where they felt they were providing what the population really needed. I tell a lot of the population, "Hey, look, you've got a belt on. Now it's time to put those tools, that you need to be successful, on that belt." I got introduced to this gentleman who was formerly incarcerated. This gentleman was awesome, he shared his testimony with the population, the female population.

Reginald Ponton: These were the types of individuals we knew, we had to put in front of our population, to win them over, and to let them know what is possible. A lot of them had a mindset like, "It's impossible. You all ain't trying to help me. You all ain't trying to give me what I need." Or, "You all ain't trying to put things in place to give me what I need." And we had to show them that we were moving forward. The DOC was moving forward with that process and had been listening to the population.

Reginald Ponton: We had sessions where we did dialogue and asked them questions. We asked what they thought we could improve on to give them the opportunity to feel more confident upon reentry. I felt that the DOC did an awesome job of incorporating and listening to them and going out and implementing new things in regard to what they said. I believe that is the reason the recidivism rate dropped from 28% to where it is today, in the low 20% range. You're correct, Mr. Coplon, it is the lowest recidivism rate, I think, in the country now. One thing I experienced while working with the DOC, is the fact that we had a lot of people from other states, even outside of the country come in wanting to learn what we were doing.

Reginald Ponton: They not only wanted to talk about what we were doing for the population, but they also wanted to hear about the training that was given to the staff. We went through an extensive training about dialogue, effective communication, equipping us with what we needed to be effective, and making this a win-win all the way around. I think the DOC is continuing to move in the right direction. They're doing the right thing. I like the fact that they have so many resources for those individuals, to where they can kick back and begin to live the life they want to live. Still, "In order to achieve, you've got to believe in yourself."

Steve Coplon: Reginald, it is just wonderful to have this conversation with you because if I weren't already doing what I'm doing, I'd want to be part of what you started there. I want to talk for just a minute about how beautiful it is that you do this from the heart. My program was a financial literacy program. My course was called *"Personal Finance and Small Business Ownership."* I would come into Brunswick and would usually teach it over a month or so. It taught an overall awareness of how money works in your life. Teaching all about money, how credit works, how money is just a tool and all those basic things,

Steve Coplon: Then, there's a whole lot of people who are incarcerated who want to start their own business. Part of the reason is because they believe that they're not going to get hired, so they feel like they have to have their own business. So, what I did was, I flipped that coin on the other side and I let them know that, until you become the world's greatest employee, you'll never have your own business that will succeed. Because if you are not a good employee, you're not going to know how to manage employees working under you. That was part of my concept. Then, I also let them know that you cannot make it in business without credit. You can't make it without having some working capital and I taught them what working capital is and all those details.

Steve Coplon: What I'm getting at is this. After they took my *Personal Finance and Small Business Ownership* course, anybody who graduated from that class, got a certificate to use if they wanted to take the *Business Plan Class*. The backbone of having your own business, is knowing how to construct a business plan. Identify all your obstacles and know what all your variables are. Anyone who got in the *Business Plan Class* at Brunswick qualified for a 30 minute one-on-one with me, where we could talk about their personal goals. Then I started doing online research for them because they did not have access to full computer research. I did hundreds of computer research projects for people who you knew.

Steve Coplon: One day during a one-on-one with a young lady, 22 years old, right at the beginning of the session, she just started crying. I mean, she was really crying, and I asked, "What is it that's upsetting you so much?" She said, "I'm getting out in six weeks and I'm scared to death." I said, "Why?" And she said, "Because I don't know how to handle money and I live in a small community in Western Virginia and there's nothing waiting for me there. It's going to be the same thing that I left. I'm afraid that I won't get a job and I can't handle money." She had a five-year-old daughter who lived with her parents while she was incarcerated. The sad thing was she and the father of the child both had gotten sent up on drug charges and she hadn't heard from the guy for three years. He is gone out of their lives.

Steve Coplon: So, the father of her child's gone, and she said, "I don't know how to handle money and I don't want to have me, and my daughter have to live with my parents for the rest of my life. I don't want to have to live with my parents." She said, "Can you teach me how to handle money?" And I said, "Yes, I can, but what you're asking me to do, everybody here needs to learn. Let me talk to Mr. Ponton about what you're asking me." Then I came to you, Reginald, and you said, "Mr. Coplon, that is wonderful." I'll never forget the way our conversation went. I said, "I want to put a personal budget class in here. I would like to add it to the *Personal Finance and Small Business Ownership* course. I want to teach personal budgeting specific to their situations." You responded with, "Well, that's absolutely wonderful that you want to do that, but let me give you an idea."

Steve Coplon: You said, "If we could do something very, very practical for them while they're here, it would be so good." Then you said, "If you could teach them how to convert their canteen spending to savings, to start looking at how to spend their money in the canteen, learn how to monitor it, keep track of it, if you could teach them how to stop spending so much unnecessary money that they don't need to spend and start increasing their savings, that would be a skill that they could carry with them when they get out that they'd have for the rest of their life."

Steve Coplon: Reginald, I just want to say thank you and God Bless you for that conversation because I did that, and it is being taught all over the country because you gave me that assignment. I want to share another story with you. I'm not going to call her by name, but there was this one woman who after I instituted and taught that program, she raised her hand and she said, "You want some feedback, Mr. Coplon?" And I said, "Yeah, that would be great," and she said, "Well, after you taught me how to pay close attention to what I'm actually spending in the canteen, I went back and got a printout for the last two years of what I had spent in the canteen." The prison keeps records of all of the canteen purchases.

Steve Coplon: I said, "What did you learn?" She said, "Well, I found out that I was spending $160 a month, every month, in the canteen." I said, "Well, that sounds like a lot of money, but would you mind telling me what you're spending it on?" She said, "Absolutely nothing. Junk, candy, sodas and potato chips." I said, "Wow, that sounds like a lot of potato chips." Then I said, "So after you learned that about your spending habit, what changes did you make?" And she said, "Well I got to thinking, I got another two years here and if I could cut that down to only $50 a month, I could save over $100 a month."

Steve Coplon: She said, "I'd have about $2,500 when I leave here." And I said, "Okay, well did you do that?" She goes, "I've saved $100 a month for the last two months." And then the following month, she said, "You want another update?" I said, "Absolutely." Then she said, "It was the last time in the month for me to go into the canteen and I had everything on the counter, and when they rang it up, it put me over $50." I said, "What did you do?" She said, "I put stuff back on the shelf."

Steve Coplon: Well Reginald, I have taught the basic program on how to monitor everything you spend and look at what you do, be conscious of what your spending habits are that you had me develop. I call it a self-motivated behavior change program. When a person becomes totally aware of what they're really doing, and you said it before, this isn't just for incarcerated people. This is for everybody, because when somebody realizes how much money they're wasting on Starbucks or junk food or whatever else it may be, they can learn to control that and start reaching goals with their finances that they didn't think they could reach.

Steve Coplon: I want to say, what you and I did together, has benefited thousands of people. And from what you have talked about on this show, people understand that the state of Virginia is successful. Number one in the country in fighting recidivism because of the dedication, the heart and the kindness of you and others like you. Reginald, I just want to tell you, you are a beautiful person. I have enjoyed you and I've loved you since I first met you. You are a kind, caring, compassionate human being and that's what it takes to reach the people who have fallen in their lives, made mistakes and don't trust anybody. They need somebody they know who respects them and treats them as an equal just like you said.

Steve Coplon: Thank you for coming on the show and sharing what you're talking about. I want to ask you, is there anything else that you'd like to say from your own personal experiences, if you'd like to give a piece of advice to all the people who are hiding the truth, or might need to hear your perspective? It doesn't have to be so exactly directly correlated, but you came on as my guest to talk about the theme of people who don't do what they say they're going to do. You went to the heart of the matter.

Steve Coplon: A lot of people do not do what they say they're going to do because they don't know what they're doing with their lives. They are going from today to tomorrow and they're saying whatever they've got to say to get by. And I've often said this. Do you ever think where the word "convict" comes from? It might have a lot to do with people who are trying to con other people. People who are not being truthful with others. If you can, take that thought and give some advice as we close the show, to whoever might be listening.

Reginald Ponton: You know, I would say the first thing you need to do is go to the mirror and look at yourself. And when you look at yourself, you need to ask yourself, if you like what you see? If you don't like what you see, you have the opportunity to change it. I want to go back to when I was talking about how you would want to be remembered. What is the legacy that you want to leave? A lot of times people don't think about this, but take the opportunity to sit down and think about that, "What is that legacy you want to leave?"

Reginald Ponton: I think that can lead you in the direction of where you can begin to do things that have an impact, wherever it may be. It can be in your community, it can be in your church, it can be in the school system, it can be in your household, it could be at your job. Wherever you want to play that role. We're here for a reason, I believe that taking an opportunity to do something where you can do good for someone else, is important. Let's not be so selfish in life. Let's understand that we all have flaws. We're not perfect, and most of all, build that relationship with God. I'm a true individual when I say that I've been through things in life and I've seen what He has done for me.

Reginald Ponton: We all are a work in progress, so we're not going to get it perfect, but we can make a difference each and every day that we have the opportunity to live. So, when you get the opportunity to get up the next day, put it in your mind that you're going to do something good to uplift somebody or uplift yourself.

Steve Coplon: Reginald, I'm going to end the show with what you just said. That is a perfect place to end. God Bless you for all that you do, for being the person you are. Thanks for being my friend and thanks for all that you do for so many people. God Bless you, Reginald.

Reginald Ponton: God Bless you too, Steve, and thank you for having me on your show. I really enjoyed it.

Steve Coplon: Oh, it was beautiful. I want everybody to have a wonderful week and God Bless each one of you.

Steve Coplon: Thanks for listening to *Right Thinking with Steve Coplon*. I look forward to being with you again next week. Remember: ***Don't Quit, Plan Ahead, It Will Get Better.*** God Bless you and have a great week!

To listen to the original interview, scan this QR Code with your camera, or visit:

https://rightthinkingeducation.com/FromtheLiptotheHip/Chapter-4/

CHAPTER FIVE

Character And Integrity Are The Deciding Factors with guest Don Price
Right Thinking With Steve Coplon - Episode 163

Steve Coplon:	Good morning. Welcome to *Right Thinking with Steve Coplon.* I'm your host, Steve Coplon. Thank you for tuning in. Let's have a great day!
Steve Coplon:	Good morning. Glad to be with you. Well, every week I say it's going to be a great show, but today is going to be an easy show for me. The reason for that is our guest today, Don Price, is one of my closest friends in the world. We've been friends for nearly 40 years. He's been on the show a couple other times, but the whole purpose of today's show, is to continue the series that we started on Episode 159 that was titled ***"From the Lip to the Hip is a Pretty Far Distance."*** I'm doing a real study with people I respect greatly. People who have good things to share with the listeners. *From the Lip to the Hip* brought out, one of the things that I have felt so strongly about my entire life, and that is people doing what they say they are going to do.
Steve Coplon:	This whole series is based on me asking people to listen to that show, Episode 159, and then come on as a guest. I believe that all the people who are guests in this series are worth everyone listening to. Today it's Don Price and we're going to start the show and see where it goes. When I say it's easy, it's because Don is a professional. I can count on him to do what he says he's going to do. You are going to see that in today's show. Sit back, enjoy it, and relax, because this show is going to help each one of you.
Steve Coplon:	Today is Episode 163. *Right Thinking with Steve Coplon* is very pleased to announce that this week's show is called ***"Character and Integrity are the Deciding Factors"*** with guest, Don Price. Tune in and be inspired by this beautiful conversation with Don and Steve. Don's 40-year banking career has helped hundreds of people to both personal and business success. Don is a man who is willing to help you in any way he can. He is a true role model. Well, Don, thanks for being a guest on the show again.
Don Price:	Steve, thank you for having me and I appreciate the opportunity to talk to you again.
Steve Coplon:	Well, Don, you are so welcome. It's exactly what I said, and I want to make it a little more personal. Don, we have known each other for pushing 40 years, almost your whole banking career. When I say you're a true role model, that you'll help anybody that you possibly can, those aren't just words or accolades. Of all the people I know, you have probably helped me more than anyone. There is a worldwide coronavirus crisis right now, but a lot of people

are starting to refocus themselves and think differently. Advice on how to better handle finances and get through this crisis is critical for everyone.

Steve Coplon: I have been in crisis off and on for 25 to 30 years. You've been with me all the way through a lot of the lessons that I have learned on how to face adversity. You have helped me more than anyone in the world to keep my life moving forward when I've had incredible financial pressures, and personal things going on. I've always said that there are two people in my life who know and understand me better than anyone else. That's you and Todd Preti, my close friend, who is also my lawyer. Both of you are founding members of **Right Thinking Foundation.** Don, I know that you have firsthand experience with what we're going to talk about.

Steve Coplon: Don, I love you and I just want to thank you for being the person you are. What I want to do in today's show is share some of your wisdom, get some advice from you, and then go a little deeper. I said you are modest, humble, and a role model. What I want people to get out of today's show, is not only the message that you give them; but also, the knowledge of how a person can become a role model, the kind of person role models are. I'd like to start off by asking you how you got to be the person of character you are today?

Don Price: Well, I appreciate that question. Before I answer that, Steve, I would like to say how much I have appreciated helping you over the years. You have had some health and financial struggles in the time that I've known you. I said this many times before, of all the people I've dealt with, you have more perseverance and passion to follow through on what you say you're going to do than any person I've ever encountered. That's a testament to you. To answer the question, how did I get to be the way I am today? I have three people I'd like to talk about who really prompted me subliminally initially, to be the person I am. The first one is my grandfather, my mother's dad. He was a dentist in Richmond for 50 years and he wasn't rich. He had four children: three sons and my mother.

Don Price: He practiced long and hard in those days. He began practicing in about 1920. In those days, the dental business was not an easy one, they didn't have all the equipment they have today as everybody is aware. He worked on many, many patients and he made reasonably good money. What most influenced me, was his work with a group called The Little Sisters of the Poor. It's a Catholic organization across the country that help old and infirm people through their last few years. There were 13 Little Sisters of the Poor, in Richmond and he became involved with them through his parish, St. Benedict's in Richmond.

Don Price: For 45 years he provided free dental care to those nuns, whatever happened, root canals, it didn't matter. Can you imagine the number of hours he devoted to these 13 nuns doing their dental care? To me that was a huge sacrifice. He didn't get paid a penny for it and that's what he loved doing. He was number one in my life, and I was very young when he was doing this. Starting out when I was six or seven years old was the first time I knew about it, but it didn't really have any impact on me until I was about 12 or 13. I always remembered that he'd come home and I'd ask him, "How was work today?" He'd say, "It was great. I didn't make any money but had a lot of fun and enjoyed the people that I was with." That's the kind of man that he was. He was the first person that greatly influenced my character.

Don Price: The second person was my dad. My dad was treasurer of Royster Fertilizer Company in Norfolk for 35 years. That was a big job, it occupied a lot of his time. He rode the bus to work every day and my mother kept the car, since we only had one car in the family, and seven children. While he was doing all of his Royster work, he was also on a lot of boards. He was a member of the Rotary Club for 45 years, served as president twice in that group. He served as a president of the Better Business Bureau on two occasions and was on that board for about 18 years. The biggest thing he did that he enjoyed the most, is that all seven of us children attended and graduated from Holy Trinity and Norfolk Catholic High School, your big rival, Steve. He loved sports.

Don Price: He was the president of the board at Norfolk Catholic on two occasions. He was on the board for 15 years and completed a lot of work there. He was also president of the Athletic Association for eight years. What really impressed me, was something that was not included in anybody's job description. People aren't aware that in the mid-1960s, Norfolk Catholic High School was having financial difficulties and was pretty close to closing. He was president of the board at that time and he started looking into it and determined that one of the biggest problems was, that many of the parents who had the ability to pay, weren't paying their tuition on time. He took it upon himself to gather a list of all those people, call them at home, and basically beg them to please pay their tuition. A good number did, but a substantial number didn't respond to his pleas.

Don Price: On his own time, he went to small-claims-court and filed against them to pay their tuition. I don't know how many hundreds of occasions, that he did this. Well, he collected a lot of money and that was one of the reasons the school was able to stay open. Most people don't know it, but that's a true story. If something would impress you, that's it. That's why my dad is really a role model.

Don Price: The third person is my mother. As I said, we had seven children in our family, and she was in charge of taking us all to baseball, basketball practice, recitals, and dance classes. I had four sisters and two brothers, so we were playing sports all the time. My mother did an awful lot of work carting us around and making sure we were available for all our events.

Don Price: She and my dad were members of Holy Trinity Parish for about 62 years. My mother took it upon herself to take one unofficial, yet most relevant job. She made sure that she took the elderly parishioners who couldn't drive, to their doctor and dental appointments, to visit friends, to go shopping, grocery shopping and so on. She did this for probably 30 years and that was in the midst of taking care of her own children and making sure everything else was handled at home. Those are the three people who really, inspired me to be what I am today. Volunteer work is not easy. It's certainly very rewarding as you well know Steve, because you've been doing it for a long time as well. That's really it.

Don Price: I have a fourth person, my wife, Barbara. Steve, you know Barbara very well. Barbara is the most giving person I've ever seen, people don't know it, and she doesn't talk about it. She started working at age 16 and paid her own way through Norfolk Catholic High School. She was one of two of her siblings to go to Norfolk Catholic. She paid her way through high school and from that point on she was pretty much independent and on her own. Her mother died in 2003, and Barbara was there every day for the last 13 years of her mother's life. Matter of fact, her mother lived with us for about two months, then we put her up in a hotel for a while before moving her into a nursing home, where Barbara visited her mother every day for 13 years.

Don Price: Nobody else in the family hardly did anything to assist with that. In addition to that, Barbara's two older sisters have some health issues, so for the past 12 years, Barbara has taken them on all their shopping trips, regardless of what the purpose was, as well as doctors, dental appointments, and everything else that they needed. Then about three years ago, one of her brothers had a serious accident and for two years she drove him around to different doctors and specialists. She's been doing volunteer work with her immediate family for the past 25 years, basically without a break. She didn't have a paying job mostly during that time period. She was employed as a copy editor for the local newspaper for 34 years.

Don Price: For her to do that kind of service for 25 consecutive years, I think is just incredible. She doesn't like people talking about it, so I did ask her before this conversation started if it was okay to mention it. She was very happy that I was going to, because she doesn't get the credit that she deserves. Those are the four people who have really inspired me, both my parents, my grandfather, and my wife.

Steve Coplon: Don, thank you for sharing all of that. I know a lot of people you know because we both graduated high school in 1969. I am humbled Don, to know a person like you and that is why I'm doing this show. I brought you on under the guise that people do not do what they say they are going to do. I asked you to listen to Episode 159 in preparation. We both have spent our whole lives trying to be there for other people and to help people navigate through life and maybe change in positive ways. If they don't need to change, then we try to recruit them to become a person who helps others. We both know, it's just plain kind to help people. I hope that people get into this series of these shows, because I am basically trying to teach them about character. Now, do you have a real definition of character yourself, that you ever use?

Don Price: I do, Steve. Character are moral and mental qualities distinctive to an individual.

Steve Coplon: Moral and mental qualities, okay. Let's break that down just for a second. You said it's distinctive to an individual, but are there any components of character that might be good or bad?

Don Price: Let's do this, Steve, let's add integrity to it because then it blends the two together. Integrity is a quality of being honest and having strong moral principles.

Steve Coplon: Now we need to talk about what moral means. I guess because that's part of the definition that you're giving for character and integrity. Let me give you part of that. In preparation for the show I found a write-up on character. What are the six traits of good character? It lists the six pillars of character and I had never seen it laid out like this before. I know you have, you probably wrote the book. Trustworthiness, respect, responsibility, fairness, caring and citizenship. Those are good, huh?

Don Price: Yeah, they are good. Very good.

Steve Coplon: Well, if I put the name Don Price under this definition in Webster's Oxford dictionary it would say, "Look at Don Price's life to understand what we just said." Integrity. What does it mean when a person has integrity? Integrity is a personal quality of fairness that we all aspire to. The dictionary says, "Unless you're a dishonest, immoral scoundrel, of course, having integrity means doing the right thing in a reliable way. It is a personality trait that we admire since it means a person has a moral compass that doesn't waver."

Don Price: Yeah, that's good. That's good.

Steve Coplon:	I looked up the word character in the dictionary, and I'm using you as a person who exemplifies it. Don, did you listen to the show that I asked you to listen to for this interview?
Don Price:	I did.
Steve Coplon:	Was there anything in there that made any sense that you think was correct?
Don Price:	That we talked about, the most recent one with Reginald?
Steve Coplon:	Oh, any of them that you want to talk about. If you want to go back, you can do it in any order you want. But the whole theme that we're branching off on is for me to have people listen to enough of these shows that they start realizing what this series is really all about. Then they can realize how to become the person they desire to be. Before we get too deep into that, I just want to sum up how the four people you admire, got you to where you are in life today. That was beautiful. I'd like to say this, you're all about family and community. For as long as I've known you, I didn't know about your grandfather. Like you said, some of the stuff you shared, you don't talk about too much. I knew your mom a little bit and it is just amazing how generous and committed she was to her family, community, all of it.
Steve Coplon:	It's in your genes, it's in your bloodline. Let me just point something out here, a takeaway for people. If you want to raise wonderful kids, you might become a wonderful person first. That's good. The other one is with Barbara. I have known Barbara as long as I've known you. She is an absolutely wonderful person. I always remember that she worked nights at the newspaper company as a proofreader. You and Barbara read more than any couple I know. I mean incredibly prolific readers. Through the coronavirus crisis, how many books did you tell me you have read since January, over these past three months?
Don Price:	17.
Steve Coplon:	17 books. You're always reading three or four at a time, I know that, and Barbara reads all the time too. Let me just say this, I've done other shows on the topic, and reading is a major key to success. Today, reading is not our topic, but reading is one of the cornerstones to a successful life. Before we get into the deep part of this conversation, for those of you who want to get a lot deeper into what Don and I have talked about, he's on the board of Right Thinking Foundation. He's in the curriculum that I've developed. It's throughout the country, in prisons, on personal finance and small business ownership. There are two episodes that we did, Episode 103, *"How to Get a Bank Loan,"* and Episode 112, *"Credit Establishing, Rebuilding and Maintaining."* We'll get back to those later.
Steve Coplon:	Before I forget, if you want to learn more about some of the subjects in those two episodes that Don's going to talk about today, you can listen to them in their entirety on *Right Thinking with Steve Coplon*, www.rightthink.org.
Steve Coplon:	Well, Don, on Episode 159, *"From the Lip to the Hip is a Pretty far Distance,"* talking about people doing what they say they're going to do. You are one of the people who always has. Now, let's talk about any takeaways you got from that episode or any of the others that you listened to. Thank you.
Don Price:	All right. I want to mention your show with Lefford Fate. Lefford is an Air Force veteran and motivational speaker and did a tremendous job. The title is, *"You Got That Right Steve!"* He had some great quotes, he said, "People don't follow through because they don't have the

courage to say no." That's true. I think we all know that and it's unfortunate. He said, "If it's to be, it's up to me." I think that's extremely strong and short, but it's very powerful because he's exactly right. If you don't take the initiative, nothing is going to happen. Another good one that he said was, "You may be done with your past, but your past may not be done with you." Meaning that other people will never forget when you don't follow through on what you indicated you'd do with them.

Don Price: This is a really good one, "If you see the man as he could be instead of the way he is, you help him become the man he should be." That's powerful too and that's exactly right. You need to treat people with respect and motivate them to the greatest extent you can. Then two very easy ones, "The best time to start is now." Once again, it's up to you to take the initiative to get things accomplished. Then kind of funny, "The two best times to plan a shade tree, the first is 25 years ago and the second is now." Meaning if you don't do it now; you're never going to have a shade tree. A lot of good initiatives there and he expressed them in a very fun way. Very, very well done.

Don Price: Another episode titled **"Start Doing it Right Now"**, by Richard Kay, a pastor in the ministry, made some very good points. He said, "There's really no difference between secular business and a ministry. Both are the same, whether in the pulpit or in the boardroom." Meaning he's in charge of his parishioners and that's a business. True businesspeople are in charge of the same thing, and that's people. You need to treat them all in the best interest possible. He said, "Honor your commitments, do what you say you're going to do." Richard continued, "God is always willing to teach us if we're willing to learn." That's critically important. God imparts his knowledge into us, and you need to share it. It's not just for you personally, share it and do the most good you can with it.

Don Price: Then the last quote that I took from him was, "It's not wrong to consider your needs ahead of others. Yours are met so that you can help others." Meaning you have a lot of abilities and should share them, not just keep them to yourself.

Don Price: Then Reginald Ponton, who is a counselor for the Virginia Department of Corrections in a woman's prison, stated his mission. He said his goal is to get the prisoners out of prison and let them go back to be productive members in society. That's huge because that's not an easy task. Steve, you've been in prisons hundreds of times, so you know this better than most. Once you get in prison, it's extremely difficult to get out. Part of the lessons you teach, is how they can become successful upon release.

Don Price: He also said he was very happy that the rehabilitated prisoners who had gotten out, and were successful, were allowed to come back and visit the prison and speak directly to the remaining prisoners. Then, they really see success can occur when you get out of prison. The last take away I got from his show was, "Treat everyone in prison as a person because they very rarely experience that." Meaning treat them with respect. You're supposed to do that with everybody. It doesn't matter where they are, prison or anywhere else. One of the keys to life is to treat people with respect and they'll respect you in return.

Don Price: I would like to make a distinction between character and integrity, Steve. I described character as being the moral and mental qualities distinctive to an individual. Integrity is the quality of being honest and having strong moral principles. The way I think of it is, if you use those two together, you can be successful. There's a lot of successful people in this world who don't really have a strong moral character. They made a lot of money through whatever means, some of them might not employ the best methods. In their minds, they're successful. But to me, in order to be truly successful and be happy with yourself, feel good about yourself, you have to have both character and integrity. There's just no way a person could be truly happy without both of these characteristics.

Steve Coplon: Don, you would know that as well as anybody. In preparation for this show, I read the transcripts from the last two shows you were on, and I have already announced the episode numbers. Don, you helped me create the curriculum on the unit of credit, which is part of my national curriculum. During your career as a banker for 40 years, you worked 50 to 60 hours on this curriculum. This was a segue from your personal life into your banking life, I wanted to read this before we go on, and there's something I want to bring out.

Steve Coplon: Just like Richard Kay said that your spiritual life, your secular life, it kind of goes hand in hand. Your personal life and your business life, you're the same person, no matter how you treat people. Whether it's at work or at home or in the community. I asked you to give me a resume so I could have it in preparation for this show. I'm just going to read through it quick, I won't dwell on it, but I just want to let people know that you found a way to have a life of service, even though you worked overtime for 40 years professionally helping people.

Steve Coplon: You approached banking in a way, I mean hey, I'm one of your clients. I have been one of your customers for most of your career, personally and in corporate life. I've got to tell you, I've always told everybody that you're the most straightforward, honest banker I've ever come across. You approached your career as a person who wanted to use whatever you had available to you, to help your customers solve their own personal problems and fulfill the needs they had.

Steve Coplon: Here is a summary of your volunteer activities. You were a 12-year member of the Optimist Club of Norfolk. You were on the board for six years and were president for two of those years. You are the one who inspired me to join and I'm happy to say we accomplished some wonderful things together.

Steve Coplon: You worked eight years with the United Way of Hampton Roads. You volunteered with a lot of these charities simultaneously. I think that you've always juggled your personal schedule and your business schedule with a minimum of six to nine nonprofits that you served on boards at high level capacities. Maybe you're one of those people who just couldn't say no, but you also learned something about saying yes. Lots of times, people need to say yes, but they think they have to say no because they don't have enough time. If you want the job done, ask the busiest person. That's another part of the dictionary that I could turn to and see your smiling face.

Steve Coplon: You talked about your lifetime, as well as your family's involvement, at Holy Trinity Church. You've been a member for 55 years, served on their council for four years, and have been the finance chairman for eight years.

Steve Coplon: You've been a board member for 12 years and Finance Committee Chairman for chair eight years at Norfolk Catholic High School, which later became Bishop Sullivan High School. At St Mary's Home for disabled Children, which just touches everybody's hearts, you were a board member for 15 years and served as board president for two years. You were one of the founding board members at St. Patrick's Catholic School and have been on the board for 17 years. You were the president of that board for two years, and the chairman of the strategic planning committee for eight years.

Steve Coplon: At Barry Robinson Center, you were on their board for 17 years, and served as board president for two years. You Don are to be applauded, as you've covered the entire spectrum.

Steve Coplon: Don, every segment of society you've given yourself to, could never be described as well as you have demonstrated. On one of our shows, we talked about credit. You used me as an example to talk about what good credit is supposed to be. I had to end the show because I was crying. You were just so amazing how you've been there for me, that's who you are, Don.

Steve Coplon: For the last 20 minutes of the show, I'd like to talk about something else. Don, you have found your own path through money, professional management, and through being a banker. Part of my whole foundation and why it's so beneficial that you're on the board with me, is because you understand that if people can get on top of their money, they can have a better life, and eliminate a lot of stress.

Steve Coplon: They can reach goals they didn't think they could reach. They can just be a better person. Through this crisis we're experiencing right now, the coronavirus crisis…I won't go on about it, but I know we're going to come out of this. The advice that I've been giving people from day one is, "Hey, we're going to be okay. The United States has got the strongest economy in the world, and we're compassionate about human life. The economy's going to rebound." I've been quoting Bob Marley constantly, "Every little thing, is gonna be all right." I like to sing my Bob Marley music. What I'm saying is, my whole purpose in life is to help other people. I finally got focused in helping people through getting their finances straight.

Steve Coplon: When we recorded our show on credit, we pretty much established how getting straight with money helps have a better life. That's why it goes hand in glove with today's show. My definition of credit is, a person honoring their good name, doing what they say they're going to do. That's the key to good credit. We spoke the entire hour, on credit and how credit ties in when you get a bank loan. We essentially gave a modified seminar, we read credit reports and explained what credit reports are. We covered all that in other shows. When you have a client, how do you look at that client when they come into your office? When they're sitting across the desk from you, how do you relate that to people who do what they say they're going to do? Because a person can't get money from a bank if he doesn't say how he is going to pay it back, generally.

Don Price: That's true. That puts a whole lot of the topics into one, Steve. When somebody came in to borrow money from whichever bank I was with, it was always interesting. What I always wanted or expected them to have is complete information. If they wanted to start a new business, then I'd ask them to tell me all the homework they had done. Send me a business plan. Show me why it will be successful. What effort are you willing to put into it? Prove to me you're a hard worker and you have character and integrity. One thing I always say is, "There's only one opportunity to make a first impression." When somebody comes in to borrow money, particularly when it's a significant amount of money, five, six, $10 million, first impressions are critically important.

Don Price: People who come in expecting to borrow money, should know, it doesn't happen easily, unless you're providing cash collateral or something of that nature. Borrowing money, is a difficult job. You need to have your homework done and you need to be willing to answer any question that I might have. You should have projections if it's a new business and you always need to have a complete business plan. You and I have had other discussions about business plans, and I think, we covered all the aspects of it. It takes a long time to put together a solid business plan. You did them for years and years. I think I told you in the last meeting, I've probably looked at 5,000 projections in 40 years. Some of them are very well done.

Don Price: Most people have bigger expectations in their projections than they're actually going to accomplish. Character and integrity are essential. What I'd like to do is give two examples of character based on real life learning situations if that works for you.

Steve Coplon: Any way you'd like to approach it Don.

Don Price: Okay, I'm going to talk about a poor case of character, which was really surprising, and then a good case. It happened in the late 1980s, four very proud businesspeople in Norfolk, very well off financially and very prominent in the community. They came to borrow $750,000 to buy an existing upscale men's clothing firm with two locations, and to buy the name. The business had been operating for about 20 years. We got all the numbers, and everything looked good and I lent them the $750,000. The interesting thing is, we get into the five Cs of credit:

Character, Capital, Capacity, Collateral and Conditions

Don Price: When I look at loans, regardless of the amount, I look at those five aspects. I thought they had character because I had already known them as being very prominent in the community. They had plenty of capital both personal and the business that they were acquiring had some capital in it. They had capacity to pay, both from the business standpoint and personally. We had collateral in the form of the inventory, the clothing inventory and the two stores. The conditions at the time they wanted to buy the stores were good. The economy was good, clothing business was good and so on. I lent them the $750,000. Each of the four was guaranteeing $200,000. Everything looked like it was in great shape and so they started operating the business and after about 20 months it did not do too well. That was attributable to two things.

Don Price: New competition surfaced in the market, and the economic environment deteriorated. They were trying to make changes to adjust and compensate for the differences in the economy and the market, and they couldn't make enough adjustments to make sense. After about six more months of that, they decided to just close the stores. Well, they still owed me $450,000. I said, "Okay, you need to liquidate the inventory and pay that down." After that was done, they still had a balance of about $400,000 on their loans. I called them all into my office and they came in and sat down. I could tell right away they weren't happy. That's what happens when deals don't work.

Don Price: I said, "Okay, you guys each need to give me basically $100,000 to pay off the $400,000." They'd apparently already had a meeting prior to meeting me, because as soon as I said that, they all said almost in unison, "We'll give you $50,000 apiece. Take it or leave it." These are prominent members of the community. I was a little taken aback and I said, "Well, that's not going to work. We're not going to do that, you owe $400,000. You have the ability to pay." They said, "Well, we're not going to, we'll give you $200,000 and we'll be done." Well, long and short of that was I thought they had all the five Cs of credit. What they didn't have were the conditions. Conditions changed because the economy changed, and competition came online.

Don Price:	The weakened market conditions weren't present when they bought the company and their character as evidenced by that, was not what I thought it was either. So, we ended up in litigation. We had to spend money on attorneys and so on. We got our money back of course, but it cost us some money to pay for attorneys. This is a case of poor character when it was not expected to work that way at all. That's the first one.
Steve Coplon:	Let me make a comment if you would. You have talked about a business situation where you came across some prominent businesspeople and it turns out they didn't have such good character.
Don Price:	Right.
Steve Coplon:	I want to say this, just prior to this show, I read the transcripts to our last two shows on credit and getting a bank loan. One was 20 pages and one was 19 pages. It just interests me so much to go back and read those. You did over $600 million in loans in your 40-year career. That's a lot of loans. You said you were extremely fortunate though, that you only charged off about $2.2 million of loans. That means that people didn't have the ability to pay and you just couldn't get your money. They might have gone bankrupt or whatever, but that's less than 1%.
Steve Coplon:	In the banking world, that's about as golden blue chip as anybody can ever achieve in their career. I want to make a point to the listeners about the story that you just told about how the four men who would not pay their guarantees. You weren't naïve and got fooled when you lent these guys the money. They just didn't turn out to be of the best character. Now, I know you're going to give another example and we've got plenty of time left. But when it comes to credit, you're saying the five C's sum it up very well. I was taught those along the way also. To repeat them, they are:

Character, Capital, Capacity, Collateral and Conditions

Don Price:	Right.
Steve Coplon:	It's made up of the five Cs, whereas in real estate the number one factor is location, location, location. In credit, it is character, character, character. If you don't have character, you can't get to the next part of the conversation.
Don Price:	That's true. Very true. Good point.
Steve Coplon:	Do you have another anecdotal story that you would like to share?
Don Price:	Yeah. This is a good character story. This was probably in 1995, I had a gentleman come in once again, well known individual in the Norfolk community. Wanted to start a new venture, a marketing-related venture. He had good credit. He didn't have a whole lot of liquidity, but he had good income. He wanted to borrow $400,000. He came in and gave me his financial information, told me the whole story about what he was trying to do. It made sense, but it didn't have enough collateral and there were concerns. You get a feel for whether a deal is going to work or not based on how a potential borrower describes it.
Don Price:	He did a good job describing it, but there were a couple of missing areas. I told him, "I can lend you the money, but I need something more. You know, a second on your house or something worth at least $200,000, $250,000 because there is a certain level of risk involved in this deal." He said, "Okay, well I can have my dad guarantee." And by law, a lender can't

designate who the guarantor can be. It's against the law to do that. I said, "Well how old is your dad?" This guy, that I was dealing with, he was about 55. He said, "He's 84." You can't discriminate against age of course. I said, "That's fine, if he's willing to do it, but keep in mind I can't require that he guarantees this deal." He said, "I understand that." He brought his dad in the next day.

Don Price: His dad comes in, he's in very good health for an 84-year-old, brought his financial statement. Pretty strong, good liquidity, perfect credit, and I had a huge amount of comfort with him. As soon as this guy's dad came in and sat down, I had a good feeling. We talked for probably 20, 25 minutes and discussed a couple of things on his statement. I told the borrower, "Sure with your dad guaranteeing, I'll lend you the $400,000." That deal went through, and his company did pretty well for a year, maybe 15 months. Somewhat similar to the previous story, additional competition and so on. He had to shut the business down. He still owed me $250,000 out of the $400,000. I said, "Well, you know what we need to do." He said, "Yeah, my dad needs to come in."

Don Price: You never like people coming in to pay that kind of money. You do on one hand of course, because they need to pay, but you hate to see the impact on them. His dad came in a day or two later, he had a big smile on his face, and he had a check in his hands. Well, I shook his hand and he sat down in front of my desk. I said, "I'm really sorry the deal has worked out this way." He's smiling. He said, "No, I don't mind it at all. I made a commitment to you. I signed the legal contract and I honor my obligations." He said, "What I appreciate is you gave my son the opportunity to be successful in another endeavor. Most people wouldn't do that."

Don Price: I said, "Well, I did it because of the trust I had in you." He just smiled some more and said, "This is just the way people are supposed to operate." That was it. That is perfect character right there. He was very happy because his son had the opportunity and he really appreciated that. He came in and gave me $250,000 and he had nothing to do with the business, didn't benefit at all from it. To me, that is one of the best examples of character I've ever heard.

Steve Coplon: That's an amazing story. It goes without saying that there's a whole lot of technique involved in how to manage finances when you're having hard times. It's very pertinent in today's world that people need to take a hard focus and really watch their finances carefully. Establishing or rebuilding your credit, these are both critical. Especially in times of crisis, and there are millions and millions of people right now having to learn these for the first time.

Steve Coplon: It's probably good that you're retired now, because bankers are getting ready to be deluged with 90-hour work weeks just to try to help people through. All the basics are more important than ever. We've been talking about what you have to do to get ahead financially and establish credit for years now. Do what you say you're going to do. Pay your bills on time, communicate with creditors when you can't pay. Everybody in the world right now is trying to give advice. "Well, just call your mortgage company and see if they'll let you defer a payment. Tell them you don't have any money. What are they going to do to you right now? Try to get a reprieve for 90 days or something." Or, call everybody you owe money to, even a bank loan and say, "Can I pay interest and just not principal right now?"

Steve Coplon: The point is people who go into this without any savings, no credit, they have to rebuild. It's kind of like the world I work in: people who either are incarcerated or who have come out of incarceration and have a hard time adjusting. They generally don't have credit, or savings, or don't have anybody who trusts them enough to co-sign for them. My whole program is really not about the financial aspect or how to understand your credit score. It's about doing what you say you're going to do.

Steve Coplon: Everything I do is built on that basic premise. I would like to go back to one thing. If you like listening to Don talk about some of his experiences, then go back and listen to the two shows about, "How to Get a Bank Loan", which is Episode 103, then Episode 153, *"Credit Establishing, Rebuilding, Maintaining."* We go over credit. We talk about what a credit report is based on and how you can improve it. We give a lot of specifics on those shows. I encourage you to go back to those shows to get more information. I'll ask you this, Don, about how many millions of dollars do you think we did with corporate clients of mine?

Don Price: I would say probably between $8 million and $15 million.

Steve Coplon: Yeah, that's a great estimate. I think that's right because we did three or four Spirit of Norfolk ships. What I also want to say is, you personally made probably 12 or 13 separate loans to me over the years where I did a refinancing, or you gave me a line of credit or things like that. If we total up all the refinance and all the loans that I did with you, I think I was into the $1.5 to $2 million range. You were always saying, "Hey, Steve. Don't worry, we're going to work this out. We're going to find a way."

Steve Coplon: I'm glad you talked about co-signers because several times it required me bringing you a co-signer. That's what my point of this subject is right now. I can relate to that young man who had his father want to help him. Your story was absolutely beautiful. Now, I want to get personal. I did two things in my life with two of my sons where you were their banker. We did a credit maneuver with my youngest son, Josh, when he was in college. With this example, I would like to teach people something that they can use. Before he graduated college, I opened up a bank account with him and I think he even had to put up the money. We put $100 into an account.

Steve Coplon: I co-signed a $1,000 loan for him and we opened a savings account that you can make up to three withdrawals a month without having to pay a fee. You sent me to your branch, I took my son in and I don't want to embarrass my son, but the end of the story is kind of funny. We opened up an account, put $100 into it to cover the interest. The interest on the $1,000 loan at whatever percent it was with 12 payments over one year only was 80-some-dollars. He didn't have any credit at all, none. I used my credit at the time to cosign the $1,000 loan with my son. The money was deposited into that savings account. We had on that day, $1,100 in a bank account at your bank. The service charges, the interest rather, the whole thing cost next to nothing.

Steve Coplon: The day we went into the bank, all I said to him was, "You've got to go to the bank with me, sign a paper." He never knew he had that loan, but at the end of that year, his credit was established. He had a credit score that was very, very high because he never missed a payment. It was an automatic draft out of that savings account to pay that loan. He forgot about it and didn't even remember, but you and I did a major maneuver for my 22-year-old son to help him get his credit established. That was just one beautiful little maneuver. I'm proud of him. He's got his own business now. Last year he did $115,000 in ticket sale revenues from his music company. I helped him with the background on the financial side a little bit. I love my son Josh. I'm proud of him. You were his banker, but he didn't even know what happened.

Don Price:	That's a good story and I remember that. That was a real long time ago.
Steve Coplon:	Well, here's another one. My oldest son, Andrew, I'm very, very proud of him. He's an entrepreneur. He's amazing. We got him into real estate, and you lent him money. I watched some real estate deals for a while, and we found one that was having a hard time being sold. He bought himself a unit. Hey, he saved money his whole life. He had $25,000 saved by the time he was around 25 years old, and with that $25,000 saved, he bought a condo to live in and then he later sold it.
Steve Coplon:	Now, he rents it. He got it at a really good price. You helped him with the initial financing. Then he moved out of that when he got married. He bought a duplex and he lived in the downstairs of the duplex and rented out the upstairs. Then he bought the house next door to the duplex. If you're going to get into real estate, that's about as good as you can get, manage a house that you live next door to or even inside of. I'm just amazed at the way he's doing this.
Steve Coplon:	The house next door is not a rental. He owns that with his wife and his baby. His baby's not on the mortgage though. He's gone from just getting his first real estate deal, to owning three rental units now and a house. The rental units pretty much cover expenses in the house that he lives in and now he's formed a business. Bottom line is, Don, in life having a banker in your family so to speak, someone who you can speak and communicate effectively with, is one of the greatest things you can do. But you can never get started if you don't have good character. That's really the main point here.
Steve Coplon:	Don, in all the years that we've been banking together, both professional and personal, how was my payment record with you?
Don Price:	Your payment record has been impeccable. As I indicated earlier, you went through a lot of difficult times and you maintained your credit in perfect order and you made huge sacrifices. I won't go into all the details, but that's one of the reasons that I really admire what you do. You're an entrepreneur, you've found a lot of different ways to live your life and to maintain your standards and character. You have character up there as high as anybody can possibly have. Your passion as I said on many, many occasions is what gets you through it. You believe in yourself, you are very, very smart. Your sons take after you and they're entrepreneurs like you are. You have trained them very well and they know what they need to do to maintain good credit. Without good credit, this is a tough life to live.
Steve Coplon:	I don't want to leave out my daughter, Lindsey. She's out in Oregon, where she's been doing tie dyes for a number of years, she's ahead of the curve with her tie dye business. I have about 27 of them. Yesterday she signed onto the IRS website to get her federal ID number. I am proud to announce that she's getting a business license. I am so proud of her. Don, I hope today's show helps people who listen to it, to understand what an example of a person who leads a life of service is. And that not only includes community and family, it also includes doing what you say you're going to do.
Steve Coplon:	I think we have tied into what the theme is. The things I try to preach every day of my life is, honor your good name, and do what you say you're going to do. The last time we did the show, when we used me as an example of the credit stuff, I got really emotional because you said with all the adversity that I've been through, I paid back every single penny that you ever lent me in all those years. That is what I want to say to people. If people think I'm

bragging or boasting, not at all. I'm trying to tell you that you don't get friends like Don Price to be in your corner, if you don't become a person of character and do what you say you're going to do. Without someone like Don Price in your life, you'll have a harder time getting through things in life. I've tried to help everybody today get one step closer to knowing what you have to do in life in order to succeed.

Steve Coplon: Don, I researched some scripture, like I usually do for my shows, and I came up with some pretty interesting ones. When I searched character and integrity, the word upright stands out to me. I'm just going to knock these out really quick.

Don Price: I have one I'd like to recite before we end the show with yours. If I could, I want to share what really is one of my favorite sayings. I don't know who it's attributable to, but it's how I would like to be remembered.

Unknown

"Live so that when your children think of fairness, caring and integrity, they think of you."

Steve Coplon: Oh geez, Don. That's the most beautiful thing I've ever heard. To raise your kids right, so that they respect you and admire you that way. Don, you are remembered that way. You will be remembered that way. You are that way. That's absolutely beautiful. Here's a piece of Scripture.

Psalm 119:7

"I will praise you with an upright heart as I learn your righteous ways."

Steve Coplon: We've got to understand what living a righteous life is.

Proverbs 14:2

"Whoever fears the Lord walks up rightly, but those who despise him are devious in their ways."

Steve Coplon: That kind of speaks for itself, get your guidance from the Lord. If I was only going to do one quote for today, I would've chosen this because you know *James Taylor* had a song,

"I've seen fire and I've seen rain and lonely days I thought would never end."

Steve Coplon: I have had a life of setbacks and adversity that we have talked about, but with friends in my corner like you, I have always been able to keep moving forward. I have not always been financially well off and I've had to use banking services a lot to get me through. Fortunately, I've kept my credit strong enough and had friends who would co-sign for me to keep me moving forward because they trust me.

Proverbs 28:6

"Better is the poor that walketh in his righteousness, than he that is perverse in his ways though he may be rich."

Steve Coplon: I just love that because anyone can experience being poor financially sometimes, but we can really be rich in spirit and that's just so beautiful. I've done a lot of talking to a lot of people about goals in life. The memory that does the most, and pulls on my heartstrings, as they say, was in a school, *Achievable Dream Academy* in Newport News. 85% of those children are at risk. Their parents are currently incarcerated or have been in the past. The school offers a phenomenal program, 98% of the students go on to college. They keep them out of trouble. I had asked around the classroom, "What are your goals in life?" I had two aspiring young kids who wanted to be NFL players. I also had a young girl who said, "I want to marry a rich doctor and have a big house and a car." We had all sorts of answers there. And I had another young lady, who said, "Less violence in my home." That just does it.

Don Price: Yeah, that's tough.

Steve Coplon: Don, I believe we're all looking for peace. I think peace is the ultimate goal and the path to peace and righteousness is what I'm trying to talk about right now.

Isaiah 57:2

"He shall enter into peace. They shall rest in their beds, each one walking in his uprightness."

Steve Coplon: Don, I just want to say again, thank you. I love you. I love your family and you are a true role model. Like I said, you're humble, and you're modest. I just thank you for allowing me to share you with everyone listening. In my work I try to teach people what it takes to be successful in life and live life properly. You are a role model. You exemplify what rightness is, what uprightness is. I'll give you the last word of the show, Don. I'll let you end the show and then I'll say thank you to everybody.

Don Price: Thank you, Steve. I certainly appreciate the opportunity to speak today. I appreciate everything that you do in the community and you're just a wonderful person and God Bless you.

Steve Coplon: God Bless you too, Don. Well, everybody, the show is what I told you it was going to be. Enjoy it. Listen to it again.

Steve Coplon: Thanks for listening to *Right Thinking with Steve Coplon*. I look forward to being with you again next week. Remember: ***Don't Quit, Plan Ahead, It Will Get Better.*** God Bless you and have a great week!

To listen to the original interview, scan this QR Code with your camera, or visit:

https://rightthinkingeducation.com/FromtheLiptotheHip/Chapter-5/

CHAPTER SIX

We Are So Blessed By Godly Women with guests Donna Coplon & Richard Kay
Right Thinking With Steve Coplon - Episode 164

Steve Coplon:	Good morning. Welcome to *Right Thinking with Steve Coplon*. I'm your host, Steve Coplon. Thank you for tuning in. Let's have a great day!
Steve Coplon:	Good morning everybody. Glad to be with you. Well, today is really a special day for me. I know I say that all the time, but today is because… well, let me just read what today is. It's Episode 164, *Right Thinking with Steve Coplon*, is very pleased to announce that this week's show is called *"We Are So Blessed by Godly Women,"* with guests Donna Coplon and Richard Kay. Tune in and hear Steve have an uplifting conversation with two of the most important people in his life, as they discuss Proverbs 31, a source of great wisdom to live your life by.
Steve Coplon:	Well, I think this is the first time I have ever done this. I actually have two guests on the show at one time. Since it is the first time, I wanted to make sure that it was Donna and Richard, two of the most special people in my life. Today is the sixth in the series that started out with Episode 159, *"From the Lip to the Hip Is a Pretty Far Distance."* Richard was on a show just a couple of weeks ago and his show was titled *"Start Doing It Right Now."* It was Episode 161. He discussed obedience from a Godly perspective.
Steve Coplon:	Donna's first show with me was, wow, it was 110 episodes or so ago, called *"The Functional Family: the Positive Model."* That started the whole thing with bringing Donna on and talking from a Godly perspective about what it is to raise a family properly and where respect fits in. She has been on five or six other shows with me. Today's show is going to be incredibly special. This series is turning out really good. It's all about character and integrity building.
Steve Coplon:	The phrase *"From the Lip to the Hip Is a Pretty Far Distance"* was taught to me by my mother when I was just a kid. And it basically means that people do not always do what they say they're going to do. You can't always know that they're going to do what they said they were going to do. We'll start by bringing on Richard and Donna. Let's do that. Richard, welcome to the show.
Richard Kay:	Thank you so much, Steve. I'm glad that you gave me the opportunity to be here and I really look forward to what the Lord is going to share with us today.

73

Steve Coplon:	Well, you graced the show with your presence a couple of weeks ago. I have had wonderful, wonderful feedback on that show. You've taught so much to a lot of people. Donna, thanks for coming on the show again, I'm always trying to get you on the show and everybody's always asking, so I'm delivering it today. Thanks for being on the show, sweetheart.
Donna Coplon:	Well, I'm excited about being on the show today and I think we have a lot of great things to talk about.
Steve Coplon:	Today we're going to get Steve out of the way really quick here, because Richard has got plenty to bring to us from Proverbs 31, and Donna is going to be sharing her thoughts with him on it. Donna, I know that you listened to the episode, *"From the Lip to the Hip is a Pretty Far Distance."* What did you get out of it and any of the other shows in this series? Did I do okay on those shows?
Donna Coplon:	Well, first of all, I want to say I think it's an absolute wonderful series that we've gone into. You've brought on some wonderful people with lots of wisdom and encouragement for others, people who have such a heart for each and every person. I would like to bring out some points that I took from the shows. One of them is about keeping your word and how the Lord says in His word, yes means yes and no means no. And if you don't keep your word, it could be a lie.
Donna Coplon:	One of the points I wrote down was, keeping your word gives people a reason to trust you. It means a lot when your word is trustworthy. Another point is about broken promises, and how they can cause people not to trust you. Lefford gave an example of that about a cousin of his who had promised bicycles to him and his two sisters. They never got the bikes. His cousin never fulfilled that promise. Things like that, you never forget. Another point that someone brought out, was learning to trust yourself by knowing who you are, and not second guessing yourself. And then Richard, from your show, it was so good what you said about being obedient to God, just putting things off is a form of disobedience. And I certainly have experienced that.
Donna Coplon:	Then one of the quotes you said is, "Slow obedience is really no obedience," which is so true. Putting things off and letting time go by, thinking it's going to go away may not be right. Sometimes it's not supposed to go away. We're supposed to deal with it. And then the last point I heard that I thought was so great, was from Don Price. He had a quote, which I would love for my children to say about me, "When your children think of fairness, caring and integrity, they think of you." I thought that was just so beautiful. Then Steve and Don talked about the six pillars of character and brought those to our attention.
Donna Coplon:	There are so many great, great topics to talk about. These are some points that I wrote down, some I have dealt with myself. And then some points you talked about in the show about people making excuses, and I think we all do some of that. Those are just a few thoughts that I have to start off the show.
Steve Coplon:	Oh, wow! Hey, did you actually remember what the six pillars of character are? When Don and I brought them out, I thought that was right on target. Do you want to share them with us?
Donna Coplon:	I did write them down, I was planning to talk more about them a bit later. Being trustworthy, respectful, responsible, fair, caring, and a good citizen. I really try to live by

these characteristics.

Steve Coplon: Well, that's why you're on the show today, Donna. You are a person with good character who has a message that needs to be shared with people. Your message will help all of us to grow. With that said, I want to tell the audience a little bit about Richard. I've said it many times before on previous shows that Richard has been on with me. He is an incredible human being and he exercises and possesses great discernment. He's a person I share a lot of time with in a very deep, personal way. Life's hard to navigate sometimes and I'm blessed to have a friend like Richard who's always there for me.

Steve Coplon: The show we did a couple of weeks ago on Episode 161 was just so beautiful. Richard was as impassioned as I've ever heard anyone when he said, "I hope that I've always made myself available to you." That's what he said when we first met. I told Richard, "Richard, you've been available to me and been there for me as much as anybody in my life, and I treasure our friendship." Richard had an international radio show that he asked me to be a guest on and then he helped me to get my own show.

Steve Coplon: Richard currently has his own show produced by the same producer as mine, Chuck Christie. But his show varies between 15 to 20 minutes per episode and it's called *"Reflections on the Word with Richard Kay"*. I urge everyone, if you like Richard's voice, doesn't matter what he says, if you like that beautiful voice he's got, go to *"Reflections on the Word with Richard Kay"*. He has around 420 episodes. It's so wonderful to listen to him for a few minutes every day whenever I can. Always a great message.

Steve Coplon: So, Richard, the reason I've asked you back today is because I thought it would be a blessing to have you and Donna and I engage in a conversation and see where it goes, see where the Spirit leads us on Proverbs 31. You had suggested that it was something you've been wanting to do with Donna on my show. Why did you want to have a conversation with Donna and I on Proverbs 31?

Richard Kay: Well, Steve, once again, thank you for giving me the privilege and opportunity to be able to speak to your audience and to just have a conversation with you and Donna. I think that in our culture today, there is so much gender confusion and there's so much positional misunderstanding about how homes are to be structured and what a family is like. I was so impressed when I heard segments of the show that Donna was on, about the function aspect of a family. And the vital role that a Godly woman has in being able to help hold and mold the family into a Godly family, a family that God would be pleased with.

Richard Kay: As I studied and as I looked more into the responsibilities of a husband and wife, you begin to understand, through the Scripture, the type of perspective we are supposed to strive for. In the apostle Paul's letter to the church at Ephesus, he writes about wives and husbands. I think that it's so important as we begin this type of discussion, that it is based in the scriptural foundation of the responsibilities of husbands and wives.

Richard Kay: I'd just like to read that particular portion:

Ephesians 5:22-28

Wives, submit to your husbands as to the Lord, for the husband is the head of the wife as Christ is the head of the church, His body, of which He is savior. Now, as the church submits to Christ, also, wives should submit to their husbands in everything.

Husbands, love your wives just as Christ loved the church and gave Himself up for her to make her Holy, cleansing her by the washing with water through the Word, and to present her to Himself as a radiant church, without stain or wrinkle, or any other blemish, but Holy and blameless. In this same way, husbands ought to love their wives as their own bodies. He who loves his wife, loves himself.

Richard Kay: I thought about that particular portion as we looked at the Proverbs 31 description. There's one part in the narrative in Proverbs 31 that is so much of a blessing. I just want to give a little bit of reference here. There's a service that is provided in Jewish homes, which I'm sure many of you are familiar with. It's a Sabbath service and for Jewish people, Shabbat. It states that the Sabbath service in the Jewish home, unashamedly, reveals the high position of women in Israel from biblical times until the present.

Richard Kay: Sabbath is primarily a home centered family celebration, which makes it only natural that the mother of the home received the honor of welcoming the Sabbath by lighting of the candles. Traditionally, the husband recites what is, without doubt, the most eloquent tribute to Godly women that has ever been penned. And that's Proverbs 31:10-31. It presents a divine challenge for womanhood, diligent homemaker, valuable helper, nurturing mother, upright and God fearing woman.

Richard Kay: The wife of noble character receives a reward for faithfulness. She is not dependent on the temporary, superficial, deceptive facade of charm, which is a mere outward varnish, easily scarred and marred by people and circumstances. She is not dependent on beauty, which can depart like an unfaithful friend to make room for wrinkles and blemishes. Rather, she crowns an enduring satisfying fear of the Lord with a reverent and obedient spirit, that makes her worthy of praise and honor from her family and the creator Himself.

Richard Kay: Homemaking is unique in combining the most menial jobs with the most meaningful tasks. It is a challenge to accommodate others without losing one's own identity. It is a demanding pursuit, but the fringe benefits are terrific. I'd like to read what William Booth, the founder of the Salvation Army, said about his own wife, Catherine, at the time of her death. He says, "To me, she has been made of God, never failing sympathy, reliable wisdom and unvarnished truth. In short, all that is noble and good, and consequently a tower of strength, a mine of wealth, and an overflowing fountain of comfort and joy."

Richard Kay: Well, when we look at this type of description of Godly women, and I'm sure there are many that we can reflect on. This portion of a wife of noble character is something to find. How much more worth is she than rubies or things that we place great value on? But I do think that one of the things that is so important, and Donna brought it out, it's one of the pillars that you spoke of, and that is trust. It's an amazing element in the love combination. Her husband has full confidence in her.

Richard Kay: I think today, women have to be placed in a position of higher esteem than society has put them in. I think women have been manipulated, and in many ways, they have been denigrated. I believe that they have fallen short of what God really wants to bring out in them, not because they desired it, but because society placed those types of demands on them. So, to be able to talk with Godly women of all ages is such a blessing, because it teaches men how to really respect what the Lord has created and placed for us to be completed by.

Richard Kay:	I know I can speak only in reference to a few women, one, my own wife. I can watch what she does, not as much just what she says, but what she does. How she reaches out to the poor, how she helps the needy, how she's always extending herself to someone else before she thinks of her own needs. That is a compliment that I can make to Godly women. And I can also say that the women I have come to know, in Donna's case, I have seen in a quiet manner, a way that she epitomizes what a Godly woman is.
Richard Kay:	The vantage point in how she takes care of her household and what she actually does methodically, is greatly appreciated even though in some cases goes unnoticed. Donna, I just want to know for our purposes, and I want you to know how much we appreciate what you do in your own household. I know it's not easy, I know that it is, in many ways, a very trying and difficult task. But I also want you to know that you have a husband who is perhaps more supportive of you than you realize, because he expresses things in a way that places him in a certain perspective with other people.
Richard Kay:	He's very pronounced in what he says, very direct, but I'm sure that he shows you the type of love and respect that is described, as a husband loving his wife as Christ loved the church and gave himself for. I really believe that your marriage relationship has gone through many, many trials. You've gone through physical trials and you've gone through spiritual trials, and you've probably experienced more than what, perhaps, some other marriages have. But in that, my prayer is that you've grown closer together and that you've been drawn closer to the Lord.
Richard Kay:	Your part, Donna, in being able to exemplify what a Godly woman is in a home, is so vital. And I commend you for it. I think that this is a part of what we need to be able to express more, not just on Mother's Day, once a year. I read something just recently, and I don't mean to be repetitive, but I read something recently that said, 'that all women are not mothers, but it says all mothers are women'. And I thought about that for just a moment and it made me reflect on my own mother and mothers throughout all time.
Richard Kay:	What you endure just in childbirth, believe me, if men were tasked with the birthing of children, the human race would have become extinct thousands upon thousands of years ago. Men could not sustain that type of pain. And I know that. I know that God has endowed women with the ability to sustain pain in a way that men, perhaps, could not even conceive. But yet out of that pain and out of that experience, such beauty comes forth in the birth of a child. And I think that that's something that can be shared. And I realized that it's not something that is easily understood.
Richard Kay:	I believe women communicate it far better than men do. But I want you to know you're definitely appreciated. And I'm going to stop and allow you to comment on how you feel about what we've discussed to this extent. How God has helped you fulfill the calling that He has on your life as a Godly woman.
Donna Coplon:	Wow, that's absolutely beautiful. Everything that you said just makes me, just as I'm sitting here, appreciate so much being a woman, a Godly woman. And just the words that you have said has uplifted me so much. I have a surrounding group of women who are Godly women. My sisters, we've learned so much from each other and I'm trying to share more with my daughter. I have a husband who probably believes in me more than I believe in myself sometimes. There might be times when he probably does push me a little more than I want to be pushed, but I believe what you said, he honors, and he respects me so much. In fact,

that's one of the qualities he told me that attracted him to me: the respect that I demand for myself.

Donna Coplon: When I was reading Proverbs 31, the Proverb woman, I look at these verses not so much to imitate this, because I mean, this woman is incredible. I mean, there's no way that one person could cover all this that is talked about in the verses. But I feel like the best I can be is what God wants me to be. And it just gives me so much inspiration when I read about the Proverbs woman. We have to look to God, that's what I do. I have to look to God to perfect me in what He wants me to be. Because, you're right, the world, social media, just what's going on out there is not where the answers are, in being the Godly woman we are meant to be. It only comes from the Lord and it only comes when you seek it.

Donna Coplon: Most women have gotten caught up a little bit in looks or fashion, but that goes away. I mean, you don't have that for the rest of your life. Your looks, I mean, it has a lot to do with what's on the inside. And that's where I try to keep my thoughts. It doesn't matter what other people think, it's what God values me as, what He values in me. For me, for the start of even trying to be a Godly woman, I have to start my day in the word with Him. It's the most important part of my day. The meditation and the time of just giving it to Him, letting all those fleshly thoughts and anxieties, and worries just hand it over to Him because it's just too much to carry.

Donna Coplon: I don't do it perfectly, there's days that it's very difficult, but I always know that He is my rock. That's where my solid rock is, is to go to Him. Trying to figure it out in this world, nothing really makes much sense until you know that you have to go to the Lord. The pillars of character that we spoke of earlier is pretty much how I try to live my life. Like you said, trust, being trustworthy for people to be able to depend on me. My husband depends on me, my family, my parents, they all depend on me. To me, that's always been pretty much the top priority in my life. Knowing that if somebody needs me or somebody needs to talk to me, I'm going to be there. I'm certainly going to be there for them.

Donna Coplon: Ever since I was a little girl, the responsibilities in the home of a woman have been important to me. I watched my mother, her mother, and my friends' mothers. Taking that whole role of being in the home, having a nice home, a comfortable home, a clean home, an organized home for your family, it's always been so important to me ever since I was very small. I just enjoyed that. The responsibility of making sure your family stays healthy eating the right foods, serving good dinners, making sure you have the things they need such as clean clothes, all that makes me feel fulfilled. Keeping things as nice as you can, has always been important to me.

Donna Coplon: A caring part of being the character of a Godly woman is helping in the community. I've done a lot of food pantries in different churches and it just gives me such a fulfillment to do these things for our community. You want to keep up what's going on in your home, and you also want to share that love and concern for other people. Also, another characteristic of a Godly woman is being fair. Just being fair to people, your children especially, because as you're raising them, they know when you're not fair, they know.

Donna Coplon: Being a good citizen is a very important part of good character. To me, being a good citizen is having respect for others and authority. Watching how I speak to people. Showing kindness and trying to understand where people are coming from. Not taking things so literally or not taking it so deep if someone said something to you in the wrong tone. Forgiving them.

These are all so important. I believe all these characteristics are what has made me the person I am. Of course, there's lots of things that I could definitely work on, there's lots of things that I wish I could do better. But when I'm focused, when I know that each day my value is in what God sees in me, it makes everything seem better.

Richard Kay: Donna, as I listen to you and I hear the experiences that have really helped you to grow and be able to pursue God, and what He really wants to develop in you, I am encouraged and I hope that perhaps women who may be listening to us today can appreciate far more that there is someone speaking, not to them, but for them. And in what you have said is such an encouragement because how many women actually do these things that you've described, and as mothers perhaps, and it is so unnoticed. In fact, in many households, it is literally taken for granted.

Richard Kay: I think about it in relation to another Godly woman, in a family I've known for many, many years. Most people would not have realized that this particular wife was such an integral part of the success of her husband's executive position. What I found to be so impressive was she wasn't doing this because she wanted others to follow her particular example, she did it out of her heart.

Richard Kay: She provided for her children, and she cared for the needy and the poor in such a way, just as you described, working in a food pantry or a clothing ministry and to help the poor. She would shop at some of the better neighborhood thrift stores, and she would outfit her family, including her husband and herself. These clothes had been placed in the thrift stores, where she could purchase them for a fraction of what they would have cost in brand new condition from a main retailer. She would do this, with the sole purpose of having her family look presentable, and not in hand me downs. No one ever knew.

Richard Kay: Some of the things that she was able to select, God just endowed her with the ability to find very fine clothing at a fraction of the cost. The importance of this was that the money she saved, she gave it up to the Lord. She provided it to Him so that He could place it in the hands and in the homes of others who had such need. I witnessed her doing this for years. I've known this family for, I would say close to 30 years, and they have never gone without, and they have always reached out to the poor.

Richard Kay: In her husband's case, it was done through an executive capacity which made it noticeable, but in her case, it went very much unnoticed. However, many of the people were aware of her generosity. One of the parts of Proverbs 31 is what you just spoke about when you were talking about reaching out to the poor, but in a portion of Proverbs 31 it says:

Proverbs 31:20

"She opens her arms to the poor and extends her hands to the needy."

Richard Kay: I think that it's beyond just taking care of your own household. That it's very good management in a household so that there is more to bless others, and without any selfishness in many cases, providing for others, rather than even providing for yourself.

Richard Kay: Donna, I appreciate what you've said; the description of how you can organize a household. In many cases, the one thing that is so impressive to me, and I know that I can speak to other men that may be listening, they talk about women being able to do something referred to as multitasking. And I have watched. I've watched so many times my own wife, how she can do four or five things at one time, make them all come out almost in the same timeframe. As I'm sure you can do as well in many ways in a home. Men don't have that same quality.

Richard Kay: Now, I'm not saying that we can't do things, but I don't think we can concentrate our focus in so many areas. We can be more focused perhaps in one area and accomplish that, maybe in two, but multitasking for men is a very difficult task. It's a very difficult thing. I'm so pleased that God gave us women so they could complete that portion of our need in life, because if it was left up to us, there'd be so many things that would be left undone. Men are essentially tasked with three basic functions in a family.

Richard Kay: One is, they are to be the provider. Now, that doesn't mean they're the only provider, but they are to be a provider. Secondly, they are to be the protector of the family. I think that a family rests in security when they realize that there is a husband, a father that is there to protect them or that his influence is there to protect them. And then thirdly, and perhaps even more importantly, he is to be a proclaimer. He is to be the one who proclaims God's word over his family. He's the one to pronounce the blessing over his family, which begins with his wife.

Richard Kay: I think more husbands need to bless their wives, so that the Lord can bring out the beauty of the wife. The longer I've been married and the longer that I can see women as we age, what I find is that their inner beauty begins to radiate far more than their outer beauty. And for me, it just epitomizes what God is saying in Proverbs 31 as He describes the virtue of a Godly woman. Again, I have brought out something from perhaps an experiential position where I've known women who unselfishly have watched the Lord develop in them the same things that you've described in many ways, the character building that is being done internally, inside as He begins to radiate through you.

Richard Kay: And I appreciate so much your willingness to allow others to come to know that, because I think it's such a vital need. In today's society, I really believe that it is not a gender position, it is a Godly position. And I don't think men can fulfill that role. Not totally, and I don't believe that God meant for men to fulfill that role. That's the reason that He created women, and I so appreciate God's wisdom in that. Also, Donna, I can say one other thing in regard to what you have mentioned and that is when you talked about being trustworthy and fair, you said you need to be fair to your children.

Richard Kay: I think children learn who they can depend on through a Godly mother, a mother who actually builds a condition of trust, and realizing even in discipline that there's fairness in what she is doing, especially when children don't understand. And when they look at an example, they need to understand at some point, young women need to understand the responsibility that they have. Fairness is something that you began to talk about. I'd like to hear you expand a little more on how you demonstrate fairness in a situation even with grown children, and that happens as we age and develop families.

Donna Coplon: Well, it is a tricky thing because I was thinking mostly of when my children were little, not just raising them, but also raising other people's children and babysitting other people's children as well. While I was a kindergarten assistant for years, I always tried to treat each child fair, no matter whose children they were. It did not matter if it was my child or not. Regardless of the situation or what they were asking for, I always wanted to be fair. I've had to ask myself that many times while raising stepchildren.

Donna Coplon: That was the direction I was thinking of when I made a note on fairness. Thinking about being fair so that if one child witnessed another situation, would they have felt they were treated the same way? Or were they treated differently because they weren't your natural born child? Situations like that. I didn't really think about it too deeply when I wrote it down, but it's just something I've always wondered about how my children felt in many situations of disciplining, did I handle it in a fair way? Can't think of a certain particular example at the moment, but that's what I was leaning towards.

Donna Coplon: I wanted to go back to something you also said when we were just talking about running a family. I think balance is the word that I've always tried to live with in my life. Being balanced in the home. I think where so many young mothers really get into trouble, especially now, is that the balance is off. It could be something as simple as maybe doing too much outside the home. They could be involved with church activities or in wonderful, Godly things, but how much time is that really taking? Is that taking away from the time that they could be home with their children, or their family, or making a better dinner?

Donna Coplon: We've all gotten caught up in it and it's easy to get out of balance. And I really have tried to live my life staying in a balance. If something seems to start to go too far and I'm feeling the stress and anxiety, then I know I've got to get back to that place of balance. I've got to center myself again. That can be many things in life. It could be your health, your exercising, your eating, doing too much. Not saying no enough or maybe saying yes too much. Keeping that balance to me keeps confusion out. It keeps the family running in a more orderly way where everybody has their fair time.

Donna Coplon: Another thing I was thinking of, is being fair in regard to individual attention in your family. Not giving too much to one and not the other. Balance to me is a big word in my life, just trying to keep everything balanced. You can't do it all, you can't be perfect. My daughter is 36 and she's raising two children and it's easy to get off balance just trying to keep up with everything. I think the social media and the stress that these young mothers try to keep up with, seems more overwhelming now, than it used to.

Donna Coplon: Just trying to keep up with everybody's ideas, opinions, thoughts, the ideas that they get on social media just to even have a birthday party, can overwhelm anyone. It goes to a place where it's almost like a competition. If there is anything that I hope everyone gets from this conversation, it is to keep life balanced. Starting with God, and beginning with Him in the morning, is what works for me. It seems to make the day go much better than starting the day with the news or stressful things that are going on. I'm not saying, close the world out, that's not the answer either. We have to live here, we have to understand what's going on around us, we should not go too far on one thing or another.

Richard Kay: Donna, I think there's such importance in what you've expressed, the ability to accomplish those things that you realize are vital in taking care of your household and yet maintaining balance. And I have to say that I don't know of too many couples who have endured the type of pressure, let's say, physical, emotional pressure that the two of you have had to endure and sustain for 16 plus years. And I'm now speaking of how you've been able to keep these things in balance and yet you've been there for your husband as he has been living with and dealing with a vicious disease that has, in many ways, would have totally debilitated many people.

Richard Kay: And yet I've seen the determination in him that is representative of very few people in being able to deal with something like Multiple Myeloma. That's an area that we could probably pursue in another conversation, but that portion of balance is something that is… it takes the wisdom and the strength of God, developed in you Donna, that helps to be there in the background for Steve. Steve is more out front, more of the, let's say the visible character. What you do, not just behind the scenes, but what you do in support of his efforts and being able to be there for him when others don't see what he has to go through on a daily basis.

Richard Kay: When he is going through very difficult periods in his battle, that part is such a strength that God places in you. I realized that we could probably continue this conversation and I look forward to being able to. I want to read the last portion of Proverbs 31 and I really believe that it does tell us what it is that you, in so many ways, have described as God has developed. It says in the 27th verse and following:

Proverbs 31:27-31

She watches over the affairs of her household and does not eat the bread of idleness. Her children arise and call her blessed. Her husband also and he praises her. Many women do noble things but you surpass them all. Charm is deceptive and beauty is fleeting, but a woman who fears the Lord is to be praised. Give her the reward she has earned, and let her works bring her praise at the city gate.

Richard Kay: I think that what we have discussed in so many ways is a growing position as we surrender to the Lord. A husband and a wife submit themselves to each other.

Scripture Says,

"As unto the Lord."

Richard Kay: The husband being the head of the wife is not her boss. He is the leader, but she is also one who guides, both submitted to the Lord. He pours in wisdom and counsel in the woman and He pours in understanding, compassion, love, and appreciation. As He develops the oneness of that marriage. That oneness is so needed in today's society, and I think that it's needed in many, many areas, but in one aspect agrees with what God says.

Scripture Says,

"Wherever two can agree as touching, anything they shall ask, it will be done for them by my father."

Richard Kay: This is Jesus speaking, and I think He is saying to marriages, "Come into agreement with what God wants to produce in your life. Come into agreement together about the balance that is needed in your home." How do you do that? You can only do it by surrendering and submitting yourselves, one to another in reference and in awe of what God develops as He brings two into one. And that oneness is not just to be able to be an example, that oneness reflects His character.

Richard Kay: It is God's character that is coming out in you Donna, and in you Steve, that is exemplified in what we have been discussing. I know that this discussion has been more in reference to the Godly woman, but for every man who develops strength, purpose in God, there is a Godly woman supporting him. There is a Godly woman praying for him. There is a Godly woman who is there for him. I appreciate so much that God has placed a woman in our lives that can be there when we are weak and helps us to develop the strength that God has poured into both of us.

Richard Kay: That to me is what we are growing into as we are transformed into His image. And I believe that in your examples, and what you've learned in your marriage, in your life, and as you said, it has not been perfect, and I'm sure in many ways, it has been messy. There have been difficult times. We all experience, but as we surrender and submit ourselves more and more to what the Lord wants to accomplish, we truly begin to understand what it means to be able to epitomize the prayer that Jesus prayed in the Garden of Gethsemane; where He said, "Not my will but thine be done."

Richard Kay: That is the supporting element in Godly women. Godly women don't ask for their will to be accomplished. They ask for God to accomplish His will through them. And I appreciate that so much in what you actually exemplify in your marriage and in your home. And I hope that this is something that can be demonstrated in marriages and in homes everywhere as we submit, and we begin to realize and surrender to God's will and purpose in our lives. It is His will and purpose that we come into agreement with Him. It's not our will that is important. It is His.

Richard Kay: And I'm so blessed to know you Donna and Steve, and to actually see God developing in you the transforming character that He has placed in you.

Scripture Says,

"Even before the foundation of the world."

Richard Kay: God knew we would be sitting here today. He knew that we would be having this conversation today before He ever formed the world. What a wonderful, amazing, all-knowing God we serve. And it's a pleasure, a joy to get to know people who through their lives have surrendered so much and are surrendering so much of their own agenda, their own will, their own plans to let God produce in them the beauty and the holiness that He desires. The two of you exemplify that in your marriage, and I appreciate so much just knowing that God can accomplish that and if He can do that for you, then there's hope for marriages the world over.

Steve Coplon: Richard, God Bless you and thank you for honoring us today the way you have. Your message is a blessing, the way that you delivered it and used Donna and the nice things you said about me and our marriage. Hopefully, many people will listen to and be able to see what can be theirs also, when they have that relationship with the Lord. I just want to end it with just one quick thought here. We're overtime now and I need to end it fairly quickly. We'll do it again sometime, like I stated at the beginning of the broadcast, "Tune in and Hear Steve have an uplifting conversation with two of the most important people in his life as they discuss Proverbs 31, a source of great wisdom to live your life by." I know we've done that today. Thanks to you Richard, and thanks to Donna. I have very few regrets in my life, but one of the biggest single regrets I can say right now, is that I never had the opportunity to have Donna know my mother. Because I've just been incredibly blessed in my life to have Donna as my wife. I asked her to marry me after only knowing each other for three weeks.

Steve Coplon: We were married two months later, and we've been married, going on 17 years. And so, if people tell me that I do things right, that I might have it right, that I'm smart, that's the proof right there. That I knew when I met Donna, I wanted to be her husband. Donna God Bless you. Thanks for sharing yourself today, and I'll give you a moment to thank Richard.

Donna Coplon: Thank you so much, Richard. I really enjoyed this discussion and I'm up to doing this again.

Steve Coplon: Well, hallelujah. Praise the Lord.

Donna Coplon: I think there's a whole lot more to talk about.

Richard Kay: I look forward to it.

Steve Coplon: Richard God Bless you, Donna God Bless you and God Bless everybody and have a wonderful week.

Steve Coplon: Thanks for listening to *Right Thinking with Steve Coplon*. I look forward to being with you again next week. Remember: ***Don't Quit, Plan Ahead, It Will Get Better.*** God Bless you and have a great week!

To listen to the original interview, scan this QR Code with your camera, or visit:

https://rightthinkingeducation.com/FromtheLiptotheHip/Chapter-6/

CHAPTER SEVEN

You Make Your Habits, Your Habits Make You with guest Lefford Fate
Right Thinking With Steve Coplon - 165

Steve Coplon: Good morning. Welcome to *Right Thinking with Steve Coplon.* I'm your host, Steve Coplon. Thank you for tuning in. Let's have a great day!

Steve Coplon: Good morning! Glad to be with you. What an amazing show we are going to have today. Lefford Fate was on the show five weeks ago, Episode 160. The show ended with Lefford saying, "Let's get on a show and talk about habits soon." So, let me jump right into today's show. This is Episode 165.

Right Thinking with Steve Coplon is very pleased to announce that this week's show is called ***You Make Your Habits, Your Habits Make You with guest Lefford Fate.*** Tune in and hear **Steve** and **Lefford** continue their conversation on *people doing what they say they are going to do* as they explore the *power of habits.* *Good habits* are so very important in being able to *gain the trust of others* so that you can be a *success in life.*

Lefford Fate: Thank you, Steve. I'm glad to be here, bro. Because habits, this is an important topic.

Steve Coplon: Lefford, everybody loves listening to you. You've been on the show I think fifteen times now.

Lefford Fate: It's a habit.

Steve Coplon: Yeah. That's what the nun said.

Today's show is the seventh show in my series ***"From the Lip to the Hip is a Pretty Far Distance."*** I am really happy; it's catching on. A lot of people are telling me they like the way that I am doing this study on character and integrity.

Steve Coplon: When I started the series, Don Green of **The Napoleon Hill Foundation,** who is a really close friend of yours, gave me permission to use actual pages out of *"Think and Grow Rich"* the masterpiece by Napoleon Hill. The last chapter of the book is titled, *"How to Outwit the Six Ghosts of Fear."* From that chapter, I used the *"Fifty-Seven Famous Alibis by Old Man IF."* I will now read the last one of the alibis:

Napoleon Hill

*IF, ***and this is the greatest of them all****

I had the courage to see myself as I really am, I would find out what is wrong with me and correct it. *Then I might have a chance to profit by my mistakes and learn something from the experience of others, for I know that there is something WRONG with me or I would now be where I WOULD HAVE BEEN IF I had spent more time analyzing my weaknesses and less time building alibis to cover them.*

Steve Coplon: Lefford, as you know, in this series I am bringing on guests that have what I consider to be tremendous wisdom that others need to hear. I want people to benefit from their testimonies and life experiences. Today as we talk about habits, please share anything that you want from your own experiences, and how you learned so much about life the hard way.

Steve Coplon: One of the best things that you've ever said on previous shows, that I love, correct me if I get this wrong, is that you've got high energy, but low intelligence?

Lefford Fate: High energy and low IQ.

Steve Coplon: Lefford, I doubt that you have low IQ.

Please share anything that will help people learn more about why they need to do what they say they're going to do, and how developing good habits and getting rid of old habits will help them have a better life. The floor is yours, or the microphone is yours, so to speak.

Lefford Fate: There you go. Well thank you Steve, I appreciate it. This whole quote about you make your habits and your habits make you came from a talk that I gave about choices. First, we make our choices, and then our choices make us. But the thing about habits, Steve, is that how you do things ultimately determines who you are. It was Gandhi and Lao Tzu said that your thoughts become words, your words become actions, your actions become habits, your habits become character, your character becomes your destiny.

Lefford Fate: But in the middle of that whole thing, Steve, is habits. What you continuously do, you become. Habits are, they're very light when they start out, but then they become heavy chains. If this is true, if what I'm saying is true, then how do you use your habits to become the person you desire to be? Because, if you keep doing stuff over, and over, and over, then it becomes a groove. Napoleon Hill actually talked about you having a groove. It's like, I grew up in the country and we used to have dirt roads. Did you have dirt roads where you were from, or are you more of a city boy?

Steve Coplon: The street I grew up on was the fourth house built on a country road that was paved. We didn't have dirt roads, but it was farmland all around.

Lefford Fate: I kind of grew up on these old roads, in Georgia you're talking about red clay. And they've got these ruts. A rut is basically if you keep going down the same path over, and over, and over, you start grooving into a thing. And that becomes a habit. The more you repeat something, whether it's good or bad, positive or negative, you start grooving. If you get to a point, where you get in that groove, then you'll stay on that same path forever, and ever, and ever. Again, whether it's positive or negative.

Lefford Fate: The reason I said I wanted to talk about habits is that if we want to do anything in life on a positive note, first we have to decide what we want to do and start working towards that.

Steve Coplon: Purpose. Goals.

Lefford Fate:	Whatever your purpose is. But again, it could be your purpose. It could be on purpose. Does that make sense? Sometimes, we do things by design, and sometimes we do things by default. All of that is based on habit. Before the show, you were talking about *Stephen Covey's, "7 Habits of Highly Effective People."* Basically, those are things that you do to be successful and to get what you want out of life. You can have habits that are successful, or you can have habits that aren't successful.
Lefford Fate:	I actually have an addictive personality. I know a lot of people say there is no such thing. There are alcoholics, and there are drug addicts. There are people in my family who do these things. Since I have a habitual personality, an addictive personality, I figured out a long time ago that if this is my nature, why not do things that are positive? Do positive things that'll get me towards where I want to go, versus slip into a rut and do things that I don't want?
Lefford Fate:	I read every day. I probably read three or four books a week. This is a habit, and because I have this as a habit, I'm continually learning. I'm continually growing. On the other side of it, like I told you before, I actually ended up divorced and lost my first wife because I had a habit of working all the time. I start working and I can work for 15 or 16 hours. She told me once that it seemed that I cared more about working and more about the Air Force than I cared about her. That was a habit. Whether it's good, or whether it's bad, whether it's positive or negative, you start making your habits, and then your habits start making you.
Steve Coplon:	I would like to make a comment about that. It is kind of personal, but you've talked about it very much in previous shows. When you were working like that while in your first marriage, you didn't realize that you were doing that. In our last show, you talked about how your habit of working all the time caused problems with your second wife. You said once she said that all she needed was a phone call.
Steve Coplon:	You were so into being the provider. I think that is what this is all about. Sometimes when a man is doing all he can to take on the responsibility of being the provider, he loses sight of some things that are important. He develops a bad habit that he doesn't realize is bad. Is that fair to say?
Lefford Fate:	It's fair to say, and you may have heard this quote before. "A person's biggest weakness is often a strength overdone."
Steve Coplon:	No, I haven't heard that before. But I love that.
Lefford Fate:	"A person's biggest weakness is often a strength overdone."
Steve Coplon:	That's another way to say, "Don't mess up a good thing."
Lefford Fate:	Right. Because I'm a worker, I'm good at it, and I enjoy it. Sometimes, I was getting my actualization, my bit of self-worth based on my ability to work and work hard. I was good at it, so I just kept doing it. Again, you've got to be careful because you can get in the habit of doing anything. You can get in the habit of doing anything positive. You can be like, Ebenezer Scrooge, you can get into the habit of saving too much. In this day and time people say, "How in the world can you save too much?" When money becomes your idol. When stuff becomes your idol, and you're a slave to your money versus your money is your slave. Does that make sense?
Steve Coplon:	Yes, it does.

| Lefford Fate: | It wasn't like it was a bad thing. It was just that it was a strength overdone that became a weakness to me. Again, it's habitual. Because, what happens is you start doing stuff, and you get into this groove. Basically, you start getting satisfaction from it. There's a guy named *Charles Duhigg*. Have you ever heard of him? He did a book called ***"The Power of Habit."*** |

| Steve Coplon: | Yeah. Let me answer you. You ready for this? |

| Lefford Fate: | Yeah. |

| Steve Coplon: | **Charles Duhigg**

Habits are powerful but delicate. They can emerge outside our consciousness or can be deliberately designed. They often occur without our permission but can be reshaped by fiddling with their parts. They shape our lives far more than we realize. They are so strong, in fact, that they cause our brains to cling to them at the exclusion of all else, including common sense. |

| Lefford Fate: | There you go. |

| Steve Coplon: | Saw you coming, Lefford. Came across him in my research for the show. |

| Lefford Fate: | He talks about there is a cue that something happens. For me, a cue is something needs to be done. We've been doing these shows together for three years now. Being that you know me, you know I'm always into achievement, getting stuff done. I'll see something that needs to be done, and then I automatically jump into, how can I get this done bigger, better, faster, and stronger? Because it's going to be positive. |

| Lefford Fate: | Then I get into a routine. I'll read about it. I'll study it. I'll look and see if there's a TED Talk about it, a YouTube video. I'll try to find out who is an expert on it. Then, typically what happens for me is, I'll do it and I'll get some type of reward. Either an attaboy, or a boost in my self-esteem. Then because of that, I get into this cycle of success. |

| Lefford Fate: | You know, even success can be habitual and can be negative. If that's all you're doing is continuously growing, going, going, going, going. And if you're doing it for the wrong reason, or you're doing it to the detriment of your relationships, to your health, to all those things, it can be negative. You have to keep an eye on things even if you're successful at it. |

| Steve Coplon: | Can I respond to that? |

| Lefford Fate: | Yes, sir. |

| Steve Coplon: | Thank you. Everything you said is absolutely true. I had a period of my life back early out where I was doing really well. I had a whole lot of friends that had very little motivation. They got into being a community of very laid back people. They used to say to me, "Relax, Steve, man. You don't have to go for all those goals that you've got. You don't need to finish college. Why do you want to be an accountant? So, you can be materialistic and get into all that?" The point is, you've got to recognize people that don't have enough ambition, so to speak, that they haven't connected the dots yet that there's nothing wrong with being successful. |

| Steve Coplon: | We've done shows on success and we can do more. The point here is that you were talking about overachievers that get hung up in their own success. Maybe they get into being too |

materialistic or something else. The hardship population that I work with are not these types of overachievers. They are generally underachievers. The overachievers, they have enough money to go see a shrink sometimes. But the underachievers, they don't have enough money to go do that. So, I need to connect with them and find out what's holding them back. Look at their habits.

Have you come across a guy named Douglas Conant in your travels of following positive people?

Lefford Fate: I heard you mention that name before. I don't think that I know him.

Steve Coplon: When I googled habits to be prepared for today's show, I came across Douglas Conant and Conant Leadership. I saw an article: **"32 Quotes About the Power of Habits."** It is exactly what you and I are talking about. It was subtitled *'Grow or Die'*. I encourage everyone listening to go to that article. Douglas Conant is phenomenally successful. He's incredibly caring about people. Let me tell you how successful he is.

Steve Coplon: He was the president of Nabisco Foods at one time. He was the CEO of Campbell's Soup Company. He was the chairman of Avon products. There is a whole list of companies that he has been involved with through his brilliant career. He started a leadership company, Conant Leadership. I picked up a great deal of great quotes from his article **"32 Quotes About the Power of Habits."**

Before I share some of them, I'm going to talk about something that is more personal to you. Lefford, you are a basketball player and you are talking about positive habits. I am shifting to another article from another person.. I'm kind of mixing apples and oranges here.

Lefford Fate: I like fruit.

Steve Coplon: That's very good. In my preparation, I found an article written by a gentleman named David Mathis. In the article, he is talking about positive habits and negative habits. He says we think about habits generally as "nasty little things." He goes on to talk about, how you've got to break that habit, quit doing that irritating thing, quit biting your lip, knock out your smoking and your drinking, get rid of your drugs. Those are all bad habits. But he also talks about how good habits can save your life, such as looking both ways before you cross the street.

Steve Coplon: You teach your little kids a habit. So, there's a lot of really good habits, and that's what we're trying to teach people right now, and it's how you develop good habits that will give you a better life. Here's the thing, he said, he wanted you to get in the habit of turning to the Lord. His article is faith-based. It is titled: **"How Your Habits Show and Shape Your Heart."** It's about getting in the habit of giving it up to the Lord. He says, "Habits make Stephen Curry, the NBA's best shooter, Mike Trout, baseball's best hitter, Jordan Spieth, the world's most promising young golfer. Habits keeps a NASCAR driver from losing control and going airborne when he's nudged going into turn three at Daytona."

Steve Coplon: The point is, Lefford, you're a really good basketball player, you're going to play it down, but you like to play basketball. You didn't develop that jump shot from the corner by just shooting it two or three times and believing that you can make it any time that you want. You developed it by practicing and developing it until it became a habit.

Now, to go back to Donald Conant. He is really amazing, and his articles are something worth reading. Lefford, you've already quoted from Mahatma Gandhi about your beliefs become your thoughts, and so forth, ultimately your destiny. That one was in Douglas Conant's article.

Steve Coplon: You mentioned at the beginning of today's show how the chains that hold us back are so hard to break. I've got two more here from Douglas Conant's article that are speak exactly to what you said. One is from Horace Mann. He is considered to be one of the greatest educators ever in America. Horace Mann goes all the way back to the 19th century.

Horace Mann

"Habit is a cable. We weave a thread of it each day, and at last we cannot break it."

Steve Coplon: That talks about how hard it is to break a habit. Now, Samuel Johnson, oh my gosh, Samuel Johnson goes even further back. I believe to the 1700s. He wrote one of the most important dictionaries in the history of the English language. Here's his quote on breaking habits:

Samuel Johnson

"The chains of habit are too weak to be felt until they are too strong to be broken."

Steve Coplon: Continuing with the theme of today's show. Here is another quote that I got from Douglas Conant's article:

Steven Pressfield

The difference between an amateur and a professional is in their habits. An amateur has amateur habits, a professional has professional habits. We can never free ourselves from habit, but we can replace bad habits with good ones.

Steve Coplon: I'm going to give it back to you, Lefford. I would like you to communicate through your own life lessons with those people that haven't reached much success in their life. Those that are stuck at a low place in their own self-esteem. For whatever the reason, they haven't developed the trust of other people. As I said in the opening of today's show, *good habits* are so very important in being able to *gain the trust of others* so that you can be a *success in life*. No man is an island. We need other people.

Lefford Fate: Exactly.

Steve Coplon: Lefford, you've undergone massive amounts of training, done tremendous amounts of reading, and possess great wisdom that have aided you in your understanding of habits. Let's hope that for the rest of this conversation, we can reach those people that haven't figured out that certain something that they need to finally make the decision that they are willing to start working on developing good habits, and free themselves up from the bondage in their lives that is tied to their bad habits.

Lefford Fate: One of the things, Steve, that a lot of people do is that they don't take a look at their habits. They don't take a look at what they are actually doing. I think sometimes we have to stop and say, "How is what I'm doing serving me? Is it serving me well or is it not serving me very well?" It's really easy for somebody to say, "Hey, break that habit." I don't really think you break a habit. I think you replace one habit with another habit. If you have a habit that's not serving you, take a look at it and say, "What can I replace that habit with?"

Lefford Fate:	If you're a smoker, I'm not a smoker, but if you're a smoker, you're not going to break the smoking habit. You can replace that habit. Whatever the reward. I was talking earlier about this Duhigg thing about there's a cue, then there's a routine, and then there's a reward. If there's a cue, you need something in your mouth. You need to feel a certain way. Then you start practicing this routine. Instead of pulling that cigarette out, you pull out a carrot.
Lefford Fate:	Instead of pulling that cigarette out, you go for a run, or a walk, or a swim. Then you get that same reward. The reality is all of us have habits. Habits are going to be there. If it were not for habits, we would not be alive. You talked about looking both ways before crossing the street. When I say left, right, left. Before you cross the street you look to the left, you look to the right, you look to the left. That's a good habit. Would you believe me if I told you one of the people that were cops when I was in England died because of that habit? This was the deal. I don't know if you know this, but in England, instead of driving on the left side of the road, they drive on the right.
Steve Coplon:	Oh, no.
Lefford Fate:	An Airman, new to the base in England, been there for less than a week. He gets ready to cross a road. He looks to the left, looks to the right, look to the left, took off. Got struck by a car and killed. Because the habit, doing the same thing over and over in the wrong environment can cause you to lose your life.
Steve Coplon:	Oh, that is so tragic.
Lefford Fate:	Yes, it was.
Steve Coplon:	That's a pretty powerful illustration of why you need to develop good habits. But be careful that the habit that you develop is what you need at the time.
Lefford Fate:	Is appropriate for the situation, and where you are.
Steve Coplon:	Wow. Yeah. You could be a guy that is in the habit of working hard to feed your family. If your family needs you for something very important, when something other than what you normally do with your day comes up, you've got to be able to modify your behavior in order to meet the needs of those that you care about. Instead of giving an excuse like, "Well, you're going to have to figure that on your own, because I've got another assignment in front of you." You have to be there for those that need you.
Lefford Fate:	Amen.
Steve Coplon:	You need to be strong.
Lefford Fate:	Amen.
Steve Coplon:	Yeah.
Lefford Fate:	Amen, and that's what it is. It's like my habit is working to pay the bills and take care of my family. Sometimes, they need you to pay the bills, there's a need there. But if that habit is so strong that sometimes your significant other needs you, if your child needs you, they need a father. They don't necessarily need a provider. That good habit can be deadly to your relationships.

Steve Coplon: Yeah.

Lefford Fate: But it's the same thing. Like some of the people that I used to work with, and you work with now who are incarcerated, the returning citizen. Some of the things that they needed to do while in the penitentiary and in corrections won't serve them well or won't often serve them well when they get out. Right? If you always have to protect yourself, if you bring that protection into an environment where you don't need to protect yourself, that habit can break you.

Steve Coplon: Not trusting people is one of the worst things about prison life. A lot of those incarcerated learn to not trust anyone. You've got to learn how to trust people. I've got a very, very close friend. His name is Steve Forbes, owner of Master's Touch Barber School of Excellence. He is the reason why I started my foundation, **Right Thinking Foundation**. He was at the church that I attended, a member of the worship team, an incredible singer. One day, I was giving my testimony asking the congregation to pray for me. The bank, that I had a large line of credit with secured by my house, was calling my loan. They had no justification to do this. This started a very, very difficult period in my life. It took about two years, but five or six of the top officials in the bank were all convicted of multiple criminal charges and ended up going to jail. That day in church, I was asking for prayer because I didn't want to lose my house.

Steve Coplon: Steve came up to me after I did my testimony and said, "Man, I didn't know you were a business guy. Can you help us with our business?" I said that I would like to help him. When I visited his barber shop a few days later, Steve was with his partner, Fred. The first thing they said to me was, "Can you get us into prisons and rehab centers?" I said, "What you mean, Willis? What are you talking about?" He continues, "That's where we learned to cut hair, and we want to be here for those people that are coming out of prison and going to have a hard time." I did an interview with Steve in November 2018. The show was called "You Gotta Stay Between the Lines Every Day." It was Episode 92.

Steve Coplon: He said something very profound on that show. He said he thought that he needed the incarceration time in his life, because he had to be reprogrammed. He said that the programming that they made him go through was necessary in his life. They told him when to wake up in the morning. They told him when to eat. They told him when to go to the bathroom. They told him when to go do this or that. They told him when to do everything. A lot of people don't have any good habits, and they don't have discipline. The process of developing good habits is called programming. Steve carried that out of prison with him.

Lefford Fate: It is programming. It's programming and discernment. To me, a habit is nothing but a behavior that you continuously do. You repeat it over, and over, and over until that becomes who you are and what you are about. This can be positive or negative. It can be an exercise routine, a positive habit. But you can overdo it.

Lefford Fate: Savings is a positive habit, but you can overdo it. Take eating. Eating is one of those things that we have to do. That's survival. But we can get into a habit of eating sweets, eating too much, and being sedentary. We need to rest, but you can get into a bad habit in doing any of that stuff. As I said, you've got to have discernment, and you've got to take a look at what you're doing and how it serves you. I think sometimes we forget that you could do something good, and it can end up bad. People say, "How in the world could that happen?" You can do something good, and it can end up being bad if you overdo it. You look like you've got a question.

Steve Coplon:	No, I'm in agreement with what you said. I don't have a question. It's a comment about something that you brought into my mind. It is something very basic. A lot of people in a relationship, they end up, where one person becomes far too dependent and needy on the other person. Someone gets hurt because they just want to be there to love on the other person, and be around them, but they end up smothering them. They haven't learned what you are saying about overdoing a good thing.
Steve Coplon:	They get in the habit of thinking that it is a good thing that they want to do for their partner. It is sad but the partner eventually has to say, "I appreciate what you're doing, but I need a little space." A lot of relationships end with this happening. "I need some space. You're smothering me." I may have gone in a different direction, but it is something that was once good that turned bad. Kind of like overdoing a good habit.
Lefford Fate:	It is. There are a lot of times that I have noticed where parents are helping their children. They are doing their work for them, doing their job for them. It sounds like a funny joke, but it isn't a joke at all. This actually can be true. Imagine you're a parent, and at five months your kid can't walk, so you carry him. Six months the kid can't walk, and you carry him. Eight months, the kid can't walk, you carry him. 18 months, the kid can't walk, you carry him. 24 months, 36 months, five years.
Steve Coplon:	Whoa.
Lefford Fate:	There comes a time that if you keep carrying the kid, then the kid loses his ability to walk. It sounds ridiculous but think about it. How often do we want so much for our significant others, for our children, for the people that we love, that we don't allow them to get strong on their own? That's a habit. That's enabling.
Steve Coplon:	You know, a big component of developing positive habits relates to a deeper understanding.
Lefford Fate:	True.
Steve Coplon:	Yeah, I think so. Wow!
Lefford Fate:	But again, even then, I'll tell you another thing. If you have a habit of doing everything yourself. Like I said, almost everything we can do, we can do it, or we can overdo it, Steve. Think about this for a second. 'If it is to be, it's up to me.'
Steve Coplon:	You said that on your last show with me. People love that one.
Lefford Fate:	It's wonderful. Do you remember when we had this conversation with Misael Diaz as part of the *Design Your Empowered Year Program*? You can overdo that also. If it is to be, it's up to me. I have to do it all by myself.
Steve Coplon:	I can't do it for you, Lefford. As much as I love you, I'd like to, but you've got to stand on your own two feet.
Lefford Fate:	Sometimes you've got to stand on your own.
Steve Coplon:	Yes, sometimes.

Lefford Fate:	But at the same time, Steve, where I want to take this is, think about it. If the only time, the only thing that can get done, I've got to do it myself, that means I can't accept help, or I refuse to take help. There are times that we need to get help. We don't need to be self-sufficient. You can get to a point where, "Hey, Steve. Let me help you." "No, I got it. Nobody else can do it as good as I can." It's a habit of you doing your own thing. That's not appropriate either. Again, a weakness is often a strength overdone.
Lefford Fate:	We have to be able to allow other people to help us sometimes. We can get too far into thinking, "I'm big, and I'm bad and I'm going to do it on my own." That is a habit too. It can easily be a negative habit, especially for us guys. A lot of us guys, we don't want any help.
Steve Coplon:	I want to speak to what you just said. People that don't have the proper trust and respect of someone else need mentors. We all need mentors at one time or another, perhaps forever. When you feel like you don't need a mentor anymore, you're going to stop growing. When you think, "I've got it all now. I don't want to receive any more mentoring from anyone," you are headed for trouble. There's always more to learn. Learning never stops. Learn from the Lord Himself and through His Word. Keep growing.
Steve Coplon:	You said something a minute ago. We're talking about people that are over independent, that don't recognize that they need to be involved with other people to help them grow. They develop a lack of trust for others. They think they've got the whole game played out. In your last show, you talked about independence and interdependence. That was a powerful part of the show. That is when you said that interdependence is where we are supposed to be. We are all interdependent.
Steve Coplon:	I was talking about your show, right after we recorded it, with a close friend that I greatly respect. His name is Ken Whitley. When I told him about the theme of the show, he said, "Well, you know, when people get to where they don't do what they say they're going to do, and they don't care what other people have to say about it, they are fooling themselves. Ken said they start living the lie where they believe that they're that good, and then all of a sudden, they're not approachable. They're not reachable. They get really deep into the mindset that they don't need other people. They think that they are right all the time. They don't care about learning from the experiences of others. How do we change a mind like that?
Steve Coplon:	All this reminds me of a TV commercial back in the '70s. It was really popular. We loved to imitate it. A defiant kid said, "Mother, please! I'd rather do it myself." The kid was really saying "I don't need your help!" He was totally wrong. The mother was trying to be there. She was being pushed away.
Steve Coplon:	Lefford, how do we get closer to people that are rejecting the friendships and the love of other people, so we can help them start realizing that they need to start changing some of their habits, and become a different person? That changing some of their habits is for their own good. They just don't understand that.
Lefford Fate:	Whew. You asked that question with 15 minutes left in the talk.
Steve Coplon:	Yes, we've got 15 minutes.
Lefford Fate:	Love them. Love them. And it's tough.

Steve Coplon:	Exactly.
Lefford Fate:	It's a tough thing, because sometimes people have lost trust, and because they lost trust, they feel that the only person that they can depend on is themselves. Some of that is, again, the social network, it's nurture, it's who they've been around. But the dangerous part about that is that no man is an island. No woman is an island. We need each other. We're social beings. You have to build up trust. The person has to know that they can trust someone to come into their lives, and to be there for them and help them. But, Steve, this isn't easy. Because again, I've been hurt before, and I've told myself stuff like, "You know what? I'm just going to do it myself because it's easier."
Lefford Fate:	People say to themselves, "I won't be disappointed even if I can't do something that I want to do, if I don't put my trust and faith in someone else." I think that's the deal. We've got to get them. We've got to let people understand that we're there for them, and we've got to love them. When we love them, we can step in and provide support. But also recognize that sometimes it's not that they are against us. It's that they are for themselves.
Steve Coplon:	I agree with that 1,000%, Lefford.
Lefford Fate:	But they also have to hear, "You know what, I'm here for you." And then you've got to be there for them. Then, you can show them where their faults are. I worked for a guy named Lieutenant Colonel James Dickerson years ago, and he used to say, "I will never paint somebody into a corner, but I will shine the light into the corner to see where they are, so they can see." Sometimes we have to bring a person up to a level of awareness to see that what they're doing is not serving them well.
Steve Coplon:	Can you give an example? I'm going to throw this at you. I'm involved with people every day that are really headstrong. People that don't trust other people. They've got to know you love them before they're going to respond to you, of course. They've got to know you care. What is it? What's the expression? Jeff Heiser gave it to me the first show that I ever recorded with him. They've got to know you care before they ... You know what I'm saying?
Lefford Fate:	Yeah. "People don't care how much you know unless they know how much you care."
Steve Coplon:	Thank you. It's been a while since I spoke that phrase. A lot of people think that when you're being truthful and honest, you have to give it to them without embarrassing them or hurting them. It must be out of love. Well, sometimes out of love means that you have to give it to them straight. We have to show people the truth. When we do that, a lot of people call it hard love. I'm not calling it that. I call it real love. What you just shared that Dickerson said about shining the light, that is so beautiful.
Steve Coplon:	I'm going to take you back into your life, Lefford. Since I've known you, you've talked about Sergeant John Gunther over and over again with me. I have to tell you, he loved you, he helped you. He became the man that you most admire in your life. He had a great, great impact on you. But in his own loving way, he put a boot up your butt.
Lefford Fate:	He did. But what he did was he recognized what I needed. Sometimes, tough love is important. Sometimes people are just tough. There's a big pause, then there's the love. If I don't know that you love me, and you're tough on me, is that helpful?
Steve Coplon:	No.

Lefford Fate:	Exactly.
Steve Coplon:	They'll reject you.
Lefford Fate:	Exactly. What I find that some people do, they come tough first without the love first. Love is always first. Love is always first.
Steve Coplon:	Absolutely.
Lefford Fate:	They've got to know you love them. Then it needs to be explained. Listen, I keep saying this all the time. More military people died in 2019 by suicide than died in combat. They lost the understanding that people love them. You can go through stuff and people can still love you. Our Father in Heaven loves us regardless. Now, we may have to be punished if bad stuff happens, but He loves us regardless. The first thing there is love. I'm not big into this fear-based religion. I'm not soft. I know you've got to be told what's up, but you've got to show that you love somebody first.
Lefford Fate:	When Sergeant Gunther loved me, he showed me that, and he told me. He showed me that first, because I knew he had my career in the palm of his hand. But he used compassion. What is the word? You're a very spiritual person. There's the law, but love is first. Right?
Steve Coplon:	Yes.
Lefford Fate:	What is it, grace before judgment?
Steve Coplon:	I'm with you there. Yes.
Lefford Fate:	Grace before judgment. So, when somebody shows you where you're wrong, versus showing you that you're wrong, you're doing wrong, but you're not wrong.
Steve Coplon:	You're helping them with their behavior. Not with their self. Because that's what we're going to change. Behavior change is what the goal is.
Lefford Fate:	Hate the sin, not the sinner.
Steve Coplon:	I'm sorry. I got excited with you there. Behavior changes is what we're trying to help people do. Not put down their being.
Lefford Fate:	Perfect. I love that. Like I said, it was said somewhere that you hate the sin, love the sinner. Right?
Steve Coplon:	Yeah.
Lefford Fate:	As I said, the reason that Sergeant Gunther was able to reach me is because he loved me first, and he showed me that love. Even though he showed tough love, he showed me that he loved me first. Let's go back to this whole thing. He had a habit of being good to people regardless. It wasn't like every once in a while, I'm good to people. He was always a good person. See where I am going?
Steve Coplon:	Yes.
Lefford Fate:	It was his behavior. And because I always saw him doing the right thing, I wanted to be like him. I saw that if you act a certain way, you get a certain result. I wanted to be like this guy. I wrote something down, and I wanted to go back to it. All of our successes and our failures

are a result of our habits. Right? Everything. Our habits determine if we get positive or we get negative results. You asked me a question a little bit earlier. How do we show people the direction to go?

Lefford Fate: I want to ask you to do this. Kind of like when we were talking about budgeting the other day on the webinar where I introduced you to Johnnie Lloyd and Chi chi Njoku. I would say take a look at what you're doing. Is it serving you or is not serving you? The things that serve you, you keep doing it. The things that don't serve you, you stop doing it. You say, "Yeah, Lefford, that's hard." Yes, it is hard. You start doing those things. You figure out where you are, figure out where you want to go. If I want to get out of debt, and I'm spending money on frivolous things that don't matter, and I look at that and say, "You know what? One of the reasons that I don't have what I need is because I'm abusing my money, I'm not doing the things I need to do, so I'm going to stop doing this."

Lefford Fate: You can't just stop without making another habit. Instead of buying this, I'm going to save this, and instead of eating this, I'm going to eat that. If you want to change a habit, I don't necessarily think you can change a habit, but you replace one habit with another. Does that make sense?

Steve Coplon: Yes, it does. It does.

Lefford Fate: That's what I think we need to teach people to do. Actually, sit down, knee to knee, talking to people and say, "Okay, how is it working for you? How can I help you? And this is the direction." Don't make people feel like they're failures because they get something wrong. It's just we need to replace this habit with this habit, because as I'll go back to say, thoughts become your words, words become your actions, actions become your habits, habits become your character, character becomes your destiny. Same thing. If you keep doing something over, and over, and over, and over, you're going to get some kind of result. See it first.

Lefford Fate: Stephen Covey, you talked about early on, 7 Habits, start with the end in mind. That was one of his premises. You start with the end in mind. You've got this look on your face. What's up?

Steve Coplon: No. I'm being taught by a great teacher. I'm just following you right now. No, no. That's my look. You've got me listening intently right now. I can obviously always come back with some thought that you're making me think about, so I'll give you one, since you paused.

Lefford Fate: Okay.

Steve Coplon: People that don't trust anyone aren't going to be moving forward. They are basically stuck. I believe that they need to take a step forward. The question again, and you have really been covering it, it has a complex answer. We've given a lot of advice to people that love other people, that want to help other people. About how to connect with them. We talked about how Gunther helped you, and how you responded. Let's assume that we are the kind of person that just doesn't really want to listen to anyone else. We know what we need to do, and we don't have to have someone else be involved. We're wrong if that is how we are thinking.

Lefford Fate: Most of us are like that too often.

Steve Coplon: Yeah. We're wrong. Napoleon Hill says that in the greatest of them all, the 57th IF. When you get there and know that you're wrong and acknowledge you're wrong. So, you've already said, and I agree with you, that we need to love someone for them to start to listen to us, to take some tutelage, some mentorship. I got that. But let's put ourselves in their shoes. We're not the person trying to help the other person. We are that person. What will it take for you to let someone into your life, to give them a chance to help you?

Steve Coplon: Because that's really the stumbling block, that getting inside. I have my ways of doing it with people, and that's why doing what I do is reaching a lot of people. I tell people when I'm loving on them that, "Hey, I know you're having a bad day, because I've been there too." Empathy is a very good connection point to get them listening. "You need somebody to talk to, I'm here for you." What would you need to hear if you're a person that's rejecting other people because you're too headstrong, and you're going to do it yourself? What are you looking for if you're that kind of person? Let's put ourselves into that frame of mind. Fortunately, we're not in that frame of mind, but sometimes we ease into it.

Lefford Fate: Sometimes I am.

Steve Coplon: Sometimes I am too.

Lefford Fate: There are some things that I can do better. I love being on stages. There are a number of people that say, "Lefford, you should get an online presence," and I say, "I don't want an online presence. I want to be on stages." Recently, because of the Coronavirus, COVID-19, four of my main speaking engagements were canceled. I've done some online stuff, some programs, but I was really stubborn and said, "Well, I've got this." Some people saw things in me that I didn't see in myself. If I would have listened, I could have been much further down the road. Really, I am that guy.

Steve Coplon: You can't do it all, Lefford. The road that you're traveling has gone very far. Don't be so hard on yourself.

I had a lot of trouble when I was 19 years old. My mother took me to a doctor. They let me know, "Steve, you can't keep working that hard. You can't do it all, Steve. You can't do it all." That's a lesson.

Lefford Fate: It is, but I'm going to interrupt you. That's what I'm saying, sometimes we're doing something, and somebody can speak into our lives, and help us change direction. My dad used to always say, "You can lead a horse to water, but you can't make him drink, but you can make him thirsty." I know me as a person, sometimes this is my way, I'm going to do things my way. I've got to be willing to listen to other people, especially when they're saying it with love. Whether I do it or not is a different story. But, being able to listen to their feedback, I think we've all got to be accepting of feedback and say, "Can what they're saying help me? If it can help me, I must be willing to listen." I'll still make my own decisions, but you must be able to be open for someone else to speak into your life.

Steve Coplon: That's beautiful. Let me try to sum things up to get to a close on today's message. If you have any major thoughts that were not presented today, help yourself, but here's one thing I'll say. The theme of this series of shows is character and integrity building. I've focused on one very fundamental basic thing, that if a person does not do what they say they're going to do in life, they're generally not going to get very far.

Steve Coplon: I've been talking with many guests about this theme who have given some great wisdom and much advice. Here's my summary of what I think you and I have said today. It's so

98

critically important to gain the trust of other people. Because, whether you believe it or not, you're not going to get very far all by yourself in this world. You can't do it alone, even though you think you can. You need to reconsider this, and you need to take a hard look at your life and look at where you're at. Do you have the peace that you seek?

Steve Coplon: Do you have peace of mind from the way you live? If you don't, listen a little more to what we are saying to you. If we are talking directly to a person that does not have peace of mind, we want to help you gain from other people who can be there for you. We can help you recognize who those people might be. You can't just listen to anyone, of course. If we get you to where you are starting to listen, okay, now you need to make a little change. If you looked in the mirror and you are unhappy, be truthful with yourself. You need to be surrounded with some people that are good positive people, and you need to get rid of bad habits and create good habits.

Steve Coplon: It's really for your own good, but we can't do it for you. You've got to do it for yourself. But know this, we love you no matter what you think. We are on your side, and we are always here for you. Let me quote Benjamin Franklin:

Benjamin Franklin

"Your net worth to the world is usually determined by what remains after your bad habits are subtracted from your good ones."

We're trying to help people; listen to people. I guess if we're still in the mind of a person that is the one that's got the lack of ability to let other people inside their lives because they just have been hurt too much in their life and they're headstrong, all we're trying to say is listen to what these others are trying to say to you, and give it a chance.

Steve Coplon: Just give it a chance, take that first step, because success builds on success. Believe me, you're not alone. We've all been through it. We're here for you. You can reach us at www.rightthink. org. Lefford is someone that I would encourage you to try to get to know deeper. I'm here for you also. What would you like to add to that?

Lefford Fate: Two sentences. One is a quote by Aristotle:

Aristotle

"Excellence is not an act, but it's a habit."

Steve Coplon: I am smiling because that one is on my 32 quotes that I got from Douglass Conant. You've used about five of them already.

Lefford Fate: Yeah, that's truth. The other thing is, and this is from me, keeping and/or breaking your word is a habit. And you will be judged on which one of those that you do. If you say you are going to do something, do it. That's a habit. If you don't do what you say you are going to do, that's a habit, and that's how you'll be judged.

Steve Coplon:	A man named Warren Bennis, said this:

Warren Bennis

"People who cannot invent and reinvent themselves must be content with borrowed postures, secondhand ideas, fitting in, instead of standing out."

Lefford Fate:	Warren Bennis. Great quote.
Steve Coplon:	Lefford, thanks for sharing everything you did. Anything else? Would you like to offer a parting thought or comment?
Lefford Fate:	As I said, first you develop your habits, and then your habits develop you. Decide what you want to do and start doing it. That's the bottom line. Simple. Not easy. Simple.
Steve Coplon:	That's great advice. Lefford, I'm sure that we are going to do a whole lot more of these conversations, because our hearts are in them. Lefford, you're beautiful. God Bless you. Thanks for being on the show today. Everybody have a wonderful week, and thanks for listening today.
Lefford Fate:	Thank you, Steve.
Steve Coplon:	Thanks for listening to *Right Thinking with Steve Coplon*. I look forward to being with you again next week. Remember: **Don't Quit, Plan Ahead, It Will Get Better.** God Bless you and have a great week!

To listen to the original interview, scan this QR Code with your camera, or visit:
https://rightthinkingeducation.com/FromtheLiptotheHip/Chapter-7/

CHAPTER EIGHT

You Are Fire When You Are Focused with guest Johnnie Lloyd
Right Thinking With Steve Coplon - Episode 166

Steve Coplon: Good morning. Welcome to *Right Thinking with Steve Coplon*. I'm your host, Steve Coplon. Thank you for tuning in. Let's have a great day!

Steve Coplon: Good morning, everybody. Today we are continuing with our eighth show in the series *"From the Lip to the Hip is a Pretty Far Distance."* The series is based on lessons that my mother taught me when I was a kid. I have been bringing on different guests who I greatly admire and respect, who each possess great wisdom. Today is no exception. I want to introduce you to my newest best friend, Johnnie Lloyd. Johnnie, are you with us?

Johnnie Lloyd: I am absolutely with you. Thank you so much. The pleasure's all mine.

Steve Coplon: Oh, Johnnie, you and I belong to a mutual admiration society. I am so blessed to know you. Today is Episode 166.

Right Thinking with Steve Coplon is very pleased to announce that this week's show is called *You are Fire When You are Focused with guest Johnnie Lloyd.* Tune in and hear **Steve** and **Johnnie** have an *enriching conversation* about how you can *maximize your potential* when you are *focused*. This show will *transform your life*.

Steve Coplon: Well, Johnnie. Lefford was on last week's show, and we can thank him for introducing us.

Johnnie Lloyd: Absolutely.

Steve Coplon: He introduced us about a month ago. What is amazing is that you and I are living examples of the Napoleon Hill principle called the Mastermind Alliance. It is basically where people surround themselves with people who genuinely care about helping one another and who share a common purpose. You and I have quickly gotten to know each other pretty well, and we've teamed up on beautiful project.

Steve Coplon: There is a local nonprofit organization called Hampton Roads Cares. Dave Richards, who is going to be my guest on the show next week, asked me to be on a panel of experts sponsored by Hampton Roads Cares, to help people navigate the coronavirus stimulus package. Johnnie, I asked you to join me on the panel. Let me tell the listeners a little about you.

Steve Coplon: Johnnie is a professional. She is a Napoleon Hill certified leader, a professional speaker, a consultant, an accountant. She's been published many times. She has years of experience working for the government in accounting before working in private accounting. Johnnie and I know that we are kindred spirits because we both serve the same Lord. We established that right away when we first met. For the next 55 minutes, you're going to hear, a conversation between two people who are just so glad to know each other.

Steve Coplon: Johnnie, what do you think about what I am saying?

Johnnie Lloyd: Actually, I want to confirm. As it's said, two or more can confirm, and I am confirming what you have said about our relationship. It is such an honor and a privilege, and I am just so grateful to Lefford for connecting us. It was a great immediate link up. Yes, we are kindred spirits. Your mission, your vision, your purpose for your organization, how you serve the underserved with **Right Thinking Foundation** is amazing, and you provide a lot back to the community. So, it is such an honor for me to be here today.

Johnnie Lloyd: You were talking about the Mastermind concept. It's an alignment. One of the most powerful things about the Mastermind is for we, as a people, to be on the same definite purpose and agreement. You and I are in total agreement with the impact that we can have, not just to the Hampton Roads area, but to the state, to our community, to this globe, to the other underserved as well as the served population. There's a lot to offer. So, thank you. And again, I consider it a privilege and an honor to be here today with you. You are one of my special friends. I'm looking forward to this time together.

Steve Coplon: Wonderful. I have a brochure in my hand of the ***"17 Principles of Success"*** from the **Napoleon Hill Foundation**. I am going to read the last sentence of the Mastermind Alliance, which is principle number two. It is a long sentence, and it's very powerful. "An active alliance of two or more minds in a spirit of perfect harmony for the attainment of a common objective, stimulates each mind to a higher degree of courage than that ordinarily experienced and paves the way for the state of mind known as faith." What an unbelievable concept! People will now know why we love the teachings of Napoleon Hill.

Johnnie Lloyd: Absolutely.

Steve Coplon: Johnnie, did you get a chance to listen to Episode 159, ***"From The Lip To the Hip Is A Pretty Far Distance?"*** If so, did you get anything out of it? Was there anything right about what I was presenting?

Johnnie Lloyd: You know what? Not only is it right, it's right now.

Steve Coplon: I like that.

Johnnie Lloyd: Because of the situation and the environment that we are currently in, what you say, is going to matter even more to what's in your pocket.

Steve Coplon: In the announcement for Episode 159, I said, "Tune in and hear Steve talk about the importance of doing what you say you are going to do. Successful people are those who accept responsibility for their lives."

Johnnie Lloyd: Oh, that's perfect. That's perfect.

Steve Coplon: Character and integrity are what it is all about.

Johnnie Lloyd: Absolutely. The show speaks so strongly to character and integrity. It reiterates the power of the spoken word, and it also reiterates the fact that we are jointly assigned, and when you say something to me it matters. When it stops mattering, there's a problem. There's a problem in the relationship. There's a problem with trust and all those things.

Johnnie Lloyd: Going back to Episode 159, *"From the Lip to the Hip is a Pretty Far Distance,"* I thought the title was really cute. It is interesting because I'm a metaphoric kind of person. I love metaphors. I teach in metaphors and stories. So, when I saw that, I said, "Oh, what is it connected to?" And most people would think it's connected to only money. It's not. It's connected to every area of our life.

Johnnie Lloyd: What we say matters. It really does. It matters to the other person, and it should matter to ourselves because when we don't speak the truth to ourselves, we stop trusting us. It was a great episode. I liked the information. At first, I did not know it was something that your mother had taught you, but it also seems like that's one of the constructs that you've used in your life when building and dealing with relationships. And that's really critical. I think the way we see ourselves and see others is really critical.

Johnnie Lloyd: Maya Angelou would say it this way, "When people tell you who they are, believe them." And that's what it is. When my lips tell you who I am and my actions don't back it up, don't believe me. In other words, if you're with a person or around a person and they say they're going to do something, but their actions don't reflect it, that action is telling you who they are, so don't believe them. You just have to address it and keep on moving forward. It was a great Episode and I encourage everyone to listen to it.

Steve Coplon: Thanks. That was a beautiful insight. You passed on a scripture to me when we were discussing how we were going to deliver a beautiful message today:

Luke 6:45

A good man brings good things out of the good stored up in his heart, and an evil man brings evil things out of the evil stored up in his heart. For the mouth speaks what the heart is full of.

Steve Coplon: I thank you for that. I just love that. Well, Johnnie, you also listened to Episode 160, the show I did with Lefford titled, *"You Got That Right, Steve!"*

Johnnie Lloyd: I did.

Steve Coplon: Lefford and I like to laugh. I enjoyed giving the show that title. What did you like about that show if anything?

Johnnie Lloyd: Actually, what I loved about the show was the interchange between the two of you. Your exchange of information and how there were so many topics. You talked about money and how a lot of people have, I'm going to call it, the spirit of poverty, because it's a mindset. One of you said something about, people can gather money, but if you don't think you're supposed to have it, then what happens is, you do something to release it.

Johnnie Lloyd: You didn't know this about me. I was raised up in the church. I was in a denomination, and they taught us right out of the Word, right out of the Word of God. They took a scripture out of the Word of God and said that basically if you had money, you were going to go to hell. Basically, if you had riches, you were … It talks about it's easier for a camel to go through the eye of a needle than a person with resources, is what the Word was talking about.

Johnnie Lloyd:	And so, I was raised with that. However, they never taught about the part that says money answereth all things. So, whether you're a profit or nonprofit organization, whether you're a single person or you have a house full of people, money is an answer. It is not "the" answer. It is an answer, especially when I build my environment around my faith and my God. I'm not serving mammon. I'm serving God with whatever I am because I'm acting as a steward. You two brought out some great points in that episode as far as confirming the importance of what you say that character is talking about.
Johnnie Lloyd:	There is one area that I absolutely loved. As a matter of fact, I made a little graph because that's the way I think. I drew two circles and I would like your viewers to do that. Draw two circles and let them intersect in the center. Steve, the two of you talked about dependence and independence. People can be both dependent and independent. There's some things we do that we're dependent upon another person. Some things we do that we're independent, that we can do by ourselves. Then where those circles connect, or overlap, is the place that we're interdependent. That's what you and Lefford talked about that greatly interested me.
Johnnie Lloyd:	In the interdependence, that area is a place of trust. It's a place that our lips need to back up what we say. I think it was Lefford who talked about his wife saying that she needed him to say when he couldn't do things. That's what I would like to address. One of the things that drove it home for me is the communication aspect of, **"From the Lip to the Hip is a Pretty Far Distance."** If, I were to mark that space, I would list it coming down to communication, responsibility, and all of that.
Johnnie Lloyd:	I made an acronym because I'm special and I have a military background, so we have acronyms. I call it the acronym RACE. There's a distance, **"From the Lip to the Hip is a Pretty Far Distance,"** right? So, it's a race, R-A-C-E.

R is for responsible and it's for respect.

A is for accountable. It's authority, activity, and accomplishment.

C is for communication. We have to communicate. What was said in that episode, communicate with the people who we make promises to, and let them know when we can't do it, so they know that they're not going to get it. C is a powerful tool. And then it deals with character, correction, and connection. A lot of faith-based people will say, "No, I just believe God's going to do it. I have faith and if I say I can't do it, then my faith is short." No, no, no. That's not the case. It's bigger than that. You have to turn around and let people know when you don't think you're going to accomplish it or update them. So, the communication is critical.

E is for us to be exceptional. For us to get from the lip to the hip, we need to be exceptional people. We need to be people of our word. We need to be people that know what we say matters. And when it doesn't, we need to be man and woman enough to make a change.

Steve Coplon:	Oh wow. Well, let me give you a quick comment on that.
Johnnie Lloyd:	Okay. I know you said, "She went crazy."
Steve Coplon:	No not at all. Hey, everyone, you know why I asked Johnnie to be on the show? She was a late addition because I had this series already mapped out, who I was going to invite to be on. Well, Johnnie was a walk-on. I didn't have to give her the sign-on bonus.

Johnnie Lloyd:	Not a walk-off.
Steve Coplon:	No, not a walk off, a walk-on. But hey, Johnnie, you had two things under the R, four things under the A, four things under the C, but only one under the E. May I add something to the E?
Johnnie Lloyd:	Absolutely.
Steve Coplon:	Good. Under the E, you said exceptional. That is positive. That's motivational. That's going to get us moving. Well, I'll just give a real quick little, simple ditty here. About 30 years ago, I was the MC at a large company banquet party. People from all over the country were invited to attend. The party was like a roast for the head of the entire organization, Richard O'Leary. I was on the executive committee and I razzed him a lot, I guess, is the right word.
Steve Coplon:	As I'm talking, I said, "Look, I just want to pass on something that all of you can take home, teach your kids this. It's something of great value and you can remember it because all three of these words I'm going to give you start with the letter E."
Johnnie Lloyd:	Interesting.
Steve Coplon:	Then I said, "Attitude, Enthusiasm, and Energy." And the vice president sitting next to me, he puts his elbow at my side, and he goes, "Hey, Steve, attitude doesn't start with an E." And I went, "What? O'Leary said it did." I've been having fun with people for a long time, Johnnie. I wish people could see the smile that you have right now. It's wonderful. So, Johnnie, let's go a little deeper here before we get past the introduction. You are a true servant. Lefford wrote a book titled, ***"Pathway to a Positive Mental Attitude,"*** subtitled, ***"The 17 Steps to Success, Conversations with World-Class Napoleon Hill Certified Leaders."***
Steve Coplon:	The book uses Napoleon Hill's 17 Principles of Success as the 17 Steps, one chapter for each principle. You wrote two chapters in the book. In chapter 10 you wrote about Accurate Thinking. We'll talk about that in a minute. You also covered in chapter 16, ***"Budgeting Time and Money."*** You understand **Right Thinking Foundation** inside and out, what I'm trying to do. I believe that if people can eliminate stress from money, in situations, that they can be better focused to deal with other things in life.
Steve Coplon:	I really like Joyce Meyer, the television evangelist, Christian author, and speaker. She is incredibly down to earth. She talks about "suddenlys in life," those things we have absolutely no control over that come out of nowhere and cause great hardship. Well, if we can get rid of the stress that's coming at us from finances, we'll be better focused to deal with those unexpected things; the job layoff, accident, injury, divorce, etc. What I do, is I try to help people get their finances straight. I have simple tools I teach throughout all the shows I do. But the long and the short of it is, if people can use the money that you were talking about and have a good, stable life and not have stress, they can use that money for many, many good things. They can do much with that money as a tool.
Steve Coplon:	We have a lot in common with our accounting backgrounds. I have a statement that I use to describe the direction of my teachings. I say. "I can teach anyone about money, how to budget. I've been doing it for a long time. But if a person doesn't know their purpose, they're going to spend their money on the wrong things." And so, what I really do, even though my program is about money, it is really only 25% about money. I'm really trying to help people find their purpose, and to live their purpose. And so, I say, that I'm trying to teach

people about finding their purpose. And where do you get your purpose from? You get your purpose from the Word of the Lord.

Steve Coplon: So, Johnnie, we share the same attitude and understanding of money. That is the heart of where we are together. We want to help people have a better life. Character and integrity are great, great components of having a good life because if you don't have them, you're not going to be trusted. You're going to fail. With that said, I want to quote from your chapter on the Principle of Accurate Thinking. You wrote, "Now, again, truth is truth and a lie is a lie, so we must look at it from that perspective, too. But, we must make it personal and see how we're going to grow from that." Where do you want to take this. Johnnie?

Johnnie Lloyd: I'm going to back up so we can go forward. Is that okay?

Steve Coplon: I love it.

Johnnie Lloyd: You talked about knowing your purpose. This is the reason I actually became a certified leader of **The Napoleon Hill** philosophy. My parents introduced me to reading his books. They were in some multi-level marketing things and they were doing very well. People in that organization were being fed ideas or concepts to change their mindset. And so, I was very familiar with Napoleon Hill. I had worked my way up to C- suite executive level positions in my career. I was considered by most, to be very successful in my career. After having gone through being homeless earlier in life, I was by all standards quite successful. So, when I retired I was at the pinnacle of my career. But that was before I went into purpose.

Johnnie Lloyd: I told the people when I left, that I retired to purpose. People looked at my life and said, "Johnnie, you're busier now. You've got more stuff going on now than you had before you retired." That is because I retired to purpose.

Steve Coplon: Love it.

Johnnie Lloyd: I didn't retire to go home and sit down. I retired to purpose. So, this is what happens with us as people, especially women. We can be good at so many things, but we don't know what we can be great at. The only place you can find out where you can be great, is to go back to the person who created you. If you're looking at anything that was created, if you want the original intent that it was created for, you have to go back to not the manufacturer, you have to go back to the creator. So, when you go back to the creator that created you, then you can find out why you're here. Find answers to those critical questions people have. Why am I here? Do I matter? That kind of thing.

Johnnie Lloyd: So, you need to find that out, and that's what you go back to. That's why I say *you are fire when you are focused*. You are fire when you know the thing that you're supposed to go after. The Bible talks about how everything will work out for my good, right? It says no matter what has happened in my life, all things will work out for my good. It's hard to think that way when you're in a pit. If you know a lot about the Bible, you know that Joseph didn't go straight to the palace, his brothers put him in a pit to kill him. Then he was sold, right? He went to Potiphar's house. He has some Ps in his life, you hear what I'm saying?

Johnnie Lloyd: Because of what he went through, it caused him to be an amazing ruler when he got there. So, the process that people are fighting is they don't want to simply say, "I want to do this.

I don't want to do that." No, no, no. Go for the best thing you know. But keep your eye on the prize. Your eye on the prize is your legacy, is your purpose. It's your transformational development. It's all of that. So, you have to go back to the Creator.

Johnnie Lloyd: When I was younger, about 15, we used to take wire hangers, because I used to lock my keys in my car, and we would unravel the wire hanger and put it through the window. Young people may not even be familiar with this, but I could unhook the lock to unlock the door. I abused that hanger. That was not the intent the hanger was made for, but I used it for my good. And we have to be careful in life when we have people in our lives who are not enriching our lives and they're using us for their good. They're using us.

Johnnie Lloyd: We have to be careful when we're in abusive relationships and we don't know who we are. There is no fire when you're not focused, not knowing your purpose. When you know your purpose, everything changes. I was involved once with a program serving Hampton City Schools. I would go in and help the middle schoolers and the teens establish what I call *Discover Your Purpose*. When you don't know your purpose, you become more distracted by everything around you. And when you're distracted, you get nothing accomplished toward the real goal in your life.

Johnnie Lloyd: That's the key with purpose. Purpose gives you a goal, a target, the bullseye. A lot of people are hitting the big target and they're doing great things, but they're still empty because they haven't searched the Word of God. They haven't gone back to their Creator and found out, what was I created for? What problem was I created to solve? Where do I add value? Go all the way to the end with your purpose. God is Alpha and Omega. Purpose may be the pinnacle for people, but it's the first thing that people need to search for, and then build on it and grow.

Steve Coplon: Johnnie, I think about finding your purpose in much the same way that you do. I share your thought about the direction that one must take to find their purpose. I just love listening to you.

Johnnie Lloyd: Oh, you are so precious.

Steve Coplon: I told you that we were kindred spirits when we started. Some of the things you said in Lefford's book in chapter 16, *"Budgeting Time and Money"*, were beautiful. You wrote, "Right now, you may not have any control. So, it's about starting where you are, and looking to see where you want to be, and then building upon that. Yes, you're not going to be excellent at it the first time. But you will learn. Just like when a child tries walking and falls but gets up and tries again and again. That child is not told, 'Okay, you can't walk anymore because you fell.'", When I read that, I said, That's pretty straightforward. You continued, "So, you need to allow yourself to go through that failing process. Failing allows us to grow and become better. As we become better, we see the results, and the results cause us to move forward. But you need to have a Definite Purpose and align everything to that purpose".

Steve Coplon: Johnnie, I couldn't have said it better myself. You actually say it better. It's beautiful the way you're presenting it. So, Johnnie, how did you get to be a person with such great wisdom? It's not because you became a Napoleon Hill coach. You became a Napoleon Hill coach because you knew by becoming a coach, it would help bring out what you already felt deep inside. So, how did you become you?

Johnnie Lloyd: Failing, failing forward, crawling. In my life, I always saw something in other people, and I always wanted to help them get it out. There was a time when I was working overseas, and I had 52 people working for me. I controlled all the money on base, billions of dollars, right? So, we were there, and I had a team and I would not accept mediocracy. I would not accept those working for me to be mediocre. I would drive them, which is not necessarily good, drive and push them to greatness. So, we were rewarded with a lot of awards and all that. However, my approach to things hasn't always been like it is today. Yes, I am a person who builds productivity and profitability. However, the main point between those two goals is the people. You can't ever hurt the people.

Johnnie Lloyd: What happened for me in my journey is, while I worked for a non-profit organization, my boss, who I greatly respect, told me this and I'll never forget it. He said, "I'll forgive you if you lose millions of dollars. I'll forgive you if you make errors and all that." He said, "But I will not forgive you, Johnnie, if you hurt the people, if you intentionally hurt people." Because of what he said to me, and what I learned from his words, I now have the tendency to go back and tell people or go back and apologize to people. Generally, they say, "No, no, no. That's not the way I took it." That was an important lesson for me that helped me grow.

Johnnie Lloyd: If I get any conviction on what I said or did to someone, I go back and make sure that we're clear. Because the worst thing I have learned from experience is falling and mistreating people, even if it is not intentional. I was in that mindset that said, "You are collateral damage. I'm good. We're going to get the task done. If you don't make it, oh, well." And that was not right. That is not success. That is not real success. You may make it to the goal, but when you get there, it needs to be with all the people intact.

Johnnie Lloyd: It's like sheep. If we're shepherds like Jesus, then we don't want to lose one. We want everyone to come. However, we also have the power of choice. That's the other thing I learned, is that people choose. God doesn't force us to choose Him. He doesn't force us to accept Him. He doesn't force us to accept eternal life. He just lays before us the choices and He tells us what is the right answer. That's one of the things I loved about Napoleon Hill. What triggered me more than anything is when he said there are two envelopes.

Johnnie Lloyd: One envelope contains all the blessings, all the positive things that happen in your life when you control your own mind. The second envelope contains the curses, all the adverse things that happen to you if you don't take control of your own mind. When he said that, it connected me back as a person who believes God and the Word of God. It reminded me of when God said, "I lay before you, life and death. Choose life." It was like, "I love you enough to give you the right answer." You don't even have to say, "Well, what should I choose, God?" No, no, no. Choose life. Choose the road of life, and that's what I had to choose. I had to choose the road of life.

Johnnie Lloyd: But that wasn't easy, Steve. It wasn't. I mean, I had to re-identify myself. No, I didn't have to just re-identify, I had to find out who I was. I knew what other people said I was, but I didn't know who I was, and whose I was. I had always been in the church, so it wasn't about my faith. It was about, "God, show me who You say I am." So that's why I'm a heavy affirmation person. I do "I am" statements or affirmations. I explain to people, "This is the way you do affirmations." They need to be an "I am" statement, and they need to be in present tense.

Johnnie Lloyd:	If they are in future tense, your subconscious mind will say, "Okay, well, we'll do that one day." But if they are in present tense, they are cued up and they force you to start making plans now because the subconscious mind never sleeps.
Steve Coplon:	I'll give an example that just popped into my mind as I listened to you. It will continue the thought.
Johnnie Lloyd:	Super.
Steve Coplon:	If a person says, "I'm a person who wants to get past this bad habit of procrastination that I've been stuck with my whole life. I've always put things off and just I want to change that," versus, "I am a person who is going to take care of business right now. And then, as I do that, I'll experience success and success grows upon success."
Johnnie Lloyd:	That's an excellent example. Current tense. See, this is the other thing, especially in the faith or non-faith community. I've had people who don't want to do any training, and someone would raise their hand and say, "Johnnie, Johnnie, I hear what you're saying, but that's a lie." I said. "Well, faith is a lie until you get it." Faith is not true. I don't need faith for a phone. I've got a phone in my hand. I need faith for something that I can't see. So, when you do an affirmation, you may not be what you affirm right now, but you're speaking it in faith and then your actions are backing it up.
Steve Coplon:	What I love about faith is that we don't know how it's going to happen, but we know that it is going to happen. That is what we believe. We can then carry on without a loser mentality, believing that we have already been defeated. Let me read some more of what you've said in those two chapters.
Steve Coplon:	I've read that book four times now.
Johnnie Lloyd:	The book is excellent.
Steve Coplon:	Absolutely. There's have been hundreds of books written by many people about the Napoleon Hill 17 Principles. Lefford has written a powerful book about those same 17 Principals that I consider one of the best because of the way that he communicates what they each mean. He really chose people to write chapters that could communicate effectively. Johnnie, you're an unbelievable communicator.
Johnnie Lloyd:	Oh, bless you. Thank you.
Steve Coplon:	I want to give an illustration of something you talked about a few minutes ago. Most people are afraid to own up and admit when they're wrong. It is difficult for most people to acknowledge when they handle something that they feel they should have done a little differently. Some people are overly sensitive. You don't want to go too far being overly sensitive, but you do want to be sensitive to the feelings of others. A person could be a really big person if they were able to go up to somebody and say, "Hey, I wanted to make sure you didn't take what I said wrong."
Steve Coplon:	I'll give the listeners an example of something that happened just the other day that you were involved in. Johnnie and I participated in a webinar for www.hamptonroadscares.org. Where we were doing a public service webinar to help people navigate the coronavirus stimulus package.

| Johnnie Lloyd: | CARES. Coronavirus Aid, Relief, and Economic Security Act. |

Steve Coplon: Thanks, Johnnie. The webinar was put together by Dave Richards. His son Bond, who I know very, very well, is about 29 or 30 now. When he was about nine or 10, I was his and Dave's wife's Karate instructor. That's how I met Dave, through his wife. I've seen Bond grow up for 20 years. He sat in on the webinar to learn how to navigate the CARES package. He owns a small company and he wanted to learn how to complete the stimulus package application.

Steve Coplon: So, at the very end, when we finished most of the presenting in the webinar, I said, "Is there anybody here who has joined in that has any questions?" Nobody responded with a question. So, I said, "Hey, Bond, how about you? Do you have a question?" My direct question to him appeared to put him on the spot, so I made a joke to ease him up. I said, "Bond, I know your dad wants you to get out there and get your company back up and running so you can make some money, so you won't have to live at home forever."

Steve Coplon: His expression was very pensive as if he were trying to think things through. Afterwards I called Dave and said, "Hey, Dave, I didn't mean to embarrass Bond when I threw that question at him during the webinar. It was meant to be loving." Dave said back to me, "Oh no, are you kidding, Steve? He learned so much from it and thanked me afterwards. Then immediately after the show he actually filled out his application, which before he didn't have a clue where to start. Don't worry about that at all, Steve. He knew you were playing." But I had thought about it because that's my personality too, just like yours, Johnnie. I don't ever want anybody to think I was doing something in a hurtful way.

Steve Coplon: Let me tell you. If you go to someone and say, "Hey, I just want to make sure that when I said that to you, it didn't come across wrong. And if so, I'm sorry for the way I said it." Well, let me tell you something. 99% of the time, if you approach another person with an attitude like that, they're going to say, "Hey, it's okay Steve. I know you meant well. It's okay." If what you said was a little bit confusing and they were not quite sure where you were coming from, they would now know that Steve is a good guy. I want people to take me as I am. I want them to know that I am a good guy.

Steve Coplon: Why does the way people perceive me mean so much to me? I don't have a problem with low self-esteem. I'm not an egocentric maniac either. But I express my love to people. I want people to receive the love that I offer them and not block me out because they don't know how to take me. I don't want to come on to people too strong or too hard and make them feel uncomfortable.

Johnnie, I shared with you my strong desire to communicate clearly with people, because I don't meet very many people who are as conscious as you about making sure that they are not misunderstood. I admire that in you. It makes me think about an old song that I bet you remember from 1965 by the Animals called *Please Don't Let Me Be Misunderstood.* The main lyric was: "I'm just a soul whose intentions are good. Oh Lord, please don't let me be misunderstood."

Johnnie Lloyd: "Be Misunderstood." Yes, I do remember it.

Steve Coplon: Johnnie, I am going back to chapter 16 from Lefford's book ***The 17 Steps to Success, Conversations with World-Class Napoleon Hill Certified Leaders.*** You wrote, "I was at an amazing job as an Executive Leader and there was something missing. I was one of those executives that was good at a million things and I did well, very well, but I had not identified my Definite Major Purpose." I'm going to hit the pause button for a second. A person who doesn't realize they haven't identified their Major Purpose, someone who has too much confidence in how good they think they are at what they do, is going to, more than likely, go off in a direction that's not going to be the best.

Steve Coplon: Then you continued to write, "I was looking for what I was created to do and become great at it. Helping people and helping them in this process of becoming greater and finding that sense of purpose, that's my lane because it's the most powerful place." Here's another one you wrote, "Because the why will continue us moving forward when times are rough and when everything is not going our way." And another powerful quote of yours from that chapter, "Don't be afraid to fail. Don't be afraid to fail and fail forward. What you do is you fail, you learn, you adjust, and you keep on going. You fail, you learn, you adjust, and you keep on going."

Steve Coplon: One last beautiful quote from that chapter, "Then you follow that process until you win. Because failing is never final until you stop." Right Thinking Foundation's slogan is, *"Don't Quit, Plan Ahead, It Will Get Better."*

Johnnie Lloyd: Isn't that where we are now?

Steve Coplon: I believe so.

Johnnie Lloyd: During this season, or any time of crisis, whether it's a personal crisis, a professional crisis, emotional or spiritual crisis that we're dealing with, we have to move forward. It's just like when I lived in Europe. It used to rain, I mean, it poured. What they would always tell us is to keep on driving because sometimes the rain is happening only right in the section that we were. And if you sit and stop, all you're going to get is rain. All you're going to get is the downpour. But when you keep moving, then you find out there's something on the other side.

Johnnie Lloyd: One of the thoughts I think about right now that is really heavy for me during this time of the coronavirus pandemic, and anytime a person's going through crisis, is to feed what you desire to grow. If you don't desire it to grow, stop feeding it. For example, if you're the kind of person who tends to be very negative because of all the stuff that's going on TV or whatever, you've got the power to the remote. Shut it down, shut it down, shut it down. You have to learn to do that because we ended up in a 24 hour news cycle after 9/11. Okay. After 9/11, we stayed in that same news cycle. So, it's almost like a cow chewing cud. We take it from one stomach and then it goes to the next stomach. They're just giving different versions of the same information. It is a constant bombardment of negativity.

Johnnie Lloyd: Now, I'm not knocking the news networks. I'm just saying you don't have to listen to them all the time. Now, the one thing I will say about this, and I just want to encourage the people who are listening to this show. If you have a senior in school or you know of someone who has a senior, please encourage that senior because they are the people who came into this world during the 9/11 crisis and they are the same people who are being impacted the most by the coronavirus pandemic. They can't even graduate from high school right now. So, please encourage them. Send them a gift. Let them know that they still matter. Do something for someone else.

Johnnie Lloyd:	And especially during this time in our history, even if they're not a senior, get on the phone, do something for someone else. That is what I encourage people to do. Remember, you are fire when you are focused. So, when you're talking about going from the lip to the hip, be a person who shows love. Serve other people. Just do something nice for someone else.
Steve Coplon:	Thanks, Johnnie. That's the message. Is there anything else, that you would like to share today, that you haven't brought out yet? I've got a question for you, but I don't want to stop you from continuing to deliver anything that you want to share.
Johnnie Lloyd:	No. I'm here to serve, Steve.
Steve Coplon:	God Bless you.
Johnnie Lloyd:	I have no agenda.
Steve Coplon:	Okay, so you're the right person for me to discuss this next topic with.
Johnnie Lloyd:	Okay, I am ready.
Steve Coplon:	I discuss this with a lot of people, but knowing you as I'm getting to know you, I think that some beautiful truth tips are going to come out now. Ways to have people get up from where they're sitting. The problem that we have in life with people that are beaten down, they don't have the strength of mind to take advice and wisdom from others because they are basically living a depressed life. They are living in a mentality where conversation doesn't reach them. A lot of people have to get to the bottom of the barrel before they can climb back up. That is what Napoleon Hill learned from 500 of the most successful people in America who he interviewed for his book, **"Think and Grow Rich,"** the masterpiece that launched his philosophy of success. He found, that almost without exception, every one of the 500 people, experienced the proverbial bottom of the barrel where their lives had gotten to a place where they had to strip themselves down to their bare naked selves and say, "I will never let life do this to me again."
Steve Coplon:	Now, I've had those experiences myself and I'm constantly trying to get better focused. Jim Stovall, one of my mentors, is going to be a guest on the last show in this series. He's helped me immensely to eliminate distractions. You and I are not psychologists. We're children of God who love our brothers and our sisters. That is better than straight psychology. Love comes straight from the source.
Steve Coplon:	Now, there's a lot of wonderful psychologists who can deal with very, very deep situations. But love is the answer. We know that. I know that we're going to love people. We're going to be there for people. We're going to have compassion for people. We all have hard times in our lives. There are times where we all face adversity. There are people we are so desperately praying for who we want to pick up, so that they can experience the riches and the abundance that life does have in store for them. The hardest part of my own journey is when I am trying to reach them but fail.
Steve Coplon:	I believe in giving of my time. I'm a teacher who tries to wake people up and help them focus, so they can start absorbing. Once you get them reading, they have a better chance to move forward, to start to desire more out of life. Johnnie, can you give us some advice? I want you to go wherever you want to go on this, because I know you have strong feelings, along with great ideas. You know a lot of truth in this area. Please share some wisdom to all

those who have people in their lives who have not lived their life the right way. Who haven't been truthful with others, who haven't developed trust, who haven't understood from the lip to the hip is in honoring their commitments.

Steve Coplon: Johnnie, I'm asking you specifically to take the remainder of today's show and give us something from your heart, that speaks directly to the people who are trying their utmost best, by praying for people they love but are still being rejected by those very same people. They are praying for those who are too down and too depressed. They are constantly hearing, "Okay thanks. I know that you love me, I hear you." Then they do nothing different. What can we do to get them to respond to attempts to help? My answer is to keep on loving them, loving them, loving them. Help us by going into some practical things that we can do to try to pick these people up and get them to start to want to seek the truth.

Johnnie Lloyd: Okay. Are we dealing with the people who are not doing it? Or are we dealing with the people who want to help them? Or do you want to deal with a little bit of both?

Steve Coplon: I want to deal with a little bit of both.

Johnnie Lloyd: Okay. So, let's start.

Steve Coplon: We are people who want to help them. How do we do that so that we're effectively helping them move forward?

Johnnie Lloyd: Okay. This is the way I would approach it. Let's talk about the people who are helping. We have to be careful that we're not enabling them. That's a real critical word, so let's use Jesus, the great physician, as our focus. I say that I want to be more like Jesus. However, I want to control what my child does. That's not what Jesus does. You know what I'm saying? So, I want to see that something gets done, but I want to do it on my terms. I want them to do it, but I want them to learn to do it for themselves.

Johnnie Lloyd: I love what you talked about on the episode I listened to with you and Lefford. You talked about a woman who was going through some stuff with her husband. She asked God to show her who this man was going to be when he got to the place where he grew closer to God and became the man that God created him to be. She stayed in prayer, stuck it out with her husband and now their relationship is amazing. Now, I don't want us to go back into that. What I want us to do is kind of use that as a springboard because what we have to know about the people we're helping, is that it's not by my power, nor my might. It is by the Lord's power and might. He has more invested in us as a person than we do.

Johnnie Lloyd: I learned that firsthand when my daughter was going through a season in her life that was terribly troubling to me back when she was attending Virginia Tech. She grew through her struggles and actually later became a very good psychologist. During her crisis, she called me and said something really crazy that was so unlike her. I started crying out to the Lord, rolling on the floor and all that. The Lord did not respond to my foolishness. You know what He did respond to? After I finished acting like I had lost my mind, screaming, hollering, and reminding Him that it's me, oh Lord, what He said was, "I have more invested in her than you do."

Steve Coplon: I want to clap.

Johnnie Lloyd: He said, "She is the gift I gave to you. You are only a steward".

Steve Coplon:	Amen. Thank you.

Johnnie Lloyd: I would encourage people to recognize that our children belong to the Lord and that we have to trust Him. Through Him all things are possible. We must all go through a transformational development. We want people to act on what we know is right for them which they will be more apt to do when they also know that the Lord is in control.

Steve Coplon: It is not our responsibility to take control of their situations. They need to take responsibility for themselves. We are walking beside them, but we cannot walk for them.

Johnnie Lloyd: Exactly.

Steve Coplon: We all have to give it up to the Lord. That's what I believe.

Johnnie Lloyd: Absolutely. That's part of it. We take those for whom we pray and hope they will find a way to move forward to the Lord. We lead them to the altar, and when we get up, we are still holding on to them. We haven't let go, we haven't given it up to the Lord ourselves. We said, "The Lord didn't see it. God, I need to help him." No, no, no. It's what you and Lefford talked about. You have to put on your own oxygen mask first when you are on a plane and the turbulence causes the masks to drop down. You must make sure that you yourself are whole. You make sure that you have changed.

Johnnie Lloyd: The people I coach for transformational development, have to sign an agreement in the beginning of the process. In that agreement, we write down what they say they want to accomplish. They define that for themselves. If their development stalls or veers off course, I go back to the agreement and say, "You're the one who said that you wanted to build another business [for example]. Has that changed?" And they generally respond, "No, I still want to do what I said in the agreement." I then ask, "Okay, then what are you doing with your time? What are you doing with your resources? It doesn't align with what you said." This is a clear illustration of a disconnect from their lip to their hip as you use that powerful expression.

Steve Coplon: Johnnie, you brought it around for me.

Johnnie Lloyd: So, yes there's a disconnect.

Steve Coplon: A disconnect from what people actually said they were going to do, from what they end up doing. I agree with you. I like the way that you show them they are not following through with their commitment to themselves.

Johnnie Lloyd: I made a note of something else that I found really powerful while listening to you and Lefford. I would encourage everyone to not judge people based on the current frame in their movie, because it is only one frame. In movie making, the end is known before production starts. The movie is based on a screenplay that has already been written. So, the director and producer go to the end and then they work back to the beginning. They have the advantage of knowing all of the details the "frames" before they even start. They know the end that they want, and they are always able to make it happen. Same as the way God does with us. He knows our end. So, he's already figured it out for us. We have to trust Him.

Johnnie Lloyd: So, what we have to do as the person who is providing that support, is we have to gird up our trust in Him, in God, to know that He has more invested than we do with those we desire to help. But it is up to each person to make the choice to let God do His thing in us, or not to let Him. Whatever their choice, you and I cannot change that choice. I can fight with a person that I believe in, who is struggling to get on the right path. I can do all that crazy stuff that sometimes we do as parents. We do some things to help other people because we see so much in them, but we can't make them choose. What happens when they have not made the choice themselves is that it will only result in change, not transformation.

Johnnie Lloyd: Transformation is like a butterfly. Once you transform, you choose as a human not to go back. Some of the things that I dealt with before in my life, still try to crawl up in my head and say, "Go back and do that, girl. You can do that." No, I can't because I choose not to. It's not because I'm not capable. It's not because I don't have the capacity or the capability to do it. That person has to choose to do it. So that's the one thing. Don't judge people based on the current frame.

Johnnie Lloyd: We need to remind people and ourselves that we are Kings and Queens, dwelling in His Kingdom. We need to stop separating our stewardship by saying, "Well, that's the world. That's the business world, and this is church." God made everything. It is His Kingdom and all of us are one.

Remember that Napoleon Hill lifted up six ghosts of fear. You and Lefford talked a little about the six ghosts of fear who appear in the last chapter titled *"How to Outwit the Six Ghosts of Fear"* of *"Think and Grow Rich"* by Napoleon Hill. Lefford spoke about how he was living with the fear of poverty throughout his early life. This is real, the ghost of poverty exists in people's minds. When you're dealing with poverty, criticism, and similar other things including ill health, the fears are real. What you have to do is, you have to change.

Johnnie Lloyd: The best way to encourage change in someone else is for us to change. If I stop giving, if I stop doing stuff, and I don't mean to not love them, it is doubtful that I will be able to help them change. However, I can love you and step back a little bit. I can love you and say, "Okay, this is a good book. You read it. It's on Audible, you listen to it. It's on YouTube, watch it." Watch our time. Watch our money. Watch it because God's going to hold us accountable for what He assigned us to do. So, remember that. It is not from a perspective of being selfish, it's from the perspective of being selfless.

Johnnie Lloyd: As a servant, we serve. And if I offer you a banquet table in front of you, all the riches and all the things that God would have for us, and you sit at that table and you decide not to partake, it is not another person's fault that you starve. It's just not their fault.

Steve Coplon: Johnnie, you are amazing.

Johnnie Lloyd: Oh, bless you.

Steve Coplon: I love the wisdom that you have shared with us today. I asked you to speak to things that are always on my heart. In everything that you said around your theme *"You are Fire When You are Focused"*, you spoke the truth. You spoke from your heart. I truly feel closer to God after listening to you today. I know that everyone listening today will reap rewards from your powerful words.

Johnnie Lloyd: May I say one thing?

Steve Coplon: Certainly, please do.

Johnnie Lloyd: I just want to thank you. Thank you for this platform. Thank you for your heart. *"From the Lip to the Hip is a Pretty Far Distance"* is a heavy subject and your series based on it

	is going to help someone. I just want you to know, if there is one person, or if there are 20 million people who you touch, God is going to honor what you are doing, and He's going to bless you. He is going to continuously bless you.
Steve Coplon:	Well, I appreciate that, but I have to tell you. He has already blessed me more than any human being that I know.
Johnnie Lloyd:	Oh, praise Him.
Steve Coplon:	God blesses me constantly. I thank you for your love. I know that you are going to be back on the show many times. I know this because we have the same calling: to love everyone and to help them have a better life. This platform is yours as well as mine, so thank you for participating.
Johnnie Lloyd:	Bless you.
Steve Coplon:	The table has been set and you are partaking. God has given us this opportunity. On the very first show in this series, **"From the Lip to the Hip is a Pretty Far Distance,"** I used Proverbs 3:6 to end the show. I will do that again today.

Proverbs 3:6

"Listen for God's voice in everything you do. Everywhere you go. He is the one who will keep you on track."

Steve Coplon:	Well, Johnnie, thank you for sharing today. Thank you for being here. Everyone, go back and listen to this show again. There is so much in it. Everyone be blessed and have a wonderful week! God Bless you.
Johnnie Lloyd:	Thank you.
Steve Coplon:	Thanks for listening to *Right Thinking with Steve Coplon*. I look forward to being with you again next week. Remember: **Don't Quit, Plan Ahead, It Will Get Better.** God Bless you and have a great week!

To listen to the original interview, scan this QR Code with your camera, or visit:

https://rightthinkingeducation.com/FromtheLiptotheHip/Chapter-8/

CHAPTER NINE

Do What You Said Even Better Than You Said with guest Dave Richards
Right Thinking With Steve Coplon - Episode 167

Steve Coplon:	Good morning. Welcome to *Right Thinking with Steve Coplon.* I'm your host, Steve Coplon. Thank you for tuning in. Let's have a great day!
Steve Coplon:	Good morning everybody. Glad to be with you. Well, I've been having a really good time for the last eight weeks on this series of *"From the Lip to the Hip is a Pretty Far Distance,"* and we've got a really special treat today. I've brought back an old cast member. I'm going to call Dave Richards a cast member, an original member of *Right Thinking with Steve Coplon.* When I started this radio show 167 episodes ago, that's a little over three years now, I depended on Dave. Dave, you'll have to be a regular. We've got a lot of stuff to talk about.
Steve Coplon:	I think this is Dave's 14th show, so he's been there for me, and his wisdom is just great. You're going to know that in a little while. Let me read you what today's Episode #167 is. Right Thinking with Steve Coplon is very pleased to announce that this week's show is **called "Do What You Said Even Better Than You Said,"** with guest Dave Richards. Tune in and hear Steve and Dave, a highly successful international businessman and humanitarian who channels his incredible energy into doing for others. You will enjoy Dave's beautiful spirit as you benefit in ways that will improve your life.
Steve Coplon:	Well, Dave I said a lot just then, but you can live up to it. Dave, thanks for being on the show, I wanted you to be part of this series because the perspective that you can bring to it is really going to be beautiful. I know that just because all the themes that we talk about are always enriching other people's lives. So, I know that you've listened to Episode 159, *"From the Lip to the Hip is a Pretty Far Distance,"* and have some comments.
Steve Coplon:	I mean, there are going to be 14 shows in this series, and as always Dave, you're going to be a little different, I know that, because you are a little different. So, get warmed up everybody. Dave and I once did a show where afterwards my wife asked, "Why do you do that to Dave? You always throw things at him that he has to go, 'Oh, wow. Wait a minute. I don't know. Let me think about that.'" So, one day, Dave got on here. I don't remember which show it was, but he said, "Steve, I want to do something different. I want to interview you, but I don't want to tell you what the show is going to be about, and I just want to get you on the air and start asking you questions." So, we did that, and it turned out pretty good.

Steve Coplon:	Nevertheless, Dave's been on a whole bunch of shows. I can maybe tell you some of them as the show goes on. Dave, thanks for being on the show today. It's just wonderful to still be here with you after eight years of doing Right Thinking.
Dave Richards:	Well, thanks, Steve. It's a pleasure to be here, with me sitting on top of a mountain in Charlottesville during a pandemic, and you sitting safely someplace. So, the fact that we're still here doing this all these years later is great. I can't say I listened to all of your shows, but I've listened to the vast majority of them, and it's fun to think that I had a tiny small piece of helping this thing keep going. So, again, it's amazing what you've done, and I'm happy to be here.
Steve Coplon:	Hey, Dave, you haven't done a small piece. In fact, for today's show, because you're so busy most of the time doing things for other people, I even volunteered that we would just play another show that we had done in its entirety. Then just add 10 or 15 minutes to it about the kind of conversation that we're going to have, concerning your feelings toward people doing what they say they're going to do, and the character and integrity issues that relate to that. We've done so much together. We've worked together in prisons approximately 17 times.
Steve Coplon:	You gave me one of the biggest tools that I teach in prisons. It came from a show that you and I did called *"Get That First Job"*. You talked about pointers you wanted to put together in a training program for returning citizens on how they can handle interviews to get a job. So, I did a whole routine on that called "Turn the Beat Around", and it's basically where you have to engage the interviewer, so that you become the interviewer, then the person takes a real interest in you. You've got to separate yourself from the pack.
Steve Coplon:	Anyway Dave, when I went back to that show, there were so many good memories and so forth and so on, and I actually pulled out a book that I have put together. I taught for a couple years at Achievable Dream Academy. It was a local high school for at-risk kids. As I thumbed through that book, it brought back so many memories of positive things I've been involved in. It has your fingerprints everywhere I've taught those principles. In fact, the website and the platform that I use for **Right Thinking Foundation** is part of Concursive. It's the Connect platform that you donated to the foundation.
Steve Coplon:	Dave, I'd never be where I am today without your involvement. I mean, you are the founding member with me. You served on the board, and then you removed yourself, so you could do other things. You're involved in so many nonprofit type things and you are a true humanitarian with your heart in the right place. When I asked you to be on the show, I said, "Well, Dave, I just need a little bit of a theme that we can talk about," and I asked you, "So, Dave, what is it? What is your passion?" I ask this to everybody before I interview them, and I said, "So, Dave, tell me," and you didn't hesitate.
Steve Coplon:	You said, "Matthew 25:36-40," and I'm going to read that now. It's on the cover of all the books that I put out for **Right Thinking Foundation** in the first four or five years. This was my cover of every book. It was my logo, and you actually gave me my company logo with this motto: You have to connect to succeed, and there's three pillars to that. Home, Work and Community. Home; you have to have a place to live. Work; you've got to go to work so that you have an income. Community; you must be a part of your community.
Steve Coplon:	Dave, I just want all the listeners to know that everything you do even with the company that you've been running for the last 25 years or so, is about community. That's your middle

name. It's about bringing people together. You can talk about that all you want to today, but first I want to read part of Matthew 25:39-40.

Matthew 25:39-40

"I was in prison, and you came to visit me. Whatever you did for one of the least of these brothers and sisters of mine, you did for me."

Steve Coplon:	And thank you for recognizing in yourself that that's where you get this from. Dave, you're beautiful. You're a true servant and thank you for being on the show today. So, where do you want to start, Dave? You got into Episode 159.
Dave Richards:	Yeah, I listened to it. I think it was great, and your mother was a very wise lady, as was mine. We were both fortunate, incredibly fortunate. To step back to what makes people successful, it's usually parents or grandparents or mentors or somebody who inspire us. Success doesn't necessarily mean making money. In fact, it almost never means just making money. It really means, "What kind of a person are you and are you a good citizen?" I can remember for many, many years, my mother always saying, "All I want you to be is good citizens of the earth. That's what I want you to be." If you have parents who tried to raise you that way, then you are fortunate. There's no perfect person, none of us are perfect, everyone's imperfect.
Dave Richards:	You're blessed to be led by people who fundamentally believe that. So again I, just like you Steve, was blessed with a pretty wise mother and father. Dad had a lot of wisdom too, but most of mine probably comes from my mother's side. So, I thought a fair amount about your mom's comment, *"From the Lip to the Hip is a Pretty Far Distance."*
Dave Richards:	The notion being what people say and what they do are not always the same thing. She teaches you that as it relates to sales. What they tell you and what they actually spend their money on, can be quite different. Then that leads to a broader concept of just your word. The impact of your word when you tell somebody you're going to do something is monumental. The impact of what you say to them, determines your own reputation. Reputations are built on this question: "Do people follow their word?" Then you challenged me with this notion of, "Okay, so there's the other side of it. It's the impact of your word on others and how we react." How do we act in an imperfect world where people tell you things and they don't always do them? How do we live our own life and how do you go forward on a practical basis given that reality? I guess when I boil it down, there are two ways to react to that reality.
Dave Richards:	So, anyway, I've thought a fair amount about that. I think it's really just rich with depth and irony of some kind. I guess when I boil it down, I get these two things. First, how is one understanding and how is one forgiving in a world where everyone of us at times, has said things and we can't live up to them? So, number one is, how can we be understanding and forgiving? Number two, we must be practical and smart and have a plan B. When people tell us things, you can't just put it in the bank. You have to have a plan B or assume it may not happen. The practical side of life is to not put all your eggs in one basket or whatever cliché you want to use.
Dave Richards:	So, that's a little bit of how I pulled it apart in my mind, and you and I talked about this a little earlier. It's pretty obvious the statements of, "If you don't do what you say, it impacts your reputation." So, my question is why don't people do that? We can talk more about that.

And then finally, I think to me at least, probably the most interesting thing is: how do you understand people when they're telling you things they're just not going to do? How do you come away being okay with it? Come away being, "Okay. I get it. I'm okay with that because they're doing the best they can," or whatever the reasons are, but I have to keep living my own life and acting accordingly.

Dave Richards: So, that's my starting point on this. I've got a few thoughts and notes all over the place because it's a topic that literally every great thinker has touched on, in one way or another. So, just for the fun of it, I was thinking back to quotes I'd heard, and I went back to see who the heck said them. Franklin has one in his ***"Poor Richard's Almanac".*** Again, this is *Ben Franklin,* and he wrote under the pseudonym of *Poor Richard.* It had all these great, great wise sayings, which I've always loved. So clever and ahead of his time, and his was:

Ben Franklin (Poor Richard)

"Well done is better than well said."

Steve Coplon: You said, "Boy, that's really wise."

Dave Richards: You can tell me anything you want, but well done is better than well said, and I just said, "Well, that pretty much captures it." Again, from a personal point of view of how do we step up? We can say everything we want, but at the end of the day, your actions speak volumes. So, anyway, that's my starting point, Steve.

Steve Coplon: Well, that's a beautiful starting point. A lot of our shows, you went back into the wisdom of Ben Franklin. You went into George Washington's virtues. I think... Was it, George Washington who listed the 13 virtues?

Dave Richards: That was Franklin, but Washington had 127 of them.

Steve Coplon: Yeah, I remember that. Yeah, ways to live by, things to live by or something. Then you also did *Teddy Roosevelt's,* **"Man in the Arena,"** which is an all-time favorite. That's powerful, and I think when you were a kid, didn't you have hanging on the wall in your living room or over the fireplace the poem *by Max Ehrmann,* **"Desiderata"?**

Dave Richards: Actually, it was in our house. My father had it in the house for years. He had two, wall hangings made. One was *Max Ehrmann's,* **"Desiderata",** and the other was *Teddy Roosevelt's, "It's Not the Critic that Counts. It's the Man in the Ring".* I now have both of those. The only two things I wanted of my father when he passed away were those two wall hangings. Due to the wisdom they contain I will gift them to my sons. I mean, it says it all in those hundred words. That's the only thing you need to read every day. You can read the Bible and lots of other good things, but in my mind, if I just read those two, they ground me. They make me feel a lot better about what I do.

Steve Coplon: Dave, I want to read the last couple lines of *Teddy Roosevelt's,* **"The Man in the Arena,"** but let me say one more thing again. We've covered all the basics; from the lip to the hip, and people doing what they say they're going to do. It's a basic truth here that if you don't live up to your word, you're not going to get real far in life. If people don't believe me, they should listen to the other 12 or 13 shows that you have been on. You've said it too.

Steve Coplon: Dave, you've got such a high level of success, and you're such a focused person. You've got a great focus on how you do what you do and still find time to do so many things for others.

It's more about living up to your full potential. How can I be a person who does what I say I'm going to do?" We're going to go into a higher level. Not only doing what you say, let's go beyond what you say. There's another expression, and I don't know who said it; "It's better to over-deliver than to overpromise." You're not going to get too far in anything you do if you promise a whole lot and don't do much of what you said.

Steve Coplon: A soft-spoken person might just be low-key about it and then blow people away with how much they actually do. That's always a better way to go. We're going to get through a higher level today. There are a couple things I thought of when you were talking about your mother and my mother. My mother had always told me, "Stevie, I don't really care what you do in your life as long as it's honest," and I just thought that was as simple and as basic as it can be. She didn't care if I was a proverbial ditch digger or a dishwasher or an accountant or whatever else along the way. She just wanted me to be honest. So, I love that she passed that on to me, and it is a personal thing, but you started it.

Steve Coplon: When you said the only two things you wanted when your dad died were the two wall hangings of "Man in the Arena" and... What's the other one? Did you say **"Desiderata"?**

Dave Richards: **"Desiderata".**

Steve Coplon: Yeah. Well, we went through a lot of struggles. I have 167 shows now. I talk a whole lot about being poor when I was coming up. My mother and I had gone through a lot of hard times, and when she died she was very proud of me. In her will, she gave all of her assets including the little money and the material things to my brothers and sisters. She gave me what I consider to be the ultimate compliment that a man can ever get from his mother. She said, "Stevie, I'm so proud of you, I'm proud that you've done so well with your life, that I'm not leaving anything at all to you except for my music collection."

Steve Coplon: She'd accumulated about 150 of these little cassette tapes and a box with all the beautiful old music, Brenda Lee and whoever, and I just loved it. She loved to watch those TV commercials and order stuff. When we moved her belongings out of her house, we found a bust of Emmett Kelly the clown with his trademark of one tear coming down his eye. It was about a foot and a half tall of just his head and shoulders. She always said, "Stevie, that's what life is. That's what life is." So, yeah, I'm just like you Dave, you didn't need a whole lot left to you because your parents knew you. So, I thank you for triggering that memory for me.

Steve Coplon: Well, Dave, with that said, when I was talking to my wife today about the show. I told her that, "No, I'm going to get Dave on here to let people know how they can reach their full potential and go even higher, because he's a role model for that. He does so much." Like you said, success isn't about money. It helps for sure. If you have it, you can do a lot with it for other people, of course. You can be a good provider. You can do good things. Your mark is what you do for other people and how you've helped other people along the path.

Steve Coplon: So, you'll do well when you get to the pearly gates because, if you hadn't done anything else in your life, what you've done for me will get you in. I promise you that. Yeah, you can look forward to that. Dave, I told Donna about people who deliver more than what they are asked to deliver. Here's an example I gave her just right away, and I hope I can do it as well right now as I did for her. So, a wife wants her husband to build a birdhouse.

Steve Coplon: He didn't just build a little birdhouse. I was looking at one outside the window when I was talking to her because I got a little teeny birdhouse. We get some birds in there, and I said, "So, what does he do?" "He builds an arboretum. He gets birds from all over the world, and he brings in a whole bird sanctuary. He imports birds and does the most amazing thing to create a whole arboretum for them." Well, that's a whole lot more than just building a bird house, isn't it?

Steve Coplon: Well, Dave, you've built a lot of arboretums and not just a lot of little birdhouses. What do you want to say next Dave, about a person who does what they say they're going to do, and then they deliver more than what they're asked? In other words, they build an arboretum instead of just a birdhouse. People know them as that person. The sky's the limit for what they can do with their life. So, why don't you just take it from there and go anywhere you want?

Dave Richards: Wow. That was great, and thanks for the story about your mother, that rings very close to me. So, that said, I think the question is, what triggers that behavior in certain people? I'm thinking back over the last 30 years of people I know who have been successful. If you really boil it down, boy they truly care. They care about what they're doing, and sometimes, it's exasperating. The people you deal with Steve must be exasperated, because you care so much about what you're doing. That's why it comes off so well, and that's why you're so good at what you do.

Dave Richards: I use the word exasperated with a lot of love. I've got people who are incredibly close to me who've been quite successful in their careers and are not making lots of money. However, they're incredibly well respected. I worked with a software developer for 15 to 20 years. He's a very smart guy, very well disciplined and he really cares. What care means in this case as a software developer is not what it does, it's how it looks. It's the flow of the software. "What does it look like on the screen?" He really cares, as opposed to some people who just slap it together to meet some kind of specification, but it's just not good.

Dave Richards: The software guys who are really good, care about that. They care about how code is written; how efficient it is. Not only does it not break, but do they go beyond it? I can remember being in business school with one of my absolute closest friends who still is one of my closest friends and godfather to one of my two sons. I remember being on a business project with him. We spent hours on it, and I was ready to move on. I was like, "I think it's good enough."

Dave Richards: We laughed about it for years later because he damn near killed me and him on this project. But here's the point, my friend, Todd cares about the job he does, and what that means is at least in business, it boils over to how he deals with his clients. His clients know that this guy will do anything for them. He will be the guy up at 3:00 in the morning. He'll be the guy staying up all night working to try to do the best job he can, and consequently, you can't BS clients. They know people who are going the extra mile.

Dave Richards: So, what triggers that? Boy, I wish I knew, I think it's somewhat mentoring. I remember my grandmother, Grandma Bond, named after her mother's maiden name, Bond. My son, Bond, is also named after my mother's maiden name. I remember exactly where I was, I was probably 10 years old, and I was just about to finish vacuuming, and grandma said to me in the nicest way, something like, "Really, it's not how fast you vacuum. It's actually how much dirt you pick up."

Dave Richards: So, I'll never forget that. I was like, wow, as a 10-year-old, I was always pretty good at vacuuming after that because of my grandmother, and I think about that, and I go, "Okay, I got that lesson at 10, and I think somehow I've applied it." Now, I'm not saying I do the best job in everything I do, because you always have to find balances, but I do take a little bit of pride in what I try to do. I see the people who are just born successful. Overall, they just care. I mean, they literally care what they do. What triggers that? And how do you teach kids to care? How do you teach adults to care? I'm not exactly sure. Maybe you have thoughts on that.

Dave Richards: Quite frankly, if you look like you care and you actually do care, it doesn't matter what job you're doing. We do a lot of the work ourselves, however, the people who do work for us and take an extra five minutes blowing the debris after it's been cut, are the ones who really care, which makes us feel good.

Steve Coplon: I think that pride is a good word. Now, you can get into the religious side of, "Pride's an awful thing." That's one of the great sins. But no, I'm not talking about that type of pride. I'm talking about taking pride in what you do, so that you can be proud to say, "I've done the best I can. I've done a good job." If a person doesn't have pride in their own work, and they just want to take the quick and easy way out, they're going to leave a lot of dirt on the floor. I learned a lesson early out when I was in college, and I was a construction superintendent. A real quick story here, I worked really, really hard. I was just a laborer in a big construction crew in a big company, and within days, they pulled me aside and said, "Hey, Steve. We want you to manage this crew because we like the way you work, and we want you to manage some other people."

Steve Coplon: So, I started doing that, and then about a week later, they said, "Hey, Steve. We got three crews out here. We want you to be the head of all three crews." So, they kept moving me up like that. Well, one of the things that I'll never forget. I went into this room. It was at Westhampton campus, University of Richmond, and we were renovating and turning it into a Holiday Inn-looking kind of place. It was a tragedy to take this beautiful 130-year-old campus and start changing it around and making it look like it was a Holiday Inn for more people.

Steve Coplon: I placed these two guys in this room, and they stayed in there while I walked around, checking on people to make sure they were doing what they were supposed to. They were in there just taking a smoke break, sitting on the floor. They had no idea that I was going to pop in the room and see how they were progressing. They didn't take any pride whatsoever, basically, they were just making minimum wage. So, the point of it was, I had to have people go into all these rooms, to take out all the debris, get all the dust out, and get it ready for the next crew to come in, paint it, put the floor in and install the carpet.

Steve Coplon: I had to teach them how to sweep everything toward the door. You'd be shocked at people who are sweepers. They're just sweeping and putting these little piles all over the place furthest from the door as possible. I learned early out, to move everything toward the door, so that when you look back in the room, it's finished. So, that's a really good concept in training people because no matter what the project is, keep the end goal in mind. And Dave, I want to apologize here to the people who are listening.

Steve Coplon: I'm not going to say that Dave is as A.D.D. as I am, however, when we were talking, I went off on another thought. I started talking about my mother. I got a few tears in my eyes, and

Dave did too. He didn't even want to go any further with where I started. I was getting ready to read the last couple lines *of Teddy Roosevelt's, "A Man in the Arena"*. I want to say, Dave, that was the most wonderful experience for you to grow up in an environment where you could read and think and meditate about this, and your dad taught it to you. I'll just pick up in this last part here.

Teddy Roosevelt

But who does actually strive to do the deeds, who knows great enthusiasms, the great devotions, who spends himself in a worthy cause, who at the best knows in the end the triumph of high achievement, and who at the worst if he fails at least fails while daring greatly, so that his place shall never be with those cold and timid souls who neither know victory nor defeat.

Steve Coplon: Dave, that's the whole thing right there. It's about putting your whole self into what you do, and we owe that to our employers. Nobody likes an employee who just gets there because he's working minimum wage. I'll let you take over now, but I train people. When you get that job, if you want great things in your life, don't think of it as a job. Think about it as an adventure. I sold that to the United States Navy about 35 years ago… Just kidding.

Steve Coplon: Now, think about it as if you are an entrepreneur in training, and this is just part of your experience training ground. Learn everything you possibly can. Be the single most valuable employee that they've ever seen. It's kind of like I was telling you. I mean, I wasn't asking for promotions, but they just kept saying, "Hey, Steve. We want you to do this other crew and then this other crew."

Steve Coplon: The point is to give it your all and give them more than a good day's work. Don't just do what you say you're going to do, do even better than you said. Dave, if you strive in life toward excellence like you've been brought up to do as a child, then you're going to be able to go real far in life. The advantage to go far in life isn't always for material gain. It's to be able to open up doors for others. So, back to you, Dave.

Dave Richards: Thanks, a lot of great stuff here. The Teddy Roosevelt quote talks to this notion of fear. So many people don't get started, don't move forward strictly for reasons of fear. I would say, "You have to get over that." Read *Teddy Roosevelt's, "Man in the Ring"* speech. If you've got fear, read it 30 times a day. What it basically says is if you give it your all, you'll feel great about it, and if it doesn't work out, who cares? At least you're not with the people who never try anything.

Dave Richards: So, get over the fear. Get started. I'm one who gets started relatively easy. For whatever reason, thankfully I've not been afraid of failing, I've got a lot of situations in my life that haven't worked out. We've tried greatly, however some didn't work out. So, again, read things like *"Man in the Ring"*, it's about fear. I looked back at it because I remembered coming upon this quote almost 20-25 years ago when I worked for a large company called Landmark Communications. I worked in the quality control area.

Dave Richards: I had sales and marketing positions. One of the part-time roles I had was to oversee the continuous improvement practice of the company. Continuous improvement is really from Japanese manufacturing, called lean manufacturing, and it's a real method. It's statistically driven by how you improve processes, lower cost, and improve quality. It's the Deming method if you want to read about it. It's fascinating, and it's really, really interesting. It's all about continuous improvement, getting better and better and better in your processes.

Dave Richards: What's fascinating about that is, I believe it's how humans have to live their lives. You have to just keep slowly getting at it. It's these thousands and thousands of little steps as humans. So, Deming is one of the big, big thought leaders in business quality. I remembered a quote from Aristotle, and I went back and looked it up for this show:

Aristotle

"Quality is not an act. It is a habit."

Steve Coplon: So, *"Quality is not an act. It's a habit."* This means the only way you get to do something well, is to make it a habit.

Dave Richards: Habits are sometimes, hard to form, and sometimes they're not. Sometimes, people can make habits really quick. Some of them are bad habits, and some are good, however, either can be learned very quickly. I'm watching my sons learn better and better habits as they get older, and I'd like to think my habits have gotten better as I've gotten older. So, anybody listening to or reading this, please realize that your habits can get better, you just have to start small. It doesn't matter if these habits are, habits like trying to spend a little bit more time on physical exercise, or your job, or your family, or the habit of spending more time with your friends. Whatever the habit is, if you can make that habit better, it drives quality.

Dave Richards: So, quality doesn't just come out of the air. It really does come from discipline and habits. Anybody can change their habits. I've seen people, as you have, Steve, who've remarkably changed their lives. I've seen a few of them in prison. You've seen them in prison. You've seen them literally have such bad behavior and such bad habits that they were incarcerated for decades, and now, they're trying to figure it out, thanks to you. "How do I change my habits and my behaviors so I can have a better quality of life?"

Dave Richards: My message is that it's really never too late, however, you have to start small. You can't worry about failure. You can't worry about it being the best approach or the worst approach. The trick is just to get started. Take that first step. There's no way eight years ago, you thought you would be where you are today with **Right Thinking Foundation.** You just got started. Now, 500 visits later into prisons, people are supporting you. You now have approximately 170 radio shows recorded, and books that are published. I mean, it's unbelievable. It's relationships you've built with men like Don Green, that started your first steps. There's nothing magical about you. The magic about you is that you got started, and you care, and that formula can work for anybody. It really can.

Dave Richards: We just have to find the influences around us who believe what we're saying, Steve. Try to surround yourself with people who will support you in getting started, and when you fail, they don't point out your failures. They say, "Okay, that didn't work. Let's pick ourselves up and start again." We'll do it better the next time. So, I'll stop there.

Steve Coplon: Wow. So, everything you said has about six different themes. I could branch out on anyone of them. For example, like surrounding yourself with people who care about you and doing well for them in exchange. But look, I've got 170 shows, give or take. I think this is 167 but listen to this. I told everybody that you were right there for me in the beginning trying to help me along, and I'm saying to everybody, "I think the greatest secret to success is being the kind of person who other people want to help along," because there's something about you that they recognize. That can be instrumental in getting you to a higher level because they're just trying to groom you, so you can pass it on to other people as well.

Steve Coplon: I think that's as fundamental in life as the Gospel is. That's what the whole gospel is, for each of us to just pass it on to someone else, so that they can pass it on to someone else. Listen to Episode five. These are just the titles of your shows, Dave. I want everybody to know these.

Episode 5, "Staying Connected"

Episode 9, "Your First Job and Pathways to Success"

Episode 14, "A Call to Action: Motivation and Challenge"

Episode 20, "Quality First: Putting it into Everything You Do"

Episode 24, "Choices: Choose to Take Charge of Your Life"

Episode 28, "Commit to Your Success"

Episode 40, "Desiderata: A Positive Model to Live By"

Episode 43, "Living a Life of Excellence"

Episode 51, "The National Online Support Network"

Episode 61, "The Connect Platform"

Episode 133, "Why Did the Dog Wag Its Tail?"

Steve Coplon: Now, I want to come back to talk about episode 133, because you thought that was clever, so I asked you the question on the air, "Why did the dog wag its tail?" Do you remember what you said? It was pretty good. Do you remember what you might have said?

Dave Richards: I remember several quips, but you go.

Steve Coplon: I think your answer was "because he can."

Dave Richards: He can. Right.

Steve Coplon: Because he can, and I said, "Well, that's the conventional answer, and I was going to challenge you on that because you're such a conventional straight-line thinker, Dave. Yeah, wrong. No. I said, "Because he can't get anybody else to do it for him." Then I launch into... I use this in prison sometime. I launch into taking responsibility. If you go around life expecting somebody else to always do it for you, you're never going to get very far. So, I think we've covered that a bit. Now, Dave, I want to share this because I read a little book that I dug up out of my files today on leadership. It's a nice little series, ***"Leadership with a Human Touch"***. It's a publication I happen to have on my shelf.

"Leadership with a Human Touch"

Benjamin Franklin's method of persuading others to his point of view took patience and endurance. It is assumed that people are won over slowly often indirectly. 'If you don't win the bargain today,' Franklin would say, 'go after it again tomorrow and the next day.' Here are some of Franklin's bargaining tips. One, be clear in your own mind about exactly what you're after. Two, do your homework, so that you are fully prepared to discuss every aspect and respond to every question and comment. Three, be persistent. Don't expect to win the first time. Your first job is just to start the other person thinking. Four, make friends with the person with whom you are bargaining. Put your bargain in terms of his or her needs, advantages and benefits. Five, keep your sense of humor.

Steve Coplon: Well, Dave, Benjamin Franklin would be proud to know that he has influenced Dave Richards as much as he did.

Dave Richards: That's funny. So, for those listening, if you aren't familiar with Benjamin Franklin, he was this guy from a long time ago. It's been 250 years...so, that's like four lifetimes of Steve and me. So, four lifetimes ago, Franklin was around. There might have been somewhat greater, more influential Americans like Lincoln and Washington. But in terms of just broad capability and impact in wisdom, Franklin, to me, stands far beyond all those. He was an incredible businessman.

Dave Richards: Steve, those words you just read are right out of every business school's leadership lessons of how to treat people. He was an incredible business guy, and perhaps one of the top two or three scientists of the entire 1700's. Literally, with his electricity, the impact from fire houses to libraries and then into political policies he worked on with the Constitution, and along with all this, he was an incredible individual. My point is, if you boiled back this incredibly successful man and looked at his lessons, they're really very simple. They are not that complex. So, you just have to figure out how to get started.

Dave Richards: Regarding jobs, it really isn't that hard to get ahead in a job. Showing up on time is 95% of the battle to begin with. Next is doing what you're told, being a nice person, letting things roll off you and understanding that everyone's fighting their own battles. So, if a co-worker says something inappropriate, let it pass. It's not a big deal, and you'll do just fine. Those people who really get ahead somehow might take a perverse pleasure in doing some of the most undesirable jobs, and you and I Steve, could be guilty of the same.

Dave Richards: So, when the boss asks, "Who will volunteer for this terrible job?" I'd wait half a second and then say, "I'll do it." I mean, because for some odd reason, I really don't mind doing it. If everyone else won't do it, I'm willing to do it, and maybe that's a weakness in my character because maybe that means I just want to be liked. Maybe I just want to be liked by the boss. Who the heck knows? But for some reason, I just find those as opportunities. I just see them as if you happen to be working in a restaurant, and someone cancels out on a shift, and it's six o'clock on Super Bowl day, and the boss needs help, 90% of the people saying, "There's no way I'm going to do that. I'm going to the party."

Dave Richards: There's 10% of the people who say, "I'll watch the Superbowl on replay. I'll go in. Somehow that'll help me. I'm helping my boss out in a tight fit, and I can always read about the Super Bowl in the paper the next day." Doing things that others won't do and helping out in a pinch are the single best ways to get ahead. I mean, maybe that sounds obvious, but it's amazing how few people will do that, and bosses completely respect it. They really do. As a boss, when those people do that for me, I say, "I'll remember that." I'll remember that when it comes time for promotions or pay raises. I will give them a good recommendation when they move on to the next job. I want people who do a good job for me. I want them to be successful, and I like forwarding good recommendations to help with their future.

Steve Coplon: I think a huge part of what you're saying, is all about the work ethic. My son, Andrew, is going to be on a show in a couple weeks, and I've got some notes ready for it that I'll share ahead of time, just because I'm so proud of it. The name of his show is *"Applied Passion: The Key to Success"*, and I wrote a little blurb on it which says, *"Applied Passion: The Key to Success* with guest Andrew Coplon. Tune in to hear Steve and Andrew, a successful young entrepreneur talk about how combining hard work with your passion will lead you to success." This is right up your alley Dave, because your whole career in the last 25 years is based on connecting things together.

Steve Coplon: "Success is defined by the strength of the community you build around yourself." So, some part of you through me is wearing off on my son Andrew because he's got that. Now, I'd like to add something really special here. This whole series has had very little humor in it that I generally like to include. I've had guests continuously on every show since Episode 159. I've been really straight with everybody. You said the word "Ahead" three times when you were talking about advancement. I've got this little story here. Listen to this:

"Leadership with a Human Touch"

Life is a gamble," a mother cabbage told her offspring Brussel sprout. "You have to weather storms and droughts. You have to fend off animals, bugs, mold, and rot, but if you hang in there, you'll grow." "I'll try," said the little sprout, but how long does this take? When should I stop growing?" "As with any other gamble," said Mother Cabbage, "quit when you're ahead.

Steve Coplon: So, Dave, I'll move on from there. Let that sink in. Quit when you're ahead. It's a cabbage and a Brussels sprout, but it's work ethic.

Steve Coplon: I think what we're really talking about here goes hand in hand to bring the theme back. Character, integrity, and doing what you say you're going to do. Those are the underpinnings of a solid work ethic, and you shared a perfect example when you said to volunteer yourself. I'm going to give you an example of part of my work ethic where I got trained as a kid. Then I'd like you to share one of your life experiences and I know you have many, just pick one.

Steve Coplon: I worked at Harrison Pier when I was 16 years old. I drove the tow boat. I got $50 a week, and it was about an 80-hour-a-week job. I went in at 4:00 in the morning and got off at 8:00 at night. I slept on the beach under boats. I mean, it was a great job because it was like a boy's home. They worked us to death. It was like reform school and we worked hard. One day I saw the owner Jimmy Harrison walking toward the bathrooms. They called them heads at the fishing pier, male and female. Jimmy had a scrub brush, a toilet bowl cleaner, and some Clorox or something.

Steve Coplon: I said, "Jimmy, what are you doing?" He said, "I'm getting ready to clean the bathrooms," and I said, "You're the owner, man. Why are you doing that? Why don't you tell one of us to do it?" He said, "I would never tell anybody to go clean the toilets," and I said, "Hey, I need the money. I'm only making $50 a week. If you'll pay me, I would love to do it. He said, "Okay."

Steve Coplon: So, I took on the job, and he gave me $2 a day, $14 more a week. I was only making $50. So, that was an incredible percentage increase. I mean, that was over 25% of my pay just like that, but here is the stipulation, and I'm in a weird mood today just because I feel relaxed with you. So, there were two heads. He says, "I'll tell you what. I'll give you 50 cents for each time you clean one, and you need to clean them twice a day each, in the morning and at night and any time in between when there's an accident. That's all you have to do." I had to clean them a lot.

Steve Coplon: I had to take a 50-foot snake out to the street at least twice a week. We didn't use gloves back then, you washed your hands really good and everything. The point is I had to put that 50-foot snake down there to clean up the clog, but here's the deal. He said, "I'll give you $2 a day and all-you-can-eat." That was terrible. I don't know if people are going to appreciate that, but seriously the point was, that I had a good work ethic, and it stuck with me for the rest of my life, and I've always taken those jobs. How about you, Dave? How about one of your stories?

Dave Richards: Yeah, so we spent our summers at a very small cottage on the water. We grew up in Vermont, and we had a cottage, and by cottage, I mean outhouses, no electricity, and no phones. I mean, literally, a tiny little cottage, and we would go there all summer starting in the late '60s until I graduated through college. When I was 10 years old, and my oldest brother was 13, my mother noticed that there were these young people in boats and wooden dories. They had rakes, and they were raking this seaweed.

Dave Richards: So, she went and asked, "What are you doing?" They said, "Well, we rake the seaweed, and we sell it. We take it down here, and we sell it to this guy, and he pays us two and a half cents a pound," and my mother said, "Well, can anybody do that?" They said, "Yeah, anybody can do that." So, my mother found a way for us to get a summer job at 10 years old, and we then each got our own little boats and our rakes and our engines, and that job I had for the next 11 years all the way through college. We all had our boats, and we would go out two hours before low tide and two hours after, because that was when we could get a certain type of seaweed.

Dave Richards: A lot of those tides were at 5:00 in the morning. We'd be up at 4:00 a.m., and you're getting your boat, and it's cold, and you're walking out in the water, so you can get into the boat, and it was so physical. It's four hours of raking the seaweed, and then we'd drive to deliver it. And I can tell you there were many times, many, many times I did not want to get up and go out there. I would like to say I jumped out of bed, however I didn't. Especially when I got older, as a 19 or 20-year-old after I'd probably been out way too late the night before. I had to get up because that's how we made money, and the more we raked, and the more pounds we collected, the more we made.

Dave Richards: Back then, the top price was like five cents a pound, and you could rake 2,000 pounds of seaweed. So, that's $100 you make in a day, which was huge money. It was way more than I could ever make working in a restaurant, and we didn't do it all the time. But I guess the point was it was hard work, in that case, that habit was greatly mentored on me by my mother and my brothers. We were also always competitive in who could rake the most. So, we competed.

Dave Richards: Every day, whoever won was called Mr. Moss. I competed daily against my brother and we would say to each other, "Who can rake the most seaweed and make the most money?" But the point is that habit was hard work. It was physical. I'd like to say I naturally came upon it. The answer's no. I had to have help. In that case, brothers and parents pushing me out the door at times, but that was a great part of teaching me that I can work probably as hard as most people and endure cold and physical stuff. I take pride in that. How does one acquire the habit of hard work? It's usually from self-interest. That's what it is, but self-interest in odd ways.

Dave Richards: So, as a 17-year-old my self-interest of doing that hard work consisted of avoiding getting yelled at by my mother and shamed by my brothers. That was my self-interest, and it worked. It got me out, but self-interest plays out in other ways. Self-interest of doing the job that no one else will do. At six or eight o'clock on Superbowl Sunday, the self-interest is, this is good. This is helping somebody else. It's helping me. Sometimes, self-interest is just ego. It's the right thing to do, and it makes me feel good. You say, "That's self-interest." You got to find the self-interest that helps you do the right thing.

Dave Richards: Steve, you've said this to me a bunch of times. You go into prison, because it's the right thing to do, and you're doing the Lord's mission as you see it. The beautiful thing is you get more out of it than you give. These people love you. They give you so much feedback. So, in some odd way, it's the most selfish thing you can do because it's in your self-interest, and it's doing the right thing. So, where there's perfect alignment and it's the right thing to do, it helps others align with your self-interest and it makes you feel good. You're gaining.

Dave Richards: So, you have to find those intersections where it's in your self-interest. If you don't find the self-interest, you're just not going to keep it up. You're not going to do it. So, you have to understand yourself. You and I have talked about this before. I exercise, because I know it's intellectually the right thing to do, and about 10 minutes into my exercise, I feel great. It makes me feel good, so I have to play this game with myself every time. I've learned that game about myself.

Dave Richards: So, again, understanding yourself and figuring out how you can build habits is in your self-interest. Find people who will help you, brothers who will guilt you into it, mothers who will throw you out the door in good ways. Find the tactics that help you create the habits that allow you to go forward and be a better and a more productive person.

Steve Coplon: Dave, that was absolutely beautiful. We're going to bring it to an end now. I want to say one thing about what you were just talking about. The greatest satisfaction I do get, is when I see other people succeed. For example, I've got a gentleman by the name of Robert Miller, and I've read many of his letters on the air. He was in prison in Baker City, Oregon, Powder River Correctional, and I started mentoring him a couple years ago. I've been out there five or six times, and he just kept coming to my classes, and I got to know him. He started corresponding with me, and he taught me a lot.

Steve Coplon: I didn't know that education is the number one deterrent to recidivism. Education keeps people out of prison more than anything else. Robert gave me some statistics. There is a 94% less recidivism rate if an inmate gets into a college correspondence course while they're in prison..

Dave Richards: Wow.

Steve Coplon: I've told this story many times. When my father died, I received a $2,000 World War II insurance policy from the Veterans Administration. So, what am I going to do with $2,000? I'll give all my kids a couple hundred bucks or whatever to pay a bill or two. No, I gave Robert a semester of college to get him started because he said, "Steve, I know you can't afford it. I know your story, but I just want to know if you would help me raise money?" Well, I just gave him the money because I didn't want him to wait. I've been in constant touch with him, probably 20 letters over the last three years or so. Last Wednesday, I got a phone call. He got out of prison, and he's traveling to Arizona as soon as the coronavirus restrictions are lifted. He thanked me for all that I had done for him and so on and so forth, and I said, "Hey, Robert. You did more for me than I've done for you."

Steve Coplon: He goes, "No, Steve." I said, "I wish I could have done more." He said, "Steve, you got me started." I said, "There are so many good things that are out there waiting for people to do, and my advice to the world is get out of yourself, go do for others, and you will be absolutely amazed at where you end up. You'll have a beautiful place where you land." And Dave, I just want to thank you one more time for always being there for me. I mean, it wasn't easy in the early stages, but you always made time for me. So, is there anything you'd like to sum up in today's show? We're at the very end of the time frame now.

Dave Richards: No. I think you've just said it perfectly. I would just reiterate the same thing; You've just got to get started. Take a lot of little steps. If you can try to put people ahead of yourself, you will feel better. People respond. So, no, I think you said it great, so thanks, and I appreciate you allowing me into your life and being a part of *Right Thinking* to the extent that I can be. So, I take great, great pleasure in watching your show develop and grow.

Steve Coplon: Dave, thank you for that. When I listened to the last show we recorded together, there was a quote that I'd like to repeat. When I first met you, I said, "Well, Dave, the difference between you and me is you do billion-dollar deals and I do million-dollar deals." So, a week or two back, I said to you, "Dave, it's a rough economy. You're doing $50,000 deals now, and I'm doing 50-cent deals." So, everybody keep that in mind. Even if the deal is not as big as it used to be, just keep giving to others, and everything's going to be okay. Dave, I love you. God Bless you. Thanks for being with me today.

Dave Richards: Love you back. Thanks.

Steve Coplon: Thanks. Everybody have a wonderful week. I hope that you got something out of listening to me and Dave have a good time together. God Bless each one of you.

Steve Coplon: Thanks for listening to *Right Thinking with Steve Coplon*. I look forward to being with you again next week. Remember: ***Don't Quit, Plan Ahead, It Will Get Better.*** God Bless you and have a great week!

To listen to the original interview, scan this QR Code with your camera, or visit:

https://rightthinkingeducation.com/FromtheLiptotheHip/Chapter-9/

CHAPTER TEN

**Perspective From A Positive Young Woman with guest Sofia Giannascoli
Right Thinking With Steve Coplon - Episode 168**

Steve Coplon:	Good morning. Welcome to *Right Thinking with Steve Coplon.* I'm your host, Steve Coplon. Thank you for tuning in. Let's have a great day!
Steve Coplon:	Good morning, everybody. Glad to be with you. Today is a really special day. I've got something going on today that is a very unique opportunity for all of you listening. The series that I'm doing on *"From the Lip to the Hip is a Pretty Far Distance,"* it's really going places. One of the reasons that it is going places is because of today's guest, who I met completely by chance. Let's get started.
	Episode 168, *Right Thinking with Steve Coplon* is very pleased to announce that this week's show is called **"Perspectives from a Positive Young Woman,"** with guest Sofia Giannascoli. Tune in to hear Steve and Sofia have an engaging conversation of how she tested positive for the coronavirus and survived it with her incredibly positive attitude. Hear Sofia share her thoughts on the complicated world that she has inherited.
	Sofia, are you with me?
Sofia Giannascoli:	Yeah, I am.
Steve Coplon:	I've got to tell you, Sofia, I appreciate you so much. We've only known each other for two weeks now. So, let's tell the story how we met because I think that will get the conversation started.
Sofia Giannascoli:	Okay, that will be good.
Steve Coplon:	I had heard that in my neighborhood, living across the street was the very first case of the coronavirus in Norfolk, Virginia. Then, one day, I'm out walking with my wife, I have my face mask on and all of that stuff. This young lady is zooming by on a skateboard, and my wife asks, "Isn't that the daughter that lives over there in the house where the dad has coronavirus?" I said, "Yeah, it is." I then said to the young lady riding the skateboard, "Excuse me a second. I'm Steve, and this is my wife Donna, we live right there." Sofia, take it from there. Continue the story, please.
Sofia Giannascoli:	So, I promptly jumped off my skateboard, as I was zooming by you really fast. I was like, "Oh, my God, what's happening?" I was very shocked. Then, you asked me if I was my dad's

daughter, I responded, "Yeah, that was us. We all had the coronavirus. All three of us, my dad, my stepmom, and I tested positive." You and I continued talking a little more about the coronavirus, and yeah, that was how we first met. Then, you asked me where I went to school and what I studied. That was what led to where we are right now.

Steve Coplon: Okay, well, that's a quick version of it. All of you who are listening, there's a lot that's going to come out in a minute, but I'm going to do this slowly, just to keep you on the edge of your seat. So, Sofia, you told me you're in college and that you go to Montclair State University, which is in New Jersey?

Sofia Giannascoli: Yes, it is.

Steve Coplon: So, part of your coronavirus story is that you left the hotbed of the United States, the area where the highest rates of infection are, and you came down here to visit your dad?

Sofia Giannascoli: Yeah. So, what happened was, Madison my friend from school, and I were supposed to take a trip for our spring break to go visit some family of mine out in Napa, California. Then, the first case in the country, I think, was in Sacramento, which is near Napa. So, my parents freaked out and made us cancel the trip. My mom was like, "We're just worried. We don't want you to get sick, so why don't you go stay with your dad for your spring break? It would be nice, you can relax." I was like, "All right, all right." So, I drive the seven hours to Virginia, I get here, and my dad greets me in the driveway. He's like, "Hey, Doutch!" That his nickname for me, "Hey, Doutch, how are you?" He gives me a hug, and he coughs on me. I was like, "Oh, that's nice." Joking around, "You probably just gave me coronavirus." And then, he did! [Laughter]

Steve Coplon: Wow! What's amazing, is that the coronavirus, it's the plague, it's the worst thing that's happened to the world in our lifetimes, and yet we're talking now, and we actually laughed a moment ago. You laughed about how your dad coughed on you and you actually got it. You went from New Jersey to Norfolk, when your mom said, "Get away from here, go down to your dad's and relax." What you did was go from the frying pan to the fire. That's awful.

Sofia Giannascoli: Yeah, yeah.

Steve Coplon: But the beautiful thing is that you have survived the coronavirus. So many people don't know a thing about what it's like to go through it. It had to be very frightening. It had to be incredibly scary. Can you share a little about what it was like?

Sofia Giannascoli: Sure.

Steve Coplon: So, once you got diagnosed, tell us a more of the history. I heard how your dad got it, but I don't know if that's just a rumor or not. You share it, then, I'll see if that's what I heard.

Sofia Giannascoli: I got to Virginia on March 9th, and I've been here since then. My dad and stepmom flew home from a trip to Park City, Utah on the 8th. So, they had just gotten back the day before I came down. My dad started developing symptoms by the 10th. So, it was like, they got home, I came down and then he was already coughing, and he didn't feel good. It just spiraled down from there. So, we found out after, I think a week or so, that Park City had experienced their first case. I think a memo, or something, went out to the members of the community where they belong out in Utah.

Sofia Giannascoli: The memo said that there was a member of the staff at a restaurant in Park City who had tested positive and was still working while having symptoms. He didn't know that he had it, but he was still going to work and stuff while sick. They happened to have gone to the restaurant on one of the days that he was working. So, that was probably cause to get my dad tested. So, he got tested, I would say, the Saturday of the first week I was here. Then, by Sunday, I had started to develop symptoms as well. Then, we found out he tested positive on Tuesday.

Sofia Giannascoli: My symptoms started with fatigue. I would say the third or fourth day I was here. I've had mono before, what I was going through was like mono turned up 50 notches. My body was so physically exhausted that I didn't get out of bed for the better part of at least two or three days, because physical exertion was so taxing in any capacity. So, that was my big thing, I had no other symptoms for a few days. So, it was super weird. I was like, "Maybe I'm just really tired. Maybe I'm depressed." It was so weird; it was such an alien feeling to me. Then, my dad started to get sicker. He was coughing, had sinus pain, sinus pressure, headaches. He was really tired. He had the worst fatigue of us all.

Sofia Giannascoli: He was in bed for probably the better part of a week, I would say, for about seven days, he could barely get out of bed. He definitely had the worst symptoms of all of us. My stepmom had the least number of symptoms. She was mostly just sinus pressure and a slight sore throat. We all had a little bit of a cough. So, then, by that Tuesday, we found out my dad was positive. Then my stepmom and I became presumptive positives. So, Wednesday, we went and were able to get tested at one of the hospital testing sites here in Norfolk. Then, by the next Friday, they told us that we were also positive.

Sofia Giannascoli: I wouldn't say I was ever really scared. It just seemed so impossible. I kept thinking, "There's no way we really all have it. There's no way that we really all have coronavirus." It felt so impossible. It really did. Then, once we were all diagnosed, it was relieving to know at least we knew what we were dealing with. I think because it happened so early on, it wasn't ... How do I explain it? The severity of the spread, just in the public eye, the severity of the disease wasn't as turned up as it is now, I would say.

Sofia Giannascoli: It was definitely a lot more like, "Oh, it's like us versus them. They're bringing this here," whatever people were saying. But it was different. I'm in the group of pre-existing conditions, people who are high risk because I have asthma. I didn't feel an impact on my lungs until after getting better and recovering, which is super weird. I definitely didn't expect that. So, post-corona, I think like a month and a half, my asthma is way worse than it has been in the last couple of years.

Sofia Giannascoli: I had developed a cough my second week of symptoms that was very slight. Having asthma, and allergies, and stuff, I'm always coughing. So, it wasn't anything new, it wasn't anything crazy or surprising. I feel more of a strain on my lungs now. So, it is unfortunate, it is still so crazy to me that we all went through this and survived and made it out to the other side. A lot of people are really struggling and losing family members. It is very tragic and scary. I am thankful in a way because I'm a big believer in "everything happens for a reason".

Sofia Giannascoli: There's absolutely nothing in life that we experience, or go through, or deal with, with no cause or no purpose. I'm a mama's girl. I love, when I'm sick to lay in my mom's bed, and be like, "Oh, just make me feel better." I had to really deal with this, for the most part, on my own because my dad and my stepmom were also sick dealing with their own things. I've learned a lot about myself from this experience. I've grown a lot and I'm just very thankful to be healthy today.

Steve Coplon: Sofia, that is absolutely beautiful how you just described what you went through. How's your dad doing?

Sofia Giannascoli: He's good. He's still coughing a little dramatically, but he's fine now. He's good. We're all better.

Steve Coplon: So, your stepmom, she's over it also?

Sofia Giannascoli: Yeah., she is pretty much back to normal.

Steve Coplon: Wow, you are in a very unique population, people who have actually experienced the coronavirus firsthand. Your family was the first case in Norfolk that had contracted the coronavirus. We had read in the paper that there was a case in Norfolk, but it didn't say the person's name. We were shocked to find out that it was right across the street from us.

Sofia Giannascoli:: Yeah, it was us.

Steve Coplon: The worst part of your experience had to be dealing with the unknown. When I told my daughter, Lindsey, who lives in Oregon, that across the street was the very first coronavirus case in Norfolk, she was emphatic when she said, "You're not getting near them are you? You don't walk on the street, do you? Because the germs could still be on the street." I said, "Well, they're quarantined. They're in the house. They haven't come out of the house." Sofia, thank the Lord, thank God that He brought you and your family through it. Your story is a powerful testimony that people can contract the coronavirus, get through it, and continue with their lives.

Steve Coplon: Well, the silver lining in the cloud though is that now that you've had it, you should have some immunities. I guess you have antibodies in your body that make it unlikely that you will get it again.

Sofia Giannascoli: Yeah that should be right. We are going to donate plasma as well, which can help other people fight the disease. I don't know all the medical ins and outs of how that works, but yeah, I shouldn't be able to get it again. And you have the antibodies forever. I think there's a big misconception that once you recover, if you donate your plasma, then, you give away all your antibodies, which isn't true. Once the antibody cells are in your body, you have them forever. They are not going to just go away. The doctor told me that, so I know it's true.

Steve Coplon: That's good. Well, I can relate to a lot of what you said. You said fatigue was the main thing that hit you. I am in a very, very high risk category myself because of my multiple myeloma cancer. It is an incurable bone cancer that affects my immune system. Because of my cancer, my immune system is compromised, and I have a very difficult time fighting infections. I get pneumonia a lot. People who have had pneumonia will tell you it feels like having an elephant sitting on your chest. You are totally lethargic. You just don't have any energy. It's the worst fatigue. Because of my compromised immune system, I have chronic bronchitis, C.O.P.D. and asthma, all respiratory conditions. My doctors have told me that my chances of contracting the coronavirus are basically the same as anyone else's, but that if I do get it, it would be very dangerous for me. I can't even fight bronchitis without antibiotics. There is no antibiotic or other known treatment for the coronavirus, so I have to be extremely careful.

Steve Coplon:	With bronchitis, if I can get on antibiotics quickly enough, it jump starts my immune system to where the antibodies that are in me will kick in and they will fight for me. Because I don't have the ability to get the fight against infections started, I need to take antibiotics. I need that extra umph to get my immune system going. Through the coronavirus pandemic, I've been isolating myself pretty much completely.
	So, that brings the blessing back around to me. I meet you on the street and you shared about yourself, and I learned that you attend Montclair State University in New Jersey.
Steve Coplon:	Last night, while I was on the phone talking to you, I found this little book on my bookshelf called **"Leadership with a Human Touch."** It's been there for about 20 years. It's a motivational book on leadership. You can subscribe to receive monthly issues. I don't know where I first came across it, but it is a great little publication. I can't say that I have ever thought about Montclair State University before, however I had heard about it. I knew it was up north somewhere. It is really kind of crazy how I meet this young lady from Montclair State University, who by the way, is taking her college courses online during the coronavirus pandemic. Sofia, you're a junior in college at Montclair, and I believe you said that you are studying broadcast journalism? What's the title of your degree?
Sofia Giannascoli:	A bachelor's in journalism with a minor in film.
Steve Coplon:	Wow, yeah. That perked my ears up because of my involvement in radio. So, I was reading this little book on leadership and said to you, "You won't believe this, but I was reading this little book on leadership, when I ran across a quote from a very, very famous person, who's one of my all-time favorites. It's about making decisions." You asked, "Well, who was it?" I said, "Well, he gave it to the graduates of Montclair State University." You were like, "Wow, who was it?" I said, "Let's wait till we get on the show." Okay, everybody who knows me, knows that I am a lifetime New York Yankees fan.
Steve Coplon:	I love my Yankees. I irritate a lot of people who don't like the Yankees. I like winners. I catch a lot of grief from people when they lose. I say, "Wait a second, wait a second, you've got to understand that we're kind. If we win more than one out of four World Series, other teams won't let us play with them anymore. We like it when somebody else rises up and wins. We're good like that."
Sofia Giannascoli:	Yeah.
Steve Coplon:	Well, right there in the book on leadership is the number one most famous quote from the great Yogi Bera:

Yogi Bera

"When you come to a fork in the road, take it."

Steve Coplon:	In the book it says, "Hall of Fame baseball player, in his address to the graduates of Montclair State University, upon receiving an honorary doctorate of humanities." I just think that it is so cool that you go to a school that gave Yogi Bera such a great honor.
	Sofia, you've said that you believe that things happen for a reason. My mother always taught me that, too. I definitely believe that. So, as I continue the conversation with you about the day that we met, I said to you, "So, are you going to be here for a while?" You said, "Yeah, I can't go home. I can't go back to New Jersey. The coronavirus is too out of control there."

Steve Coplon: So, I asked "Are you looking for anything new to do?" Your response was, "Well, I don't know. What do you mean?" I said, "Would you like to make some money?" Then, I threw a dollar amount out there, and you went, "Yeah." Then, I said, "Well, here's what it is. I'm doing a series of shows starting with Episode 159 on the theme *"From the Lip to the Hip is a Pretty Far Distance,"* and I am going to have transcripts done for each of the shows in the series. I've done a curriculum that is being marketed into prisons across the country. Meagan, who is a PhD, English major, attending graduate school at William & Mary, proofed 30 transcripts that I used in the curriculum. I get the transcripts from a company called REV. They're 99% accurate.

Steve Coplon: I upload the file to REV of each show that I want to use. I get the transcript back within a day, but it still needs proofing. So, I said, "Would you like to proof transcripts for me? Could you do that?" You said, "Yeah." At that moment, you and I were standing across the street from each other during this conversation, about 15 feet apart, practicing social distancing. Then I said, "If you're interested," here is my business card with my email on it, which you took and entered into your cellphone. "Just send me an email and we can talk tonight, and I'll send you the first transcript when you are ready." An hour later, I got a beautiful email from you.

Steve Coplon: Your email said, "Hey, I left you a voicemail, but I'd love to take a look at one of the transcripts and the audio of the show tonight!" I could tell that you were enthusiastic, but I loved your message because the series that I am doing is about people who do what they say they are going to do. You took action. You took affirmative steps to seize an opportunity that was presented to you. The series explores, why do people say things that they don't do? Why do people lie to themselves? Why do people say yes and don't really do things that they said yes to? I immediately respected you because you followed up on what we talked about. So, I knew about you immediately. I said to my wife, Donna, "Wow, this is incredible. I've been looking for someone and here she is." Meagan could not do the transcripts for this series because she is back in school and has some health issues. I needed to find somebody to assist me, and I wasn't sure when I would find that someone. All of a sudden, you presented yourself. So, I sent you a transcript to review and here we are.

I want to continue with the story of how we met and where we are now. You're a college kid, you stay up late at night studying, get those creative juices flowing. Later that first night at 11:12 pm, I receive an email from you. The subject was, "Currently Working." And you wrote:

> *Hey, Steve, I'm sitting here in the office listening and marking up the transcript document, and I just felt compelled to say I really think God brings different people into our lives for a reason. He shows us what we need to see when we need to see it. I'm sitting here, really listening to what you talked about in the episode, and a lot of it resonates with things I have been thinking and realizing about life, and trying to better my mindset, and therefore, my life. As well as affirming what I have been praying about. I'm on page four, the William James quote that said about concentrating on what you wish and not '100 other incompatible things.' This is what really resonated with me. I've been coming to terms with where I want to go in my career path after college and focusing more on my health. So, I just wanted to take a second to reach out, because I am really enjoying the episode. Sorry for rambling, but also, thank you. Looking forward to speaking tomorrow.*

Sofia Giannascoli

Steve Coplon: Sofia, that was the beginning, for me, of an amazing new relationship. You are such a wonderful person. You're only 21 years old, with a wonderful maturity level. Another thing that we have in common is that you have your own talk radio show. So, I knew that your personality was going to be great for me to connect with. Is your talk radio show on campus at Montclair really three hours?

Sofia Giannascoli: It is. [laughs]

Steve Coplon: That is so wonderful! I can really appreciate that. I want to get deep into who you are and how you got to be the way you are, but let's stay on the surface for just a second. How did you get into doing a talk radio show, and what do you do on your show? I listened to 30 minutes of one of your shows. You're incredible. You're natural. You know how to flow.

Sofia Giannascoli: Thank you. So, I was in, one of my journalism classes, and I sat next to this guy. His name was AJ, he's one of my good friends now. He was always very outspoken in class and he's a big free speech kind of guy. So, we would always get into discussions in class just about different news topics and stuff. He and I usually had similar opinions on things, and I would be like, "Yeah, that made me think of this thing and that thing." So, we always just had good conversations. Then, he said to me one day, "You should come to one of the WMSC general meetings."

Sofia Giannascoli: I was like, "What is that? I don't even know what that is." He said, "Oh, well, we have a radio station upstairs." I was like, "Stop, no way. Like a real one, like a real radio station?" He was like, "Yeah, it's great. I have a show with a buddy of mine, and you can maybe get one, too, if you go to the training and stuff." I was like, "Sounds pretty cool. Maybe I'll go check it out." So, I went to a few meetings and last year was really about just diving in headfirst to more college experience type things. Because I didn't do a lot my first semester at Montclair.

Sofia Giannascoli: I was very nervous. So, then, my second year, I was like, "All right. This is my time. I'm going to make a bunch of friends. I'm going to do cool stuff. I want that college experience." So, I went to a couple meetings and I signed up for what we call ADJ training. It was four weeks, where I would go observe and hang out in two shows a week. The DJs, who were doing those shows, would teach us different stuff each week of what we needed to know. How to run the whole soundboard, how to queue songs and commercials from the computer system, how to use the computer system itself, just all technical aspects.

Sofia Giannascoli: Then, how to really conduct a show. Because you can do shows on whatever you want, but if you're not engaging, if you're not entertaining, if you're not making the audience want to come back and listen to you each week, then you might not be a good fit for the radio. So, I took my test after the four weeks, and I'm probably not supposed to say this, and I won't say who told me, but I found out that out of the whole group I think of 30 or so of us who took the test, there were only seven of us who got approved to be DJs. I was the only person who got 100 on both parts of the test, the technical aspect, and the talk aspect.

Sofia Giannascoli: So, that was really cool. That was a big boost to my ego, I was like, "Oh my God, this is crazy." Then, I became a real DJ for WMSC Upper Montclair. I started with my own summer show where once a week last summer, I would drive an hour to campus every Thursday morning and I would conduct a three-hour show all by myself. It was really important to me to do the summer show because I was like, "Okay, I committed to becoming a part of this organization. I really want to prove myself." A lot of people don't do summer shows, because no one's on campus and there's not a lot happening up in Montclair.

Sofia Giannascoli: Someone had told me that if you take the opportunity to do a summer show, a lot of people, will give you credit, because it's like, "Okay, you really want this. You're really committed to this." Because it's boring and it's just you alone for three hours, if you really commit yourself to it, then it's really good. So, I did. I really took that time each week to learn as much as I could and teach myself as much as I could about everything that I have to do. So, then, this year I have a show called *"Confused by the Muse,"* currently not running because I'm stuck in Virginia.

Sofia Giannascoli: But it's me and one of my best friends, Madison, and we talk about everything, entertainment, music, movies, TV, art. It's just our commentary on everything in the entertainment industry that's happened in the past week up till the current show. It's super fun. We developed this, what do you call it? Not like culture, but our show is like the hangout show. All of our friends come on Thursdays, one to four. So, it became this time where we always have at least 10 people crammed into this tiny little studio room.

Sofia Giannascoli: We have big, everyone-in-the-room, involved conversations, about astrology, or everyone's favorite Avenger, or everyone's favorite movie, just silly stuff, but it's a lot of fun. It's definitely one of the most rewarding things I've done in my college career so far, 100%.

Steve Coplon   While I was just listening to you talk about your campus radio show experience, you made me think, in another life, if I ever get another chance, I should go back to college and get some training like you in how to do a radio show. Because you're like a professional musician, I'm like a garage band. I just figured out how to use Zoom and start doing recordings and talking all the time and getting guests on that I think people want to listen to.

Steve Coplon: I was totally right about you. I caught onto you in the first two minutes when we met. My wife said, "How did you know?" My response to her was very simple, "I just knew." Part of the reason that you're on the show, whether you know it or not, is because you are a role model for young people who are trying to approach life, figure it out, get educated, and whatever they need to do to move closer to who they want to become. You've already demonstrated, through the approach that you've taken, that you are going to get where you want to go. What you have already said, about how you took an opportunity or two, is inspiring.

Steve Coplon   My wife shared with me an expression that is so much what's going on with today's youth. She asked our son, Michael, a question the other day. His response was very non-committal. He said, "I'm not sure yet. Probably not." It was like, "I don't know, but I probably won't." Well, she heard someone else recently say, "Absolutely maybe, but probably not." Now, how is that for a wishy-washy non-committal statement? Absolutely maybe, but probably not. Many young people just don't know what they are doing. But, Sofia, you're not like that.

Steve Coplon: So, let's transition into something here. I've asked 11 people to let me interview them in the series that I'm doing with people I respect, people who have a lot of wisdom. The series addresses a subject that is universal: people who say things that they don't ever end up doing. It then explores the subject from many angles. Having Meagan work on the transcripts of 30 of my radio shows for my prison curriculum and becoming an expert on what I am involved in, was a rare treat for me. To have so much conversation, so much feedback was very special. Knowing that Meagan would not be available for this project was weighing on my mind, because I didn't know how I was going to replace her. I needed an assistant. But then, all of a sudden, you popped in. Your incredible enthusiasm and your interest in what

I am doing, made me feel really good, as well as, it gave me a huge sense of relief to have found a qualified assistant.

Steve Coplon: You've now worked on the transcripts of 12 of the episodes. It is a blessing for me to have you be so incredibly tuned in with such an intelligent approach to the project from a different perspective. That is why I came up with the title for this show, *"Perspectives from a Positive Young Woman."* You're very positive. Did you get anything out of working on all those shows? Is there anything that you can you relate to in the shows?

Sofia Giannascoli: Yes. I value so much this experience of getting to work on these transcripts. I really have taken something from each episode. One of the most impactful things for me was the William James quote that I thanked you for in the email that I sent you the night we first met. It was in the first episode that I listened to and read, Episode 159. What was it? It was something like, don't put energy ... Do you have it?

Steve Coplon: Yes, the William James quote that you are referring to is about concentrating on what you wish and not 100 other incompatible things at the same time. It's about focus, it's about eliminating distractions. I'll read it right now:

William James

If you only care enough for a result, you will almost certainly attain it. If you wish to be rich, you will be rich. If you wish to be learned, you will be learned. If you wish to be good, you will be good. Only you must then really wish these things, and wish them exclusively, and not wish at the same time 100 other incompatible things just as strongly.

Sofia Giannascoli: Yeah, thanks. When I first read that in the transcript, it was like a direct line of communication from a higher power or something. I'm very big into, like I said earlier, "God shows you what you need to see when you need to see it." I believe in guardian angels, who are always helping us out and stuff like that. So, for me, that quote, was so affirming because I feel like, for so long, I've been so conflicted about what I've wanted to do in my career. I'm studying journalism. I'm doing stuff with the radio. But I have this passion for creative writing, and filmmaking, and acting.

Sofia Giannascoli: I finally realized, I would say, probably like two weeks before I came down to Virginia, that I don't really want to work in broadcast news. I don't want to edit the news. A big part of the program at Montclair State is broadcast news. It's like almost entirely what they teach us, and I realize that it's not where my heart is. It's fun, it's an interesting, ever changing, fast paced job, which I enjoy, but it's not where I see myself settling in. I want to go down my own creative path with acting, writing and filmmaking. That's something that I had talked about with my parents, even before college.

Sofia Giannascoli: I took acting classes in New York City. That's always what I've wanted to do, but I never fully allowed myself to really accept it. It was always something like, "Yeah, oh, I do that during the summer." Or, "Oh, maybe one day." But I accepted that that's what I feel I'm meant to do with my life, and it was like, this is crazy because I believe that we don't have one purpose. I feel that we can have many and any number of purposes. It's wherever you put the most energy, the most thoughts, and the most of yourself into, that will manifest and become a reality for you.

Sofia Giannascoli: So, reading the William James quote was super affirming of that thought for me. I'm not like unrealistic about it either. I'm not going to drop out of school and just go and figure it out. I have a plan. I know where I want to go with it post-graduation. So, that was really cool for me.

Steve Coplon: I remember last week when I was just getting to know you, I was asking you a lot of questions. You gave me an ultimate compliment. You wrote in that first email that you sent to me that reading transcripts and listening to Episode 159 was making you think about things. Then, when you told me how you felt, you said, "Oh my gosh, Steve, I feel like this show was done just for me, that you're talking just to me." What you told me, Sofia, is everyone's hope in any kind of communication field, particularly in radio. When you have someone who is reading something that you wrote or listening to something that you broadcast tell you, "you are talking directly to me," that makes you feel so good because you know you are reaching someone. So, I said to you. Sofia, "Thank you. You're amazing."

Steve Coplon: Sofia, when you mentioned to me that you are interested in becoming an actress, you spoke with a great deal of passion. You said, "Oh my gosh, yes, I am." It is wonderful how you opened up and became so alive when you talked about how you would like to go into acting. In the shows that are being done in this series, keys to success that keep coming up are to know what you want, be passionate about it, and follow your dream. Last night, you listened to the show that hasn't aired yet, *"Applied Passion: The Key to Success,"* with my son, Andrew.

Sofia Giannascoli: Yeah, I did.

Steve Coplon: You liked that one?

Sofia Giannascoli: I did. I liked that one a lot. You and your son are very, very similar, it was so funny. It was really cute. [Laughter]

Steve Coplon: He probably doesn't want to hear that, but I love it when I hear that. [Laughter]

Sofia, when you and I were discussing the transcript of Andrew's show, you said something to me that I thought was very interesting. I told you that my guests in this series are a very diverse group of people. The series is about character and integrity development. It is about helping those who are in the group of people who are in the habit of not doing what they say they are going to do, to recognize how they are and help them start making changes. Sofia, you are blessed to not be in that group of people. You are very focused and a person of your word.

Steve Coplon: You have great initiative, you follow up, you're a role model, that's why you are here on the show with me. So, I told you that I had a lot of diversity in the people who are doing the shows in this series. I want people to not have to listen to me over and over again and hear only my thoughts. I want to give the listeners an opportunity to hear people that I respect and admire. Well, I told you that my son, Andrew, was going to be the only younger person participating in the series. Most everyone doing the interviews and expressing their wisdom on the subject are older, they are all middle-age and up.

Steve Coplon: Then, I said to you, "Sofia, I asked Andrew to do a show in the series because he's young, he's 34 years old. It adds to the diversity." When I realized that you would be a great addition as a guest in the series, I asked you, "Sofia, would you like to do a show in this series? I think it would be great for you to share your point of view. You are already a radio personality, you'll be great. People will love you." You said, "I would love to, I think it would be really good because even your son, Andrew, at 34, he's in a different generation than me." I got the biggest kick out of that. I never thought of Andrew as being in an older generation.

Tell me more about you being in a different generation than Andrew. Your comment was absolutely priceless.

Sofia Giannascoli: So, first of all, I'm so honored to be a part of this series and to be included with all these incredible people that you've been talking to and interviewing. As I listened to every episode, I don't know, it's like it really is such ... How do I explain it? Like "a one of a kind" type of experience, I like reading and listening to everything that everyone is bringing forth on the shows. It is giving me an opportunity to hear about all of these different parts of life from all these amazing people. I think that it is so important, especially for people of my generation, of my age, to understand that we are capable of connecting with and learning things from people who are older than us and have different life experiences.

Sofia Giannascoli: I feel that a lot of people my age feel alone, or feel so different, like we are the odd man out from everybody. People my age and younger, feel so separate and so different, because we have experienced so many different types of tragedies in our lifetime. Such as this coronavirus pandemic and social isolation, 9/11, swine flu, the rise in school shootings, the wars in the Middle East, all of it. It's a strange environment to grow up in, all this chaotic energy. These chaotic events have been taking place during our lifetime pretty consecutively. So, when you try to find yourself, find who you are, find your passions, figure out what you want to do and who you are at your core, all that mass panic and uncertainty make it that much harder.

Sofia Giannascoli: I struggled with it. I still struggle with it. I'm not claiming to know any crazy magnificent thing, but I think it's really important to compare and contrast perspectives with people my age, as well as, with you, with people your sons age, and with anyone at any age. I think it's really important to be open to learning and growing at all times from any experience, any avenue. Does that make sense?

Steve Coplon: Oh, yes it does! What a beautiful attitude. What you said is exactly what Napoleon Hill said in *The 57th of the Famous Alibis by Old Man IF*. I'll just read it now:

Napoleon Hill

If I had the courage to see myself as I really am, I would find out what is wrong with me and correct it, then, I might have a chance to profit by my mistakes and learn something from the experience of others.

Steve Coplon: I think that's just exactly right. A smart person learns from others. They have an open mind and they get more educated, but they learn from other's experiences. Sofia, it is wonderful that you do all of that. Thank you for listening to the shows. Thank you for all the feedback that you give me. It's very, very wonderful for me to receive it, and I am so enjoying all of our conversations. Have you ever gone through any struggles in your life that were really hard to get through, struggles that were extremely difficult? You have already talked about the coronavirus. Can't be much more difficult than going through that.

Steve Coplon: What are some of the things that you've gone through that life has thrown at you? When we came up with the description for the show, we said, "Hear Sofia share her thoughts on the complicated world that she has inherited." 9/11, just to get started, how old were you when 9/11 took place?

Sofia Giannascoli: Three, I think? Three or four.

Steve Coplon: So, you're a child of the 9/11 aftermath. When President Bush said immediately after the attack, "Life as we know it will never be the same." We were invaded on American soil for the first time. Everyone knew that future generations were going to experience something that the rest of us had never experienced, after being attacked on our own homeland. We knew that there was going to be an insecurity bred into our children and future generations. So, you're a product of that era. The technology that's taken over, all of the social everything, social media, it's just a whole different world for you than from mine.

Steve Coplon: Speaking as an older person, it's hard to embrace it sometimes. So, what are some of your perspectives on things that you've had to face in your life that are deep? I thank you again, you're young, I am old, but yet we're communicating, and I am enjoying it. I'm enjoying it a great deal. Sofia, I am certain that everyone listening to this show is going to really enjoy your perspectives. That is another reason why you are here. You are demonstrating that you are doing things in a very beautiful way. You have my respect. That's my wife's main thing, respect. She's done several shows that always come down to respect.

Steve Coplon: With that said, is there anything you'd like to talk about? What are some of the challenges that you have faced in your life, the world that you were born into?

Sofia Giannascoli: Yeah, okay. So, I definitely haven't had a "difficult life". But I actually thought of this the other day, when you and I were talking about what we were going to discuss on the show. I didn't have a difficult life, but it was difficult for me. I grew up, my parents were never married. My dad lived in Virginia, and then Pennsylvania. I grew up with my mom in New Jersey, and we had fun. We were hanging out. We were a couple of best pals. We lived with my grandfather and it was fun. But I think I didn't realize until I was older the kind of effect on my ... when you grow up in a two-parent household, you have this inherent sense of structure and stability.

Sofia Giannascoli: We moved around a lot and just kind of ... it was unpredictable. It was fun, but it was unpredictable. So, that sense of non-stability throws you off a little bit without directly knowing it. So, at, I think, age four, I was diagnosed with generalized anxiety disorder. So, that's always been a part of who I am. I'm just like, I'm anxious, I have anxiety, I have A.D.D., I'm always like vibrating at a certain level of "What's going on, what's next? Let's move to the next thing, let's jump around."

Steve Coplon: In my world, you're completely normal. [Laughter]

Sofia Giannascoli: Thank you. [Laughter] So, growing up with intense anxiety like I did, had its own challenges. I don't know. My biggest things as a kid were emotional. So, in the grand scheme of life, it's not terrible but certainly, it wasn't great. So, as I got older, my anxiety progressed into social anxiety and depression once I got to high school. I don't think anyone has a good time from middle school to the middle of high school. You're just kind of in this weird era of your life.

Steve Coplon:	I did. When people ask, "If you could be any age over again, what age would you be?" I always answer, "I would like to go back to junior high school and high school, because I just had a great time."
Sofia Giannascoli:	That's so funny. [Laughter]
Steve Coplon:	You know that I spend a lot of time in prisons. I joke around, that I would like to be 17. My perfect age to go back to is 17. If you ask, "Why 17?" I would say, "Because you're still a minor, and anything that you do wrong would be expunged from your record when you turn 18."
Sofia Giannascoli:	That's true. That's so funny. [Laughter] Yeah, and I don't want to sound all like sad and whatever. I really believe that as I said, everything happens for a reason. Growing up the way I did, my internal issues and stuff, it's really helped me develop myself into the young woman, the positive young woman that I am. There's not one experience, one aspect, any part of my life that I'm not in some way grateful for, because I truly, truly believe that I am meant to be exactly who I am in this moment. I wouldn't want to be anybody else.
Sofia Giannascoli:	So, the biggest thing that we talked about before the show from my past, was what I went through my freshman year of college. I took my spring semester off to attend an outpatient eating disorder rehabilitation program. I had always had issues with self-esteem, body image, and food my whole life to that point. It finally reached a point where I was like, "Okay, this is something I'm really dealing with in actual time. It's time to grow up and face my reality." I think that part of my life was one of the first times that I was like, "Okay, there's nothing I can do better for myself than accept the conditions of my reality." I needed help to figure it all out.
Sofia Giannascoli:	Okay. So, I went through this program in North Jersey. I drove 60 miles a day in total to get there and back to this program, because I didn't stay at the hospital. I definitely learned a lot while I was there. I don't want to say that it's one of the most impactful experiences I've had, because I feel every experience is an impactful experience. But it definitely changed my perspective on a lot of things in my life. So, on my last day of treatment, when you get discharged, they give you an award. Some of the counselors, whoever was on your team, give you an award.
Sofia Giannascoli:	It's like secret, it's just for you. They go in a room, and they're like, "Okay, we just wanted to give this to you to show you how much you mean to us." So, the "award", it was a little piece of paper with a cartoon star on it, it's like, "You're *the blank* at this thing." So, mine was "Most likely to brighten up a room." I realized during my time in the program that what made me feel the best was trying to make everybody laugh, because it's like such a gloomy situation. There are like 10 or 12 people in the room, all saying things like, "I'm sad because of this thing, but today is a good day." It is group therapy. My favorite thing to do was try to make people laugh and make people smile.
Sofia Giannascoli:	I was like, "We're here, but it's a good thing we're here. We're all in the process of healing. We're all in this process of growth. This is a great place to be." I remember a conversation I had with my therapist in the program and one of my other counselors. It was like during my first couple of weeks or something. They said, "How are you doing?" We got to talking and the conversation basically was me saying to them that, I felt obligated to the other people in the program, to myself most of all, and to the counselors, that I needed to get better. Like I felt obligated to everyone else that I needed to get better even if it wasn't fun to face yourself.

Sofia Giannascoli: It shocked me because she was so taken aback. She was like, "Wow, I need to sit with that for a second. I can't believe that. I wish more patients thought like that." I was like, "What? What do you mean? Don't people want to be better? Don't they want to get better?" She was like, "They don't know. They don't realize that it's the best possible thing they could do for themselves." I've always felt, in any kind of situation, since I was younger, this obligation to be the best whatever it was for myself, first and foremost. So, once I left the program, I realized the not so great aspects of it, and the parts of it that needed to improve, insanely, for the benefit of the patients.

Sofia Giannascoli: You had asked me last night, what is something that you could see yourself either advocating for, or being passionate about, or wanting to support people, however you worded it. It really took me back because the first thing I thought of was improving and advocating for the betterment of eating disorder treatment programs. Because I think while I was there, I was given what I needed, but I was also given a very generalized version of a treatment program. I think they really need to be more, not even personalized, but just more in-depth. I think the program that I went to was maybe not the most funded or the biggest.

Sofia Giannascoli: We were in this little half of a hallway in the corner of Robert Wood Johnson Hospital in Somerset, New Jersey. I just think that at least for the general treatment guidelines in New Jersey, I think they could be so greatly improved. So, when you asked me if there's anything, I would ever be an advocate for, it's absolutely that. It's something I've thought about for a few years now. I don't know what the logistics of that are, or whatever, but if one day I decided that was a cause that I care about the most, and say, I had to go back to school for it or something so I could better be prepared or capable, then, I 100% would.

Steve Coplon: Sofia, you're amazing. You're a shining star, a bright light, and for people of my generation, or whatever generation, we are so thankful that there's a young person like you out there who's going to carry the mantle into the future. You're just wonderful. I want to say something about what you just said you felt you had to do. You almost quoted Shakespeare:

William Shakespeare

"To thine own self be true."

Steve Coplon: A lot of young people, don't even know who William Shakespeare was, but you do. I have three pieces of scripture that I want to share today. Sofia, you inspire these three pieces of scripture.

Proverbs 16:3

"Commit to the Lord whatever you do, and He will establish your plans."

Steve Coplon: You've shared with me that you do daily prayer, daily meditation, and then you seek guidance and counsel, and you serve the Lord.

Jeremiah 17:7

"But blessed is the one who trusts in the Lord, whose confidence is in Him."

Steve Coplon:	You're a beautiful, young woman both on the inside and the outside. There is an inner quality in you that is shining right through you.

Psalm 5:3

"In the morning Lord, you hear my voice. In the morning I lay my request before you and wait expectantly."

Steve Coplon:	That's what you've told me you do. You've told me that you have that relationship with the Lord. I hate to end this show because I'm enjoying you so much. We'll have to do some more sessions. I told my wife that in the next couple of years, Sofia is going to have her own national TV talk show, and that I want to be a regular guest on her show. She said, "She probably will." Sofia, is there anything at all that you would like to say as we end this conversation?
Sofia Giannascoli:	Yes, I would also like to give a piece of scripture that I learned from listening to the different episodes of the show. I had never heard it before, and you've said it a few times. I believe it's Proverbs 3:6 and it says:

Proverbs 3:6

"Listen for God's voice in everything you do, everywhere you go. He's the one who will keep you on track."

Sofia Giannascoli:	My whole life, that's always been the through point. It's like, you know what? I don't know what's going on, but He does, and that's enough for me.
Steve Coplon:	Wow, Sofia, God Bless you in all that you do. Thanks for being part of my life.
Sofia Giannascoli:	Thank you, Steve.
Steve Coplon:	You're welcome. So, hey. I'll see you in the neighborhood. [Laughter]
Sofia Giannascoli:	I will. I'll see you later. [Laughter]
Steve Coplon:	Yeah, that's good. Well, everybody, thanks for sharing your time with Sofia and me today. I know that you've been inspired by listening to her and getting to know her. God Bless each one of you and have a great week.
Steve Coplon:	Thanks for listening to *Right Thinking with Steve Coplon*. I look forward to being with you again next week. Remember: ***Don't Quit, Plan Ahead, It Will Get Better.*** God Bless you and have a great week!

To listen to the original interview, scan this QR Code with your camera, or visit:
https://rightthinkingeducation.com/FromtheLiptotheHip/Chapter-10/

CHAPTER ELEVEN
Don't Want To, Don't Do It with guest Randey Faulkner
Right Thinking With Steve Coplon - Episode 169

Steve Coplon:	Good morning. Welcome to *Right Thinking with Steve Coplon.* I'm your host, Steve Coplon. Thank you for tuning in. Let's have a great day!
Steve Coplon:	Good morning. Glad to be with you. Another very special day because I've got the Aloha man himself back on, Randey Faulkner. Randey, how are you doing?
Randey Faulkner:	I'm doing fantastic on a grand scale, Super Steve. How about yourself?
Steve Coplon:	Well, Randey, I'm doing great. I'm doing this series on ***"From the Lip to the Hip is a Pretty Far Distance,"*** and I've invited some of my best and closest friends that I admire and respect to share their wisdom, with people that could maybe benefit from hearing some words of wisdom on the topic. I wanted you particularly to be in this series that I'm doing.
Steve Coplon:	You're the 11th episode in this series, but you're in it because, out of everybody I know, you've got the most positive attitude that hardly ever lets down. I've only seen you once or twice where you were just a little bit stressed, so to speak, but it only lasted for about 15 seconds. And that's better than me because I proclaimed years ago that people would say, "Steve, aren't you ever down?" I said, "Yeah. If it goes over a minute, then I just kick myself hard and jump right back up." I don't like to feel down more than about a minute. I've got a lot I can learn from you.
Steve Coplon:	We've done two shows in the past. I did show Episode 157 called, ***"Reflections of Optimism and Hope,"*** where you shared something you wrote about 10 years ago that was just absolutely beautiful. I built my show around that and then the following week you came on and I actually titled that, ***"Aloha with Randey"***. I'm just going to read what that show was before I read what today's show is because that's who you are.
Steve Coplon:	It says, "Exhilarating conversation with guest, Randey Faulkner. A man whose life is a living example of Aloha, the Hawaiian word for love, affection, peace, compassion, and mercy. Meet the force behind Reflections of Optimism and Hope. You will be inspired as you learn how you too can be an ambassador of Aloha." Randey, God bless you. Thanks for being my friend.
Steve Coplon:	Randey, I'm going to just announce today's show now, so we can just get into what we want to talk about.

Randey Faulkner:	Sounds good.
Steve Coplon:	It's called **"Don't Want To, Don't Say It."** Right Thinking with Steve Coplon is very pleased to announce it. This week's show is called **"Don't Want To, Don't Say It,"** with guest Randey Faulkner. Tune in and hear Steve and Randey have an insightful conversation on breaking that awful character trait of saying you will do something when you just don't want to do it in the first place. Your relationship with others will be so much more positive when you eliminate this negative behavior.
Steve Coplon:	Randey, that's pretty much what we're going to talk about today. I've asked you as I have all the other guests in this series if you would listen to Episode 159, **"From the Lip to the Hip is a Pretty Far Distance,"** which talks about people that don't do what they say they're going to do. Did I get anything right in that episode that you listened to?
Randey Faulkner:	Yes. I'd like to comment on that. First, I want to thank you for asking me to join in today to comment on this most important topic. I also want to thank your listeners for tuning in today or listening from the archives.
Randey Faulkner:	First of all, how are you doing on this glorious IRS day 2020? Are you feeling wonderful today?
Steve Coplon:	Yeah, I'm doing great because I'm trying to get a positive message put out there so that everybody knows, "and this too shall pass" and it's bringing people closer together, people appreciating their families more.
Steve Coplon:	My sister will kill me for saying this, but my sister and brother-in-law, they needed this quarantine together. They're playing Rummikub every day. They're having some massive tournament because they're not able to see their family. I told my sister, "Arlene, would you and Bob hurry up and get it straight so that this period of separation can be ended for the rest of us?" I told her, "This whole thing is because of y'all. This gave y'all a chance to get your lives together and be closer once again." That's what we're going through. Everybody's trying to be more kind and more patient, aren't we?
Randey Faulkner:	Oh, yeah. I like what Reverend Robert Schuller said, I've been saying this quite a bit lately. He made the statement:

Reverend Robert Schuller

"Tough times never last but tough people do." That's me and you Steve, and the rest of America. We're tough people and we'll get through this together.

Steve Coplon:	We're doing very good.
Randey Faulkner:	I did listen to your inaugural show Episode 159 when you first introduced **"From the Lip to the Hip is a Pretty Far Distance."** I also listened to another show you suggested, which was phenomenal. It was Episode 164 with Richard Kay and your darling wife, Donna Coplon.
Randey Faulkner:	Let's see. Donna said something that was so simple yet very powerful. She said, "Keeping your word gives people a reason to trust you." I thought, "That is quite a concept," my thoughts immediately dominoed into thoughts surrounding a husband and a wife for example. I thought to myself, let's say a wife does not trust her husband. This means if she doesn't trust him, she probably doesn't respect him. After all, how can you respect someone you can't trust? Therefore, I think that marriage would most likely be on a downhill spiral.

Randey Faulkner: Those words that Donna said, "Keeping your word gives people a reason to trust you." I think those are powerful words. People can learn just from that one simple sentence alone.

Steve Coplon: I'll tell you something real quick on that. I was talking to my wife this morning and she's always so caring and loving and just wants to do the right thing. She's like that. What a blessing she is. And by the way, the name of that show, it was Episode 164 which you said and was called, **"We Are So Blessed by Godly Women."** Richard Kay really wanted to take Proverbs 31, which is all about Godly women, and just preach it.

Steve Coplon: I was so honored and so was Donna that he wanted to use Donna as the example, but she said to me today. She goes, "I've been listening to all these shows on the series. I don't know that my show was really on the subject of doing what you say you're going to do that all these shows are about." I said, "Sweetheart, let me just tell you. Character and integrity is all about doing the right thing, doing what you say you're going to do, honoring your good name. To be able to have a whole show, about what a Godly woman is, embracing that kind of character that you have, and other Godly women have, that's really the point. It's exactly what we're trying to talk about because this whole series is about character and integrity."

Randey Faulkner: Yeah, I agree. Richard Kay made a statement that really touched my heart too. He said, speaking about Donna, "A wife of noble character is hard to find." First, let me comment. I know that you and I both have wives who are of noble character and in turn that makes us two lucky men. Don't you agree, Steve?

Steve Coplon: Beyond luck.

Randey Faulkner: Yeah, beyond luck.

Steve Coplon: Blessed. Most blessed.

Randey Faulkner: Yeah, I sometimes like to refer back to what Eleanor Roosevelt said. "A woman's intuition is better than a man's best judgment." I have quoted that so many times and some men don't particularly like it, however, it is so true. For example, I love it when my wife is right. I tell her that gives me a chance to learn something and a chance to grow. A woman's intuition really is, sometimes better, than a man's best judgment.

Steve Coplon: My mother was an 11th grade high school dropout. She's the one that gave me that phrase. I have a friend that I was hoping was going to do one of these episodes but I saw him the other day and when I told him about what I'm working on and when I said **From the Lip to the Hip is a Pretty Far Distance"...** His name's Dave. He said, "Oh, yeah, man," then he holds his elbow up and he goes, "Yeah, to come out of your mouth and go all around the front of your elbow all the way back down your hip pocket. When you do what you say you're going to do because my mother told me that when I was nine years old when I was trying to sell magazine subscriptions in Young Park." He is an old buddy of mine. I've known for 40 years, but I loved it that his mother taught him the same expression.

Steve Coplon: My parents were divorced, and I've told a lot of stories about my dad and so forth. He died a year ago at 95 years old. But we got really close at the end and then we had some breaks in the middle. He was an engineer and he graduated from Virginia Tech, and he had a really expensive, powerful lawyer that punished my mother during the divorce. My mother barely could afford a lawyer and she had a younger lawyer that wasn't experienced. And those lawyers had a lot to do with the direction of my life because we were quite poor, and we didn't get a lot of support from my father.

Steve Coplon:	But my mother used to always talk about... My father's name was Sidney and hey, I love my dad so don't get this wrong. We came around greatly. But she said, "He didn't have a bit of common sense. All that book learning that he had but he didn't have common sense. He didn't understand people."
Steve Coplon:	That's deep rooted in me. I appreciate book learning and education greatly. But I love that the core of me came from my mother, in the way that she loved other people. Because of my mother, the dedication in my curriculum in the prisons is: "I dedicate this course to my mother, Rose. She taught me how to love. She was the original 'Never met a stranger.' and 'Give you the shirt off her back.' She passed these on to me." We are so blessed by Godly women and I put my mother right at the top of the list right up there with my wife, your wife, and Richard's wife.
Randey Faulkner:	Yeah, I think your mother did a fantastic job. She created an exceptional person of character.
Steve Coplon:	She loved me. I loved her so much.
Randey Faulkner:	Oh, yeah. She's the one who gave you *"From the Lip to the Hip is a Pretty Far Distance,"* and that's what we're going to talk about today.
Steve Coplon:	Pretty far distance, yes.
Randey Faulkner:	That's a pretty far distance. As you know, Steve, I'm a pretty simple guy. I always go back to the basics. I asked myself the question, why would someone say they were going to do something and then not do it? Of course, there's lots of reasons. However, the number one reason, I think, is the fact that they "simply don't want to." Want is a magic word here that I'll be concentrating on today. It's a powerful little four-letter word that contains the problem as well as the solution. Again, they simply don't want to.
Randey Faulkner:	When they agreed to do whatever it might be, it probably sounded like a good idea at the time. However, as time passed, for one reason or another, they decided they did not want to carry through. Sometimes they keep putting it off and hoping the other person will forget. Other times it takes them out of their comfort zone and they subconsciously say to themselves, "I don't really want to do it." There's that word again, 'want'. Regarding whatever it is that they're trying to get out of, they say to themselves, "I don't really want to do it,". Then there are others who simply do not know how to say no.
Randey Faulkner:	Anyway, I always try to go back, and I break my thoughts down to the basics. Like I said, I'm a pretty simple guy. I asked myself, how could I possibly help Steve's listeners today? In other words, if you have a listener that realizes that he or she has this character flaw, of not doing what they say they're going to do, and they really want to get a grip on it, what could I possibly say to help them today? As you stated in one of your previous shows, this flaw of not following through, is a form of lying, and in today's world, who wants to be tagged as a liar? Not you, and certainly not me.
Randey Faulkner:	In all honesty that's one reason I'm on your show today. When you asked me, first of all, I was honored and secondly, my gut reaction was to say yes because after all, you are Steve Coplon. You are trying to make a difference in people's lives and I greatly respect that and therefore it inspires me to 'want' to do the same thing.

Randey Faulkner: Did I have second thoughts? Did I consider calling you back and saying, "I think I'll take a pass on that one"? Yes, I did, Steve. However, given this exact subject matter, how could I? How could I tell you, "Yes, I want to do it," and then all of a sudden come back and say, "I'll pass"? Therefore, you have already helped at least one person and that's me and I thank you.

Steve Coplon: I didn't want you to feel any pressure.

Randey Faulkner: Thank you and no I didn't.

Steve Coplon: I wanted people to be exposed to you.

Randey Faulkner: Thank you.

Steve Coplon: You're Mr. Aloha and you bring a dimension to this series that we're doing just like you said. We've had so many wonderful conversations where we just laugh and talk about something we did when we were young or some music that we like or whatever. You've got a very, very upbeat communicative nature, and you care about other people. I knew that there'd be some real good to come out of this. I'm just complimenting you and saying that you exemplify what this series is all about. Thank you for accepting.

Steve Coplon: Hey, I want to tell you when I talked to my wife about what we're going to do the show on, and I read her what you first wrote me. Now, your title might be better than mine. Mine is "Don't Want To, Don't Say It." That was just like... I don't know what you call it, like a real quick kind of hit, a catchy phrase for a title. "Don't Want To, Don't Say It": If you don't want to, then don't say it in the first place. That's what I'm trying to say.

Steve Coplon: But yours, when I told her what your point was, that you got out of Episode 159. She said, "Well, that's exactly right." She says, "People say things that they don't really want to do and then they just blow it off." Like, "Well, I am not going to do it. Because I didn't really want to do it in the first place." The underlying question is why do you say it in the first place? Learn to control that.

Steve Coplon: But here's what your title was after you put some thought into it. You suggested, "Making Want Work For You, When You're Not Wanting To". That's really what we're going to get into here. If you really don't want to do it, but then you end up doing it anyway, it may have a positive benefit for you and others. That's what I guess you're trying to say, is that you're pretty busy these days and you weren't sure you really wanted to do it. But you knew that I'd asked you, so you wanted to do it for your buddy, Steve. But what does it really mean? Making want work for you when you're not wanting to.

Randey Faulkner: Yeah, okay. Let's talk about that. Let's go back for a minute. First, we have a person who realizes that he or she has this character flaw of not doing what they say they are going to do, and they consciously hope to practice ways to overcome this flawed personality trait.

Randey Faulkner: The next step, I believe, would be to realize the possible number one reason they do not want to follow through, which again, is because they don't want to. There's that word again. Want is going to keep popping up all the way through this. Because as a rule, people will do exactly what they want to do. We both know that.

Randey Faulkner: The first question, I believe, they must ask themselves if they want to get help is, "How can I make myself *want* to carry through with this obligation?" Once they realize they have this problem, they might say to themselves, "Okay, I said I would do this, but now I don't want to, because for one reason or another, I honestly don't want to." In order to come up with a method that will work every time, I think, first, he or she must look at what motivates them. They will need to perform an internal search that might yield some personal motivators. They will need to ask themselves, What motivates me . . . and, what am I motivated by?

Randey Faulkner: I have made a quick list of four simple forces that motivate people. There's hundreds of them, of course. But let's take number one. These are very simple and basic. Usually, at the top of the list is money. However, that does not always work, nor does it always apply, but money can be a powerful motivator. Number two, making someone happy could be a factor. Some are motivated by the fact that they can make others happy like their spouse, for example. Number three, some are motivated by a feeling they get from helping someone. This can also be a factor. Number four might be for recognition. For example, some people are motivated by the thought that they're going to be recognized. Like I said, of course, there's hundreds of examples depending on the person.

Randey Faulkner: First we're going to look for the benefit. Here is a question they have to ask themselves, "What is my benefit, or in some cases, the overall benefit of me following through with this obligation?" As I said, Steve, I'm a pretty basic guy and personally, I learn best by example. Therefore, I'm big on examples no matter how simple. Actually, the simpler the better.

Randey Faulkner: Let's say you're a person who's motivated by making someone happy. They just love to see folks smile after what they've done. A simple grade school example is: your wife asked you to take the trash out by 5:30. You look up and it's 6:00 and it's raining and you say to yourself, "I don't want to," there's that word again, "I don't want to take the trash out. I just don't want to." Stop right there, and you look for the benefit.

Randey Faulkner: In your mind's eye, you might see your wife smiling when you come back in a few minutes, possibly dripping from rain? Sometimes it can be that simple. In my case, her smile alone would make me 'want' to do it. It makes me 'want' to go take that trash out and come back and see her smile rather than the alternative. This is just one little simple example.

Randey Faulkner: Let's try another one. Let's say that you're a person who's motivated by helping others. Another simple, grade school example, might be that your neighbor asked you if you would mind helping him move a swing set in his backyard this coming weekend. Maybe it's a big, giant swing set and requires taking some part of it to be disassembled before moving. Friday night comes along, he calls, and says, "Can we move it tomorrow?" And you say, "Yes, sure. Happy to help."

Randey Faulkner: Then Saturday comes along and it's a really nice day. You have something else you'd much rather do. The normal thing would be to start searching around for excuses to get out of the commitment. Stop right there and remember, you're motivated by helping others. One of your motivating factors is helping others. However, suddenly you have something you would rather do.

Randey Faulkner: As you look for the benefit, you might want to try and hear, in your mind's ear, your neighbor saying, "Thank you so much. I could never have done this without you. Let me know if there's anything I can ever do for you. Thanks again." And he's smiling. This could be the motivating force that makes you 'want' to follow through with your commitment. Sometimes it can be that simple. However, it's the visualization of the benefit that counts and sometimes moves you forward. Steve, is what I'm talking about making any sense thus far?

Steve Coplon: Again, like I said I'm trying to do a study on this with a lot of people who I respect their opinions and their wisdom, but you cut right through the mustard. Picture that. Picture mustard and a knife and cutting right through it. It's a mess.

Steve Coplon: You got it distilled down to... I thought that what I was talking about people don't always do what they say they're going to do was about as basic as you can get. Anybody can relate to that. Anybody can relate from one angle or another. But what you're saying is what I think is the most basic part of the whole equation. If somebody doesn't want to do something, they're probably not going to do it. There are people though, that I wanted to respond to, that put others first. Even though they don't want to, ultimately, they do want to because it's for others.

Steve Coplon: It wouldn't be something that I really feel like doing, like going to a chick flick with my wife. It's just this real emotional, girly movie. Do you want to go to this real nice movie that girls generally like? Take out a tissue and cry. Maybe you wanted to go see a different kind of movie. But you know what? My advice to all the young men out there, old men too, do what your wife wants to do because you'll be a lot happier. You're a country western kind of guy. When Mama's happy, everybody's happy. You know what I mean?

Steve Coplon: You ultimately may do something that you didn't really want to do at first because it was for someone else. I'm going to slip in my first scripture of the day because it's important here.

Philippians 2:3-4,

Do nothing from selfishness or empty conceit but with humility of mind, regard one another as more important than yourselves. Do not merely look out for your own personal interests but also for the interest of others.

Steve Coplon: I think that's the most beautiful thing when you're selfless you do for others. That's really what we're talking about here, is how do you break the cycle of, "I only do what I want to do," if a person is like that.

Steve Coplon: Hey, some people didn't like it when I did the first show and said, "People that don't do what they say are going to do." It's a form of lying. And then other people came along and said, "Yeah, I know, Steve, but they just didn't know how to tell you no," and stuff like that. All that's true but if somebody says they're going to do something and they don't, then that's a falsehood and a falsehood is an untruth and an untruth is a lie. So, I can keep on that conversation.

Steve Coplon: But in this case, I'm not saying that everybody who doesn't do for others is completely selfish, but maybe they are. I'm introducing the concept that if you only want to do for yourself and not put others before yourself, then maybe you're somewhat self-centered and selfish. What do you think about that?

Randey Faulkner: Yeah. First, I'd like to comment on your scripture because that ties right into the last motivating factor of helping people and receiving that feeling of importance. You inserted your scripture at a perfect time because, some people are motivated by the fact that they do get a thrill, a feeling of importance by helping other people.

Randey Faulkner: Let's try another one here. Let's say that you're the person who's motivated by recognition. Let's get down to another grade school example so we can try to figure out how one might motivate themselves and make them 'want' to do something that they said they would do, and now, all of a sudden, they don't want to. For example, let's say a colleague asks you to volunteer at a food drive. He tells you right up front that there's going to be a dinner given for the volunteers.

Randey Faulkner: Here, you have the same scenario. The day comes around and all of a sudden you have something else you would rather do. So, you start thinking of excuses. Stop! Stop right there. In your mind's eye, you want to picture this dinner, and even picture them possibly calling your name and you get to stand up so everyone can recognize you. Now, you're having that feeling of importance and sometimes that feeling of importance is just as, or more valuable than recognition.

Randey Faulkner: Most people love to feel they're important. I forget who said it or how it was said but it goes something like this: "Some men and women will do more, and work harder, for recognition and the feeling of importance, than they will for the wage itself." I think it's actually been proven. That feeling of importance, when it comes to helping people, as well as being recognized, can be an incredible motivational factor.

Randey Faulkner: I sometimes use the example of a homeless camp where you have a bunch of homeless people. Even in a homeless camp, you have a leader. This leader has that feeling of importance that he's helping his people, so it doesn't matter what walk of life you're in, everybody likes the feeling of importance.

Randey Faulkner: Now, I saved the motivating factor of money for last, because as I said in the beginning it doesn't always apply. However, it's pretty cut and dry. If you're a person who's motivated by money and you can see a financial gain in any way, then you can use that for your motivating factor. It's easy to visualize the benefit of your bank account swelling.

Randey Faulkner: While on the subject of money and want, I'm going to share a personal example of something I wanted. Money played a role, however, not in the normal sense of the word. It's a little story I'll just throw out here. I hope I don't bore you. There was a certain rock and roll band who had just released this beautiful lithograph of a concert they gave at the Red Rocks Amphitheater in Colorado. It was large and very impressive.

Randey Faulkner: I called the purveyor. He was in Oklahoma or Kansas or somewhere. Anyway, I asked him if I could get one of the band members to inscribe it to me in a certain way. He replied, "No, no, no. We've already asked him to do that. He won't do it. He already said no. He's not going to sign any of them. Just send us your 150 bucks and we'll send you the lithograph."

Randey Faulkner: That didn't sit too well with persistent Randey. I did what Abe Lincoln did. You probably heard this story 1000 times, but I'll share it again. Back in the day, they handed Abe an axe and said, "Abe, we're going to give you six hours to cut down that tree. What are you going to do?" So, Abe said, "Well, I'm going to take the first four hours and sharpen the axe." In other words, what he's saying is, he's going to think about this situation first and he's just not going to take the axe and start chopping down the tree.

Randey Faulkner: In other words, before we jump into a request or into some type of task, let's sit back and give it some serious thought. That's why I hung up with the purveyor that day. I knew it would not do any good to start arguing with him or trying to persuade him in any way. So, I said, "I'm going to give this some thought." I'm working on my four hours with Abe Lincoln here. I'm going to give this some serious thought. After a week or so, I came up with a plan.

Randey Faulkner: Here's where the money part comes into play. I knew I could not offer money to the person that I wanted to sign the lithograph. After all he lived in Monaco, which would be an obvious indicator, that he didn't need money. Therefore, it was not a motivating factor.

Randey Faulkner: After thinking about it for a couple of weeks and working with my four hours there with Abe Lincoln, I finally had a thought to call a guy who worked for the band. I said, "Hey, I'm trying to get so and so to sign the Red Rocks lithograph in a certain way. My question for you: Does he have any charities that he donates to?" He said he would check and get back with me. A couple weeks went by and he called back and said, "Yeah, this person's mom had died from leukemia and he donates a portion of his concerts and music and so on to the Leukemia Foundation." I said, "Thank you"

Randey Faulkner: I thought aha. So, I gave it a few more days to think and I called the purveyor back. I said, "I would like to donate X amount of dollars to the Leukemia Foundation if he would sign this lithograph in a certain way." The purveyor again was negative. He said, "I don't think he will. It really won't do any good to ask. He's just not going to do it." And I say, "Well, could you just please ask him? Tell him I'll donate to Leukemia Foundation." So long story short, a week or so goes by and he called me back. He said, "Well, oddly enough, he said, if you give him proof that you donated what you said, to the Leukemia Foundation, he will sign it."

Randey Faulkner: Again, long story short, I was happy to receive the signed lithograph. I displayed it proudly for several years but where is it today, it's in the storage. So much for that. But nonetheless, I share this with the listeners who might not be able to think of a benefit that would make them want to do something that they really do not want to do. That's just another little insight, to maybe sometimes, dig a little deeper.

Randey Faulkner: And then the last insight I would like to add is the ever-present motivating factor for the person who wants to overcome this character flaw that we've been talking about. They should be able to see a huge benefit right in front of them. The benefit being the fact that they can smile at themselves. Why . . . because they have figured out a way to make themselves do something they did not want to do. Therefore, they are well on their way to overcoming this challenge. By realizing this, I believe it puts them safely on the road to integrity, trust, and respect. Does this still make sense to you, Steve?

Steve Coplon: Randey, I'm loving it. You talk about being so basic and I don't know... People talk about people who have incredible wisdom, like that sly old fox kind of thing. But Randey, you didn't get to where you are with as many people who love you like I do by not doing everything that you said you would do. That's who you are. Now, you're talking really basic to try to help other people understand the different breakdowns of what it might entail, with your characteristics and so forth.

Steve Coplon: When you did your **Moody Bluegrass Project**, you got 50 of the top people in bluegrass music together. Including all five original members of *The Moody Blues*, that you were doing the tribute albums to. As well as Vince Gill a member of *The Eagles*, Ricky Skaggs and Alison Krauss and some other top people from the world of bluegrass.

Steve Coplon: Why did they commit to your project, Randey? Is it because you might have been a person who has done some things, but didn't do other things that you said you'd do? No, Randey. It's because you're Randey Faulkner. People know you as a person who's honorable, trustworthy, and has all the qualities that we're talking about. We're kind of playing some of these things down a little bit. I don't want to embarrass you by talking too nice about you but, Randey, you're a really good person. Many people look to you and say, that's a man of character and integrity. That's why I asked you to be on the show today. I do appreciate the humbleness that you're trying to break this down into its very basics.

Steve Coplon: Did that answer your question? Am I getting anything out of what you're doing? Randey, you do the things that you're talking about.

Randey Faulkner: I appreciate that. Thank you much, Steve. Thanks for the nice compliment.

Steve Coplon: Well, it's true.

Randey Faulkner: I'm not sure what you're talking about some of the time, but I'll sit here and take it. I'll take it like a man. Ha!

Steve Coplon: Yeah, that's good. Knowing how to take your compliments of virtue, by the way.

Randey Faulkner: Yes, that's true, very true. Let's see, you had also asked me to possibly think about a couple of examples of a type of person, in my life, who didn't do what they said they were going to do. You asked me to give you a couple examples. I thought I would give you the bad one first. I call it the bad one anyway. For example, we had a tenant in one of our houses and although he was a very positive guy, he kept saying he's going to do something and would not follow through. He was a little late starting the rent and then he kept promising he's going to get caught up. Then he said, "Within two months, I'll be caught up." This goes on and on.

Randey Faulkner: Over a period of a year it just went on and he never, got caught up. He never did what he said he was going to do. He would always say, "I'm going to put in so much on Friday. Then on Friday he would be $50 short," or whatever. It was just one of those constant things for over a period of a year. When it came time to renew his lease, we told him, "We're not going to renew your lease." And he said, "Why?" My answer was exactly what we have been talking about here today on your program. I said, "because you don't do what you say you're going to do" That was the exact reason. There was no other reason. That was it. Plain and simple. He never got a whole month behind, but he just wouldn't do what he said, therefore it would almost make me stress out.

Randey Faulkner: It wasn't the money. It's just the idea that he didn't do what he said he was going to do. And he couldn't figure it out. He still said, "Why aren't you going to renew my lease?"

Steve Coplon: Can I give you a comment though?

Randey Faulkner: Sure.

Steve Coplon: That's a perfect example. Absolutely perfect. You made me think at least two or three thoughts right off of that. There's a lot of people... I went to my high school 50th reunion last October. We all know that some of the most popular good looking people that everybody wants to hang out with in high school, they peak way too early. And by the time they get a little bit older, they're way over the hill. You know what I mean? And then some of the sleepers that were just the little shy ones who nobody paid any attention to, they're like phenomenal human beings. They did great things with their life. They blossomed later which is such a beautiful thing.

Steve Coplon:	I wrote down while you were talking about the guy who just never did what he said he was going to do. He's always short on his rent, always talking a good game. Some people just don't understand that your looks and your charm will only carry you but so far if you don't follow through. A lot of people are still playing that high school thing where they think that just because I'm Mr. Popularity, I'm the good looking person here that that's all they need in life. No, that's very, very superficial.
Steve Coplon:	The other one is much more serious. Napoleon Hill, when we did the, **"Fifty-Seven Famous Alibis by Old Man IF."** I haven't read it in a couple shows in this series but I'm going to read the 57th, one more time because it's all we're talking about.

Napoleon Hill

IF, ***and this is the greatest of them all***

I had the courage to see myself as I really am, I would find out what is wrong with me and correct it. *Then I might have a chance to profit by my mistakes and learn something from the experience of others, for I know that there is something WRONG with me or I would now be where I WOULD HAVE BEEN IF I had spent more time analyzing my weaknesses and less time building alibis to cover them.*

Steve Coplon:	Randey, this is one of the most serious things I've said in a while. One of the things that is the hardest thing for us to see in life is the proverbial deadbeat father. The person who hasn't accepted the responsibility of providing for his family and being the kind of person that his family needs to be supportive and loving and raise good kids and take care of his wife.
Steve Coplon:	When you talked to me just now about that simple example of your tenant that you didn't want to renew his lease because he wasn't a person of his word that kept doing things, I find that to be somewhat of a selfish person, someone who is just looking after what they want, not what others want, and this is what this show's about. We're trying to break the character flaw.
Steve Coplon:	But a deadbeat father's a tragedy in this life because children are exposed to a parent who's not taking care of what he's supposed to do, and the children are going to suffer accordingly.
Steve Coplon:	Last scripture, as I throw it back to you:

Proverbs 18:1

"An unfriendly person pursues selfish ends and against all sound judgment starts quarrels."

Steve Coplon:	Now, somebody that's not doing what they said they're going to do will very often end in a quarrel and argument, something that's just not going to go well.
Steve Coplon:	That young man or that person who was your tenant that you just said, "Hey, I appreciate you and everything, but we just don't want to deal with it anymore." If he didn't really understand his own character flaw, people like that have a tendency to blame it on somebody else because they're not accepting responsibility yet and just because a person is selfish… I'm not saying that they're necessarily going to be unfriendly, but my definition of a friendly person is a person who's kind and nice to other people and considerate of others. So, if a person's very selfish and they've overlooked how they treat other people, then that can be interpreted by me as being an unfriendly person.

Steve Coplon: With that, Randey... It's very deep what we're talking about. We can talk about it in simple examples here or there but when it comes right down to it, it is basic. It's very simple. Are you going to be a person who only does what you want to do and puts yourself before everyone else? I'm going to throw it back to you because you're moving my thinking along and I greatly appreciate what you're doing today to take this time to delve into this basic human nature.

Randey Faulkner: Thank you. I appreciate that.

Steve Coplon: You're welcome.

Randey Faulkner: Since I gave what I called a bad example. I'd like to give a couple of examples of people I do admire. The first one who came to mind when I started thinking of people who do exactly what they say they're going to do, is our mutual friend, Don Green, the CEO of the **Napoleon Hill Foundation**. His mother drilled into him at a very early age to always do what you say you're going to do. Don't say it unless you plan on following through. That's what Don told me time and time again. I will ask him something, and not only does he say he's going to do something, he does it immediately. You probably noticed that about him too.

Randey Faulkner: It's not the fact that he said he's going to do it and maybe he'll get it done tomorrow or the next day, he does it immediately. And then when I compliment him on that most positive character trait, and he always refers back to his mom by saying, "My mother taught me at a young age to follow through with what I said I would do. For me, the best way to accomplish this is to do it right now. So that's why I got it done so quickly." Steve, I know we both admire that in a person.

Randey Faulkner: Another person I greatly admire is my mother-in-law, Carmen Marquez. She's a beautiful 86-year young lady and she's been raising two small great grandchildren for the past 10 years. Now, they're teenagers. However, she's so busy tending to their needs as well as her husband, Andy, who's 90 this year. She has all these other responsibilities, yet she's the exact same way. When she says she's going to do something, she does it and she does it right now.

Randey Faulkner: For example, just last week, she said "Oh, my lemons and my oranges are ready. I'll send you a box." Three days later we received a huge box of lemons and oranges in the mail. She's a woman I truly love and admire that does exactly what she says she's going to do, when she says she's going to do it. I do have one more person, I just happen to think of as I'm sitting here talking to you.

Randey Faulkner: This would be a gentleman by the name of Steve Coplon. Although I've only known you for a year or two, you never fail to call when you say you're going to call, or email when you say you're going to email, or text exactly when you say you will. I know you're busy and you say you will send me a link to something, within five minutes I have it. So, you too are to be applauded. You're one of the people I admire as far as doing what you say you're going to do. This show is going to help me too, because when it comes to human nature, I'm just like everyone else.

Randey Faulkner: There are so many reasons people make excuses. Some people just don't like to leave their comfort zone. That's a big reason people will change in the middle of the stream and say, "I don't think I want to do that," because they suddenly realize, "Oh, I'm going to get out of my comfort zone." They want to stay nice and comfortable where they are and therefore, they start making excuses as to why they don't want to do it.

Randey Faulkner: I think that is all the comments I have on today's subject; however, I do have a little story to share if we have time? I'd like to make mention of the four candles all aglow in a quiet little room. I don't know how much time we have left.

Steve Coplon: We have five, 10 minutes anywhere in there.

Randey Faulkner: Okay. First of all, I hope your listeners get some good out of today's chat and this crucial topic you have chosen to dwell upon. Possibly the main take away a listener might gain from this topic is say, "Okay, here I am. I'm a person. I realize I have this character flaw; a lot of times I tell people I'm going to do something, and I don't do it because of one reason or another." Here they should stop and just ask themselves very seriously, "What motivates me? What am I motivated by?"

Randey Faulkner: Make a list. Understanding your own personality, let's write down the ways in which you are motivated. As the days and weeks pass by, keep adding to the list. If suddenly you hear yourself saying "Oh, I really like this or, I feel motivated by this" then immediately go add that to your list of motivators. Then every time one of those situations come along where you start thinking about making an excuse, Stop! Then just look at your list and say, "Which one of these motivating factors is going to make me follow through, so I can carry on and be a person of integrity and trust?" Then just do it! You will be happy and feel good about yourself. That's it in a nutshell

Randey Faulkner: Somebody sent me this the other day. I just thought it was beautiful. I'd love to share it with you and your listeners, and it fits right into your show.

The Story of the Four Candles:

They're all aglow in a small tranquil room.

The first candle says, "I am peace. I am peace. Since the world is full of anger, no one can keep me lit." So out she goes.

The second candle says, "I am faith. I am faith. I am no longer indispensable. It doesn't make sense that I should stay lit for a moment longer." Out she goes.

The third candle says, "I am love. I am love. People today do not understand my importance, so they simply put me aside. They sometimes even forget to love those who are nearest to them."

Then suddenly a child enters the room. He asked, "Why aren't these three candles burning?"

The fourth candle speaks up. It says, "I am hope. As long as I'm burning, I can relight the peace, the faith, and the love." She says the greatest of all these is love. However, your flame of hope should never go out of your life. With hope each of us can live in peace, faith, and love.

Randey Faulkner: And there is a little prayer attached to it. That said:

Prayer of the Four Candles

Dear God, you are my light and my salvation. You are my hope. Please come into my heart and forgive my wrongs. Help me be an instrument of Your love. Let me cause Your candlelight to shine on others through me today. Amen.

Randey Faulkner: I just thought that was beautiful, Steve. The Story of the Four Candles.

Steve Coplon: Randey, it is beautiful. That's absolutely beautiful. Everything we've talked about today it's so important. First of all, I want to thank you for your kind words, because you included me with people who do what they say they're going to do.

Randey Faulkner: It's true.

Steve Coplon: Even if I'm not as good at it as I should be, having someone who I respect and love, say that to me is going to motivate me to do it even better. See that's another thing about, as we surround ourselves with people who we trust and love and admire, it's the concept of we don't want to be the smartest person in the room because if you're surrounded by people who are smarter than you are, then it'll raise you up. I thank you for the encouragement that you're giving me, and I hope that everyone listening gets a lot of encouragement also.

Randey Faulkner: You're welcome.

Steve Coplon: Thank you. I actually had you on for Episode 147 to introduce you and then I brought you on the following week. ***"Reflections of Optimism and Hope,"*** it had a tagline in there that said, "And remember, you can rise above your circumstances and grab hold of your dreams." Randey... I encourage everybody to go back to that episode and listen to it in its entirety; ***"Reflections of Optimism and Hope,"*** that you wrote some 10 years ago. But I just want to read one little piece of it just so they'll get a sense of what your message is.

Steve Coplon: This is near the end. You've said a whole lot of incredible things, positive affirmations. You've covered so much, and you've given the glory to the Lord throughout.

Randey Faulkner

We're not supposed to talk about the way we were. We're supposed to talk about the way we want to be. God said, 'Let the weak say I am strong.' He didn't say let the weak talk about their weakness. Some say I'll never rise any higher. I've gone as far as I can go. Those words claim them. Sure enough, they will be stuck at the same place year after year. Or some say, I'll never break this addiction to alcohol or drugs, I've had it too long. It's too hard. And just like that, they've said them. Those words will control them. Some need a new attitude and to speak. This may be the way it's been in the past. But this is not the way it's staying. I may feel weak but my declaration is I am strong. I may have had this addiction for years but I'm declaring I'm free. If we keep saying the right thing, if we keep speaking victory, speaking favor speaking health and wholeness, our Lord is faithful and we shall reap those seeds we have sown. In due season, we will eat the fruit of our words. I am thankful He is surrounding me like a shield and also opening doors that no man can shut. Nothing happens unless we speak and believe. I am blessed. I am prosperous. I am favored. I am healthy. I am free.

Steve Coplon:	Randey, Don Green did a wonderful thing when he introduced us over the phone. He said, "Randey would like to hear that interview that you and I just did, Steve. Would you share it with him?" He gave me your number. I called you about a year and a half or so ago and you're just a breath of fresh air to me because you're just a real person.
Steve Coplon:	In closing for what our message is today, do you feel comfortable, satisfied that whatever you had on your heart that you'd like to share that people might go back and listen to a little bit that will help them move forward and know the extreme importance of doing what they say they're going to do even if they don't want to, that they shouldn't have said it in the first place, but if they said it... I'm not a card player or gambler but Kenny Rogers was, and God Bless him. He passed just last week. But the gambler, it comes back to, a card played is a card laid. You know what I'm saying?
Steve Coplon:	I'm asking you to put a closing spin on the message today if you would, about just only doing what you want to do, and try not to let people down.
Randey Faulkner:	Yes, Thank you. Like I said, I'm a very simple person and its actually basic simplicity that the magic word, is want. Like I said in the beginning it's a powerful four-letter word. It's the problem here, but it's also the solution. If you sit down and you realize the reason you're not doing what you say you're going to do, is because you don't want to, you have to make yourself either... Either you're going to remain a person of no integrity and untrust or you're going to find a way to make yourself want to do it. Whatever the situation is, you have to find a way to make yourself want to do it and once you find this way, you'll not only do it, but you'll do it happily and you'll do it completely. You might even go the extra mile in doing it because now all of a sudden, you found a reason that you want to do it.
Randey Faulkner:	I just encourage people to look inside and find what motivates them and grab ahold of that and not only use it for this practice but use it for everything in their life. That's what I got for you, Steve.
Steve Coplon:	Randey, thanks for sharing that. It's been a beautiful conversation that we've had. Thank your wife for the time that she allowed you to break away from the honeymoon that you all have been on for a long time now and share your wisdom with me and the listeners. Randey, thanks again and God Bless you for being Randey.
Randey Faulkner	Wow Steve. I can't believe you said what you just said about our honeymoon. No one knows this, so since you said what you did, may I share something really personal with you?
Steve Coplon	Randey, the listeners and I would love that. Go for it.
Randey Faulkner	I consider the luckiest day of my life to be August 19, 1989. This is the day at the Grand Cayman Island Airport, God blessed my vision with Cindy Rae Pardo. I then consider my happiest day to be June 8, 1996. On this happy day we celebrated Cindy's 40th birthday with over 250 guests, consisting of family and friends. At 9pm the festivities were interrupted, and we announced a surprise wedding, which only the Pastor had knowledge of.
Randey Faulkner	From here we opted to forego the honeymoon. However, since we met on 8-19, we opted to enjoy 819 mini-moons. At this writing in 2020, we have completed a little over a third of them. Cindy and I highly suggest this style of honeymooning, due to the fact that it lasts a lifetime, therefore, keeping that fire of love ablaze. I would also like to say, "You know you are in love when you can't fall asleep at night, because reality is better than dreaming." I haven't slept for over 30 years.

Randey and Cindy Faulkner

We firmly believe in this little rhyme:

> *"Love is one of the only things in life, whereas, the more you give away, the more you receive in return. Always live a life of love, laughter, and continuing to learn."*

Steve Coplon: Randey, you're incredible! That was the best advice on how to keep a marriage filled with bliss I've ever heard. Thanks for sharing that with us.

Randey Faulkner: God Bless you, Steve and Donna for your good work, and please keep it up.

Steve Coplon: Thank you so much. Everyone, I hope you go back and listen to this a little more closely because there's a lot there today and I'm here for you. Randey's there for you. Just God Bless each one of you and have a wonderful week.

Steve Coplon: Thanks for listening to *Right Thinking with Steve Coplon*. I look forward to being with you again next week. Remember: **Don't Quit, Plan Ahead, It Will Get Better.** God Bless you and have a great week!

To listen to the original interview, scan this QR Code with your camera, or visit:

https://rightthinkingeducation.com/FromtheLiptotheHip/Chapter-11/

CHAPTER TWELVE

Applied Passion, The Key To Success with guest Andrew Coplon
Right Thinking With Steve Coplon - Episode 170

Steve Coplon: Good morning. Welcome to *Right Thinking with Steve Coplon.* I'm your host, Steve Coplon. Thank you for tuning in. Let's have a great day!

Steve Coplon: Good morning everybody. Glad to be with you. Well, I say it on every single show, what a special show we're going to have today. Today is incredibly special because I've got something we're going to be doing, that I've been waiting to do for a long time. I've got my oldest son, Andrew, on the show today. Andrew, how you doing?

Andrew Coplon: Hey Dad, good morning. I hope you're having a good day so far. Thanks for having me after, what, 150 episodes so far?

Steve Coplon: Yes. You're actually the 170th episode..

Andrew Coplon: Oh my gosh, wow.

Steve Coplon: I want to thank you, Andrew. When I first got started, you listened to every one of my shows, critiqued them for me, and I value your opinion. I've been wanting to get you on the show for a long time. I'm going to read what today's show is for the listeners and then we can start. I will talk about why I asked you to be on the show.

Andrew Coplon: Sounds good.

Steve Coplon: This is Episode 170, *Right Thinking with Steve Coplon* is very pleased to announce that this week's show is called ***Applied Passion, The Key to Success***, with guest Andrew Coplon. Tune in and hear Steve and Andrew, a successful young entrepreneur, talk about how combining hard work with your passion will lead you to success. Success is defined by the strength of the community you build around yourself.

Steve Coplon: Andrew, I came up with the title for this show after I discussed with you what the theme of your message was going to be. I love the title: *"Applied Passion, The Key to Success."* I hope that people will quote me for the rest of my life and long after for coming up with that expression. Combining hard work with your passion will lead you to success. Powerful!

Steve Coplon: Andrew, it really describes who you are. I am so proud of you, always have been, your whole life. Especially now that you're married and you have Max, my eighth grandchild. Having such a beautiful family is the most wonderful thing. It gives me purpose. You have always been incredibly disciplined and really focused. I've been wanting to get you on the show to use you as a role model and as an example of a young person who ends up having a very successful life. I want to get deep into who you are, why you're like you are. I obviously know a lot about why you are the way you are because I'm your dad, I've watched you grow up, I've been involved with you your whole life.

Andrew, you're an entrepreneur. You started working when you were 16 years old. On today's show, I want to go back to when you were that age and talk about the things that influenced you and shaped you into the man that you are today.

Steve Coplon: I asked you to listen to Episode 159 *"From the Lip to the Hip is a Pretty Far Distance."* You know from listening to earlier shows in this series that the title comes from an expression that Grandma Rose taught me as a kid.

Andrew Coplon: Yes, I do know that she taught it to you and yes, I did listen to it.

Steve Coplon: Do you have any thoughts about the show? Did I say anything that made sense?

Andrew Coplon: Everything you said did make sense. Just a real positive motto to live by.

Steve Coplon: Originally, you were going to be a guest on a future show to talk about what it is like to be a young successful entrepreneur. I decided to invite you into this series instead of just doing a solo show, because you deal with people who don't do what they say they're going to do on a daily basis in your career, as much as anyone that I know.

Andrew, we haven't told people yet what you do, so now is a good time to share what you do. When you were 16 years old you started working for Flamingo Joe's, a food vendor.

Andrew Coplon: Yeah. I remember when I was 16, we were in the kitchen, I think it was slightly before I even turned 16. We had a neighbor who worked at Harbor Park, the baseball stadium where the Tides played. At the time I really liked baseball. After nearly 20 years of being around baseball, I don't watch it as much as I used to, but at that time it was a really cool idea to have the opportunity to possibly work in a baseball stadium. I called the owner of the company, a guy named Emory. I met him for an interview outside of Scope, which is the local arena here in Virginia. I got hired right before I turned 16. I remember at that time I was getting ready to travel to Spain on a school trip. So, it's kind of crazy how times have changed. I went to Spain and upon returning, I started working at the baseball stadium selling snow cones, walking up and down the bleachers, it was a great summertime job. That was my first job and I still work for the company today.

Steve Coplon: Andrew, you're my son, and you're also the hardest working disciplined person I know. It makes me proud to be able to say that. You've been with that company for 18 years now, right?

Andrew Coplon: This would have actually been my 20th baseball season if opening day hadn't been canceled due to the coronavirus pandemic.

Steve Coplon: Were you actually 16 or 15, because you're 34 now?

Andrew Coplon: I think I probably worked a couple days when I was 15. It was right before I turned 16 when I really got going.

Steve Coplon: So, you started off, doing what? Hawking snow cones, cotton candy in the stands, vending.

Andrew Coplon: Yes, my position was to walk up and down bleachers, interact with all the customers out in the seats, selling everything from snow cones, cotton candy to lemonade. Selling the snacks people really enjoy while they're at a baseball game in the summertime.

Steve Coplon: So, you quickly were promoted by Emory to the general manager. How old were you when he promoted you to general manager?

Andrew Coplon: Well, let me step back a sec. The cool thing about the job that really got me working hard was the fact it was commission based. I got paid based on what I sold. I believe when I first started, I would make 30 cents for every snow cone I sold. So, if I went out there on a hot summer day and only sold one snow cone, I'm only getting 30 cents. That's pretty ridiculous. It would be kind of a waste of my time. But if I went out there and sold 200 snow cones, that would be a quick 60 bucks. In that angle, I was making more over the course of a baseball game than most people my age working wherever they were, whether it's fast food or working somewhere else. But I believe it was gradually over the first couple years that I took on more responsibilities, whether it was from just helping set up for the baseball games or doing a lot of behind the scenes work. I think by the time I turned 18 or so, I was helping schedule and run events. At that point in time, I was just graduating high school, going into college, so it was a really cool opportunity for me to take on more management responsibilities.

Steve Coplon: Everyone knows I love baseball and especially my Yankees. I did enjoy watching the Tides play, but to be honest, what I really enjoyed was sitting in the stands with Josh and Lindsey, your younger brother and sister, and watching you work. Lindsey and Josh both worked for you too. But I'll never forget how I would be sitting up there in the stands and point out to people who were with me or sitting around me, "See over there. See the guy way over there vending, moving so fast? That's my son." Then they would watch you for a couple minutes, observing how you would do it. It was as if you were insane, the way that you were so focused, moving so fast. That was amazing to watch. I'll never forget the time that you told me you were shooting for 300 units. No one had ever sold 300 units in one game. Was it snow cones or cotton candy that you were selling that day?

Andrew Coplon: It was snow cones. I think it was on Father's Day probably in 2002. It was a while ago.

Steve Coplon: It was a while ago. You're right, I remember it was Father's Day. I'm telling you. I'm a proud papa now, and I was proud daddy then, wasn't a papa yet. There were about 50 people sitting around me. I was on the third base side. It was getting near the end of the game There were 10 or 15 minutes to go. You came by and I'd said, "How many you got?" And you said, "270." I remember standing up and I yelled, "Hey, everybody. My son needs to hit 300. Buy some snow cones." And I got you over the hump. Andrew, there's a male alpha thing that's always been between you and me that we can share. You have always been incredibly focused, and you've never really needed me to tell you what to do, because you've always done whatever you put your mind to. I mean, you're the only kid I ever knew that when you were in elementary school you made your bed every day. You got up and you were disciplined.

Steve Coplon: Andrew, I don't want to embarrass you but I'm going to get this out now because it will always be here on the recording of this broadcast. Do you remember when you were in the Field Lighthouse Gifted and Talented Program, you went one day a week. Do you remember that program?

Andrew Coplon: Yeah, I still live near where that school used to be.

Steve Coplon: Yeah. What was the school called?

Andrew Coplon: Stuart Elementary. It's not a school anymore. They're actually turning it into apartments now. It's interesting to see how the building has changed.

Steve Coplon: Oh, wow. So, you'd go over to that school once a week. It was part of the City of Norfolk gifted and talented program. I don't remember the teacher's name, but when you were in the third grade, your mom and I sat down with her for the parent teacher conference. What happened is what every parent lives for, dreams for. Your teacher said, "I just want to tell you about your son, Andrew. I've never met a child like him before. He can do anything he ever wants to in his life." Then she said, "If he wants to be the Governor of Virginia, he'll be the Governor of Virginia." And then she went on to say, "We get new students throughout the year transferring from other schools." She continued and told us that every time they get a new student brought into the program, she sits them next to you because she wants you to be their point of entry to understand what the program is all about. That was amazing, Andrew. I thank you for being that person, the person that you are.

Steve Coplon: Andrew, when you were young, you read a tremendous amount. What would you say molded your personality the most to get you to be the disciplined person that you are today? You always do so well with whatever you put your mind to?

Andrew Coplon: I think there's a couple things that probably molded that. First off, I always enjoyed learning. I liked reading books, learning weird trivia, and today, I still love watching Jeopardy. Using that trivia, I probably learned in third grade to answer questions on Jeopardy. Just merely the fact that learning was pretty fun, but I also liked to see the reward I would get from learning that information. If I could apply it in something and use it in other parts of my life, I would see that it's valuable having those skills. So that taught me early on that I could put the time in to learn something and the hard work would actually pay off because I'd be able to utilize it in some other aspect of my life. It was exciting to see that happen.

Andrew Coplon: I remember when I was in elementary school, we had a program called Accelerated Reader. You could get points for reading books and then taking quizzes on the books. So, if I read a biography of Abraham Lincoln, I'd take a quiz on Abraham Lincoln. If I got X out of 10 questions correctly, I would get a certain number of points put on to my account. I would quickly find out, just like selling snow cones, that the more points I had, the higher I would climb on the rankings. It was fun to see. The program gamified reading books. So, it wasn't just reading a book. It was making it fun to read a book. I've always enjoyed doing things, whether it's work or reading, that I've considered fun. If it's not fun, then why are you doing it? Whether it's reading, working, or whatever it may be.

Steve Coplon: Don Price, my close friend who had a 40 year banking career, was on the show as part of this series seven episodes ago. You know him pretty well. He helped you with the first condo that you purchased and with some of your rental properties. He reads more than anyone I know, with maybe the exception of you.

Andrew Coplon: No, he probably reads more than me right now. I haven't been reading as much as I normally do. I've been working on a few big projects.

Steve Coplon: I know. We'll talk about some of your projects in a few minutes. I know you haven't had as much time to read lately. Don said on the show that he had read 17 books by the second week of March this year already.

Andrew Coplon: Wow, very impressive.

Steve Coplon: He reads around five books at a time. He'll read anything that I ask him to. He's an amazingly quick reader. Andrew, when you did all that reading when you were young, you were laying out your foundation for success. I'm glad you brought out that reading is one of the keys to your success. I've done so many shows trying to get people to understand that. I've read a lot all my life also. I've always read a lot of comic books in addition to real books. You and I read comic books together as a kid. I still have some of the collections. There's a lot of information in comic books. Here's a big one, Andrew, this is a flash to the past. Do you remember the *"Prince of Persia"* computer game that you played so much of?

Andrew Coplon: Yeah. I think they made a movie out of it a couple years ago even. Yeah, I remember it.

Steve Coplon: One of the benefits that I think paid off greatly for us was that I became very involved with *"The Learning Company"*, *"Broderbund"*, *"Sierra"* and dozens of other educational software companies. I figured out how to become a VAR, Value Added Reseller. Then I was able to get demo copies of their software for either free or usually just $5. I created a peer to peer computer network in my office upstairs. No one else had one like it. You and Lindsey both had your own computer. I had a library of over 500 educational titles. We had nearly every popular educational computer game out. *"Where in the World is Carmen Sandiego?"* was one of your favorites. You developed great computer skills. You might remember, I don't, which grade you were in, when you actually wrote a newspaper article that was an entire double section. It was two whole pages in the Virginian Pilot, the local paper. You were interviewed about the computer literacy skills that you had acquired so early on in your life.

Andrew Coplon: You can still find that article if you google. It's out there.

Steve Coplon: Well, I'm going to google it after the show.

Andrew Coplon: Yeah. I think I found it a couple years ago just for fun.

Steve Coplon: Well, that's a good memory. Yes, and then you wrote for that newspaper also. I think they called it *757*. You did a music review column. You were selected into the All City Jazz Band. You were the keyboard player. You were good in music. Yes, you did a lot during your school years. I've already said it. You were very, very self-motivated. You were highly competitive also.. Okay, I want to get this out quick. I think this is my best memory of something that you did that I laugh about.

Andrew Coplon: Wow, let's hear it.

Steve Coplon: You got into karate at a really early age. I trained you your whole life and that was a thrill for me. You competed in tournaments and you won a lot of competitions in both kata and sparring. When you were, about 14 years old, one night in class at the YMCA I taught you a new technique. You had just made second degree black belt. When I teach a technique, I break it down. As an instructor, you know this because you're an instructor, you pay the price sometimes because you give the student the opening. You want to see if they've learned the technique well enough to see the opening when it is there and take it and score with the technique. It was a combination I'll never forget. It was a slide in, back fist, reverse punch, roundhouse kick to the head. So, I said to myself, "Okay, I'm going to give him the opening." So, I went a little flat-footed. Do you remember kicking me in the head that night and how you couldn't wait to get home?

Andrew Coplon: Yeah. I remember that story.

Steve Coplon: Yeah, it was terrible. You just about knocked me out on my feet. You kicked me right across my jawbone and ear. I kept my balance, my knees wobbled. I was all right. I remember telling you, "Okay, Andrew. You got the technique. I'm never going to give it to you again." And we came home that night and you rushed out of the car, flew the front door of the house open, and said, "Mom, mom, mom, guess what I just did? I just kicked Dad in the head so hard I almost knocked him out."

Andrew Coplon: Yeah, I remember that one.

Steve Coplon: Yeah, well, let me give some advice that will motivate a lot of kids. Get your family to become a karate family and beat your dad up. Just kidding. But working out does get good aggression out.

Andrew, do you remember the name of the program that Barry Einhorn, Marty's dad, invited you into? It was an interfaith, interracial program.

Andrew Coplon: It was called Operation Understanding.

Steve Coplon: Can you talk about that for a moment?

Andrew Coplon: Yeah, I believe I was a junior in high school, I don't know if it still exists, but it connected African American students with Jewish students. They would talk about diversity, talk about differences, talk about faith, and look at the civil rights and the similar struggles that both groups of people have been through. We did a lot of fun activities to learn about one another. Some were social activities. Some were more educational. I remember at the peak of the one year program, the big graduation present was that we went down, I believe it was to Alabama. We went to a lot of historical sites from the civil rights movement, which was really powerful and awesome to experience.

Steve Coplon: I remember that it culminated in a walk across the Edmund Pettus Bridge, where the famous march across the bridge took place.

Andrew Coplon: Yeah, that's correct.

Steve Coplon: Yeah, I was very proud of you for being involved in that. You were also selected in elementary school to be on a quiz show they made up, that was on African History month.

Andrew Coplon: The competition combined Virginia, African American, and local history. It was almost like an elementary school version of Jeopardy. We had buzzers and everything. The teachers running the program would give the contestants a set of trivia questions to study. I would just memorize the answers to the questions. I probably still know most of the answers. Yeah, then we would compete against other schools. It was a lot of fun. Like I mentioned earlier, I still love trivia. It's fun. I have got a little Jeopardy game on my desk right now.

Steve Coplon: Yeah. I think knowing all that trivia is very helpful to keep a sharp mind. So, as you got older you got more and more into deciding what you might want to do with your career, and you started traveling whenever you could. You went twice to Nike Running Camps in Asheville, North Carolina. I will never forget when you got your driver's license at 16 years old. Do you remember what we did the day after you got your license?

Andrew Coplon: Yeah, so the day I turned 16, I got my driver's license. I was really excited to drive, having the freedom of being behind the wheel. The next day we started driving to San Antonio, Texas. We made a lot of stops along the way, you probably remember better than me how many places we visited. I think the trip was almost three weeks. It was really a fun adventure to go on. Actually, speaking of San Antonio, I was supposed to be in San Antonio five days from now, but I had to cancel the trip because of the coronavirus pandemic.

Steve Coplon: The coronavirus is really unbelievable. The driver's license story tells a lot about your personality. I've said a couple times today that I've never had to really get behind you to motivate you, you're very self-motivated. So, I taught you how to drive, and we got on the highway and on that trip we went to an Atlanta Braves baseball game. I remember they were playing the Cubs, and the Cubs pitcher, I can't remember his name, maybe you do.

Andrew Coplon: I'm not going to remember that one.

Steve Coplon: I remember now. It was Greg Maddux, a Hall of Famer, and he was pitching. It was the worst outing of his career. The Braves got something like eight straight hits off of him in the first aiming. He got knocked out even before the second inning was over. This is where your love of highway started. Your present career has you driving unbelievable amounts on the highway. So, on that trip when you were 16, you got behind the wheel, and you did not want to let me take back the wheel. We started doing a minimum of a three hour stretch. You just wanted to drive. Letting you drive was fun for me. I just relaxed in the copilot seat, riding shotgun. We did an amazing piece of driving together. We left Norfolk and drove straight to Atlanta. That was the first of many historic road trips that we've both done. We arrived in the parking lot, went into the game, and saw the second pitch. We missed the opening pitch because of the parking situation. It was a 12 hour drive from Norfolk to Atlanta. We watched the game, and then we continued on to San Antonio. We drove 4,169 miles on that trip.

Andrew Coplon: 12 hours to Atlanta is a little slow. I can do it a lot faster today.

Steve Coplon: Yeah, I know. When you went to college at James Madison, you would come into town, work events all weekend for Flamingo Joe's, and then drive back to James Madison at 2:00 am in the morning. You used to do that midnight run, Harrisonburg to Norfolk quite often. You drove too fast, Andrew. You drove way too fast.

Andrew Coplon: I probably did drive a little fast then, but I don't drive that fast now.

Steve Coplon: That's good. Okay, so Andrew, I've laid out a little bit about your childhood and your upbringing. We've talked about your love of reading, your self-discipline, how you started working and developed a strong work ethic at a young age, and some of the other things that you did in your early years. I've always been very pleased with the kind of person that you are.

You've had a lot of experience around diverse groups of people. Before we move on to what you are doing now, I would like to go back to our Karate days at the YMCA. You trained very seriously with me your whole life. We used to have what I call Wednesday night fights at the Y. We would have as many as 22 black belts from all over Norfolk, Virginia Beach and Portsmouth visit us at the Y to work out with us. You were always the youngest one there. We would pair off in maybe 12 different one-on-ones going on at the same time. I would clap my hands to start everyone sparring and then clap again when it was time to stop. Then we'd switch to the next guy. Everyone would spar at least 12 or more different people on those Wednesday nights. At first some of them didn't know why you were there participating with all adults. You were just a 14-year-old kid, only weighing about 125 pounds. When you would drop that axe kick on their face, they caught on pretty quick why you were there! You earned their respect. It made me very proud as both your Karate instructor and your dad.

Steve Coplon:　　Okay Andrew, now let's talk about what you do now. You are currently, among other things, the general manager for Flamingo Joe's. I want to tie your work ethic in to **"From the Lip to the Hip is a Pretty Far Distance."** I said at the beginning of the show that on a daily basis in your career, you deal with people who don't do what they say they're going to do, as much as anyone I know. You work at major events all over the country. You can talk about how you progressed to this with Flamingo Joe's. You drive 50,000 miles a year to places like the Indianapolis Superdome and the New Orleans Superdome, or whatever they are called now. You vend at events held in these types of places. I want you to explain how in order for you to have 75 or 80 vendors working in the stands, you've always told me that you have to hire about 150 people because half of them…

Andrew Coplon:　　Let me take it from here. I'll kind of explain, give a little more background on this one.

Steve Coplon:　　Please go for it.

Andrew Coplon:　　The food service that I run, started off working mostly local baseball games. Then we would do some college sporting events, hockey games, and other events in the Hampton Roads area of Virginia. About a decade ago, we got involved with working really large motor sports events. Things like monster truck shows and supercross. Events that I really had never been to and never really watched. But the real fun part about getting to work these events is that they were really large operations, which posed a huge logistical challenge for me. That's part of what I really enjoyed about doing them. I didn't really care about the monster truck show, or the silly souvenirs that we would sell. I really enjoyed the aspect of having to make it happen; going into town three days before the event, having to get it set up, having to find a large staff and making it work, and coming out after the event knowing we did as well as we could.

Andrew Coplon:　　For these events, I would go all over, from up north into Indiana to down south into Alabama. Sadly, I never made it to New Orleans, but some day hopefully my travels will take me there. I would go to these large stadiums, and let's say I was working at the Atlanta Mercedes-Benz Stadium, which is a 60,000 person stadium in downtown Atlanta. A monster truck show, for example, might draw 50,000 people. Just imagine a stadium usually used for football, full of 50,000 people for a monster truck event. These stadium crowds were really impressive. I would take with me somewhere between 15 to 20 people from Virginia who knew what was going on, who had skills in these operations. Then I would have to hire local staff to make the rest of the operation work. Part of the local staff that I would hire were the people who would walk around and sell the souvenirs. It is a lot of people. Imagine you are at a baseball game. There is the beer guy, the hot-dog guy, the snow cone guy like I once was. I used to be the guy walking up and down the bleachers selling those products, but now I am the guy responsible for hiring all of these local people that are necessary to make the event run smoothly in Atlanta.

Andrew Coplon: What I would do is, I'd post an ad on the internet on Craigslist, Indeed, and other job sites that you've probably heard of. I'd have hundreds of people apply. The first challenge was getting them on the phone. I would call in advance and say, "Hey, I'm Andrew with Flamingo Joe's. You applied for a job with us." I'd give the quick rundown to the people that I actually got on the phone. Out of say 200 that may apply, I probably only get half of them on the phone. Even though they applied for the position, they don't return my calls, they don't return my emails. They took the initiative to apply, but they don't end up following through and answering my call or calling me back. If I talked to 100 people, let's say out of those 100 people, I hired 80 of them. At the end of the day when it's the time for the event, only about half the people would normally show up for the job. So, 200 people applied, talk to 100, 80 people got hired for the position, 40 people might show up for work, and out of those 40 who show up for work, just a small percentage were what I would deem quality workers.

Andrew Coplon: For me, it became exceedingly tough to find quality staff, because just as you said in the statement, *"From the Lip to the Hip"*, people don't always do what they say they are going to do. I met a lot of interesting workers, out of those people I would meet. I met people who were like myself who really want to work hard. Those are the people that I remember. But I would also meet a lot of people who might not have had the skillset or motivation to actually make it to work or even show up. So, it gave me the opportunity to interact with people from all walks of life and to see and observe different people's work ethics, which became really quite interesting and fun.

Steve Coplon: You learned so much about managing people through all this, that you later had an idea where you could use all that you had learned. I said earlier that you are an entrepreneur, but I haven't mentioned yet that you were a marketing major in college. It would probably be good now to transition into how that skill of being able to recruit people combined with your passion helped you to start a business. Today's show is about applied passion. So, let's phase into what you've done in your life that is of great note; that has grown into a huge success with unlimited opportunity. One of the reasons why you're on the show today, is to share this part of your story. It will inspire many people. You know that I am a business consultant. You've watched me work at it your entire life. So, when I told you when you first shared with me your new business idea, that it is one of the best ideas I had ever seen with close to unlimited potential, you knew that I had a strong basis for my comment. What's great is that you are realizing that potential by the month. Every month is better than the month before. That is what businesses dream of happening. You were smart to connect with the Old Dominion University Entrepreneurial Center. This is like a mystery show. I am sure the suspense is killing everyone listening. How about telling the listeners what you do?

Andrew Coplon: While I was running the food service business, I was always enjoying the challenge of it. In the back of my mind, I was always thinking of other really fun ways that I could put my skill-set to use. It is also nice to make a little money while you're doing something. I am always thinking of new business ideas, so I created one that I thought was pretty cool. I'm a big craft beer fan. There are breweries popping up all over the country right now. I know you don't drink, but you know that they are becoming a big part of communities everywhere. They are social gathering spots. So, as the craft beer industry was continuing to grow, I knew that these breweries had to do more than just make great beer. I mean, right now there's over 8,000 breweries in the country, and if you're not making really good beer, then no one is going to go to your brewery.

Andrew Coplon: So, I wanted to take the skills I learned through Flamingo Joe's, the food service company, while I was working at special events and apply them to another business idea. I learned that whether you're at a baseball game or a monster truck show, you're not just there for the baseball game or the monster truck show, whatever it may be. You're there for the overall experience. People like to experience fun and exciting things. So, I wanted to create a mystery shopping company for breweries and help them maximize that customer experience. Because when you go to a brewery, if you just go for a beer or you go to a restaurant just for a hamburger, you're not just going for that, you're going for the staff interaction, you're going to learn about the company. You're going because you enjoy the community aspect that you feel while you're there.

Andrew Coplon: As you know, dad, my wife, Stacie, and I, created a company called **Secret Hopper,** which is a mystery shopping company for breweries. As I mentioned, we wanted to help breweries maximize their customer experience for two reasons. One, the guest would spend more money while they're there, and two, they would also come back. At the end of the day, it's about creating really positive memories at these community establishments.

Steve Coplon: Andrew, I'm going to read something that you wrote. When you and I were talking about what we were going to try to bring out in this show, we agreed that it would be basically about you being a young entrepreneur and how you have brought together all of your life experiences, but mostly your tremendous passion. Andrew, you wrote this, and then what I wrote for the title and description of the show came out of this. You said you would like to mention something like, "Andrew started working at the age of 16 selling snow cones at minor league baseball games. He quickly learned the value of hard work and building relationships. Now Andrew runs two similar, but different companies and he is passionate about helping others succeed while providing them with the means to better themselves as well as their businesses. He believes in the value of creating memorable positive experiences, whether at a baseball game or while at a brewery. Success is defined by the strength of the community you build around yourself." I think we're doing what we set out to do today.

Steve Coplon: Andrew, you've been fortunate to be in a leadership position, being the boss wherever you've worked. You've always given people a chance whenever you could. I know a lot of people. I bet that I've sent you 15 or 20 people whose parents said, "Oh wow, your son does that. Would he let my son work for him?" You have a philosophy that I'll let you explain, why you always say, "Sure, Dad. I'll let anybody work."

Andrew Coplon: Well, everybody deserves a chance. If you can come to a job with no skills needed for that job; and learn the skills and have a positive attitude for something like selling snow cones, and you put the effort into it, you're going to see results. One of the biggest characteristics I look for when I train someone isn't necessarily hiring someone with experience but hiring someone with a good positive attitude. Because you can take someone with a good positive attitude, who might be unskilled and train them, and teach them, and get to know them. Just by motivating them and helping them out, they're helping you out. So, it becomes a really mutual relationship because you're both seeing a benefit from it. I'm getting a hard worker out of it and they're getting a place of employment where they enjoy being. That ties into the passion aspect. If I'm passionate about what I'm doing, whether it's helping a brewery out or helping someone sell snow cones at a baseball game, that passion is contagious. If you can get excited, you can get someone else excited about their job. When you do that, that energy is dangerous in a good way because it catches on to someone like a wildfire, and when they start enjoying that environment, they're going to be more successful.

Steve Coplon: I couldn't agree with you more. One of the central themes that we're bringing today is building whatever you do around your passion. So, you do have some passions, Andrew. You love to travel, and what you do now is filled with travel. When you travel for a Flamingo Joe's event, you take four or five people with you to set up. What do you call it when you arrive a couple days before the event and open up the 18-wheeler that holds all of the inventory that you will be selling? Stocking up?

Andrew Coplon: Setting up.

Steve Coplon: Setting up. Well, I'm pleased that as hard as you work, as hard driving as you are, literally, you take books with you to read. You do a lot of hiking in national parks, and state parks, and catch some interesting sights along the way. What are some of the places that you have seen in the last few years that stand out in your mind?

Andrew Coplon: Stacie and I have been to quite a few interesting places. Utah was an amazing place. Montana was fantastic. We really enjoy the Western United States because when you go to these places, it's almost like you're on a foreign planet, just the way the landscapes are so different and unique. It's the freedom of being outside and exploring that's great.

Steve Coplon: You sent Donna and I to Galena, Illinois when we drove back from Oregon in 2017.

Andrew Coplon: Yeah, I remember. That wasn't a national park, but it's just a really cool quaint small town. Stacie and I love visiting small places where you can experience their culture over a couple days.

Steve Coplon: So, I'd say that as hard working as you are, you find ways to relax. Hey, as driven as you are and as driven as I am, it is always difficult to be able to slow down a bit and relax. But what are some other ways that you relax?

Andrew Coplon: I like to drive. So, even though I've driven a lot in my life, I enjoy the time while I am on the road. I especially like going to national parks. I like traveling. I enjoy good food and good drink, reading books. These are ways that I can escape and take my mind off the work that I might have spent a lot of hours on that day.

Steve Coplon: Relaxing is so important, but you use your time productively. I mean when you're on the road, staying in hotels or camping out, you're always reading. That's a beautiful thing. Andrew, your mystery shopper company, Secret Hopper, you've had it for three years this May. Do I have that right?

Andrew Coplon: That's right.

Steve Coplon: The coronavirus pandemic that we're going through right now, has really slowed things down. I'm sure that it has affected your business. You told me once, that except for one month early on, you have experienced a higher gross each month over the previous month.

That upward climb is unbelievable. I mentioned earlier that you went to the Old Dominion University Entrepreneurial Center in the very beginning. They welcomed you and embraced your product. What was it like going to them and getting some help from them?

Andrew Coplon: Well, I've always been a firm believer in outside feedback. It's nice to hear someone else's opinion, their ideas. When you're working in your own business 24 hours a day, you're just seeing it from one angle, but when you talk to someone else about it, they're looking at it for the first time and giving you a fresh perspective on something that could be beneficial for you. The ODU Entrepreneurial Center has become a community that I'm part of. I still meet up with them weekly for about an hour. We communicate now virtually to talk about business ideas. The basic philosophy is that when you get involved in an entrepreneurial community, even though you're talking to other people whose businesses may be completely different than yours, when you listen to them talk about their businesses, there might be one little takeaway that you could apply to your business that could help you succeed even more. So, it's really about the spirit of community and just participating in conversation that can help you and others better yourselves and your own businesses. The Old Dominion University Entrepreneurial Center has been really a great resource for me.

Steve Coplon: The ODU Entrepreneurial Center would never have worked with you, and many of the other opportunities that you've developed in your life would never have advanced, if you didn't do what you say you're going to do. That is so basic with you. You make a commitment, you fulfill it. Four episodes ago, I interviewed Johnnie Lloyd, one of my newest best friends. She talked about the importance of punctuality and said that if she's on time, she's late. That's how you are also. A great character trait.

Steve Coplon: Let's go back to your childhood for a moment. I have a note here about something you did in elementary school that has a lot to do with your current approach to your business. It's about passion and making things fun, something you and I have in common. If you're going to be really good at something, you've got to love doing it. We did a fun project for a science fair that both Lindsey and Josh were able to later use. Do you remember the foul shooting project that you did for science fair that we put together?

Andrew Coplon: Yes.

Steve Coplon: Let me hear what you remember about it, because that was the best we've ever done.

Andrew Coplon: Oh, that was a long time ago, but I remember it was me shooting at the basketball hoop in our driveway, to see what percentage of shots I would make. I believe it was from certain distances.

Steve Coplon: Yeah, yeah. We did layups, foul shots, and three-pointers.

Andrew Coplon: Yep.

Steve Coplon: I remember coaching you on a team in the YMCA Youth Basketball League. You and your friend, Jonathan Meyerholtz, both loved to shoot three-pointers. You didn't want to give him the ball because he would be under the basket and then he'd dribble back out to three point range and hawk it up there. That is what gave me the idea for your science fair project. We wanted to prove through the hypothesis method that the closer you are to the basket, the higher the percentage that you're going to make the shot. So, every day you would shoot 300 shots; 100 layups, 100 foul shots, and 100 three-pointers, and we would chart the number that you made and the number that you missed. It proved beyond the shadow of a doubt that if you are right under the basket and can shoot a simple little layup, you're probably going to make around 90% or higher of your shots. Foul shots, maybe 40 to 50%, and three-pointers maybe 10%. I enjoyed that, we had fun doing that project. You had science to back you when you told Jonathan to take the layup when he was under the basket. Josh couldn't believe it when it came time for his science fair. I said, "Why don't you use Andrew's?" It was a no-brainer for him. You also combined your love for baseball with a school assignment when you wrote papers on Jackie Robinson breaking the racial barrier and Curt Flood pioneering free agency. You have always found ways to mix the handling of responsibilities with things that you are interested in.

Steve Coplon: Let's go back to Secret Hopper. You talked about creating an experience. Basically, what you do is, you pair people that like to go to craft breweries and have them do a mystery shopper report. You developed a questionnaire with 25 questions that your secret hopper fills out and then you share it with the owner of the craft brewery. The owner learns a great deal that will help to better manage the business. It shows things that could be done better. The feedback that you provide to the owner will increase profits. An example of a question is: "Did your server offer your patron something to take home?" You told me that the survey doesn't grade the beer. You don't tell them that their beer is good or bad. I think I've got a fair understanding of your business. Your goal of creating a positive experience is really something that any business can benefit from. Please tell us about more about the concept behind Secret Hopper.

Andrew Coplon: Well, it goes back to that foul shooting science project. When you do something 100 times and you start to collect the data on it, you prove it scientifically that certain things can be a certain way. Obviously, when you do the layups, you're going to make a higher percentage of layups versus the three-point shots, but you're actually proving it. While it might seem like common sense, it's nice to have the data behind it. So, through Secret Hopper, what we've done is kind of take the same foul shooting approach and apply it to breweries. While it might seem like common sense, if you offer a guest a recommendation or make a suggestion at a brewery, they're going to spend more money. When you have 5,000 people go to breweries, you find out that when the bartender or server offers the suggestion, they're spending 25% more than when the bartender or server doesn't offer a suggestion. It's a way that they can improve their business. So, what we do through Secret Hopper is pay attention to the little things that can ultimately make an experience more profitable for a business, but also more memorable. When a visit is more memorable, the customer is more likely to become a repeat customer.

Steve Coplon: It's absolutely brilliant, and I'm sure it's going to continue to grow. So right now, you hire a part-time person every now and then, but mostly it's just you and Stacie running the whole operation.

Andrew Coplon: Oh no. I mean, it's not typically me and Stacie doing it. Unfortunately, we're not the ones going to the breweries.

Steve Coplon: Oh, I'm sorry. I'm talking about the administration, the management.

Andrew Coplon: Okay. It's been a fun process with regard to running the company. Stacie, my wife, is the only actual employee, although I had to let her go recently, which is unfortunate due to the coronavirus slowdown. But we actually found other people to use as subcontractors. My brother, Josh, is one of them. We have a student at the University of Virginia who helps us out sometimes as a subcontractor. We found people who are also really hard workers able to help us out. I don't know if you knew this, Dad, but we actually have someone we use, he lives in Bangladesh, who is pretty much my assistant through all of this. He lives over there, and I just give him lots of fun projects for him to work on that are really helpful to me. It takes things off my plate and it helps him out because he has a source of income that he gets to use just from working from home.

Steve Coplon: Dave Richards, a founding member of Right Thinking Foundation, who recorded an episode on the show three weeks ago, found out about partnering with people in India years ago. That's wonderful that you are doing that.

Andrew, I think we've covered a whole lot about you today, about where you came from and how you got to be the way you are. I have always made it a point to not ask many questions or make comments about your relationships when you were dating. I am thrilled to share that when you got engaged and introduced me to Stacie, ever since then, just about every time I ever see her, I tell her that she's my bonus daughter, the love child that I never saw coming.

Andrew Coplon: Yeah. Stacie is fantastic!

Steve Coplon: I thank you for all of the wonderful things you've done in your life. The two best that you've ever done, is marrying Stacie, and now bringing Max into this world!

Andrew Coplon: Max is awesome! They're downstairs playing right now.

Steve Coplon: Through the coronavirus separation, the hardest things for me to go through has been having to cancel the trip to Lindsey's in Oregon for Stella's first birthday, not seeing Willie while I was going to be there and not hanging out with Max. I was really enjoying taking him for walks and playing with him. It was great the other day seeing him on Facetime, watching him standing up by himself with such good balance. Yeah, he'll be a great athlete like you.

This is interesting for me. I never get to ask you these kinds of questions. Andrew, look at your life for a minute. You're an entrepreneur. You've worked hard. What's changed now that you're a husband and a father in your outlook towards your future?

Andrew Coplon: Well, I've had to move my office upstairs, that's the first thing.

Steve Coplon: That's a good response.

Andrew Coplon: I don't know how I'd be as productive as I need to be if I had my office in the living room still. So that's definitely changed. I think I'm always trying to find ways to grow my business, but at the same time, be able to spend more time with my family. The goal is to find success and work less, which I think is everyone's goal. And also, to travel more. I'm actively taking steps to get there.

Steve Coplon: What do you think Max's world is going to look like when he's your age?

Andrew Coplon: That's a question I don't think any of us know the answer to right now. I think on my end, I'd like for him to be comfortable with whoever he is. Not have to worry about finances, but also have a brain where he's constantly thinking and wanting to create things himself. I think creativity is something we definitely want him to be passionate about.

Steve Coplon:	That's beautiful. Andrew, I've been asking this next question my whole life to many, many people, and I'm going to give you my answer after you give me yours. If you were to leave this world right now, what is the most important thing that you want to make sure that you pass on to your children that will help them succeed in life?

Andrew Coplon: I think that's really already been summed up in this episode so far. Honestly, staying positive. That's the most important thing you can do, stay positive, and also hard work. You're not going to get anywhere just by sitting back and watching the world. I hope Max grows up knowing the value of hard work, and also having a really positive attitude to go along with it, because if he has those two qualities, he'll be able to do whatever he wants to do.

Steve Coplon: Beautiful answer! That is very close to what my answer is. I'm going to tell you, before I tell you mine, that Max has already got it. I have never seen a child as happy as he is. Every time that I am around him, he just gives me that ear to ear grin. He is just an absolutely adorable, happy child. You and Stacie are doing a beautiful job with him. So, my three things that I've always said that I would like to pass on to my children are one, enthusiasm.

Andrew Coplon: Definitely.

Steve Coplon: Yeah, and you've got it. Two, politeness, and three, to smile. Now, these aren't any particular traits of intelligence or anything like that, but I tell you, Andrew. If you drop a person off at a truck stop or at a bus stop somewhere, any part of the world, and they've got those three things going for them, they're going to be able to take it from there and make it. Being enthusiastic, having that passion like you've got, being polite and respectful of other people, and giving a warmth and a radiance to other people with a smile that's welcoming, people will feed you. I've learned that myself, people will pick you up, take you in and help you out.

Steve Coplon: Andrew, you know I always like to bring a piece of scripture into the show. I'll do some Old Testament in honor of you being here today. I've actually chosen two:

Proverbs 21:5

"The plans of the diligent lead to profit as surely as haste leads to poverty."

Steve Coplon: I guess we could say truer words have never been spoken.

Andrew Coplon: Yeah, very good.

Steve Coplon: This second scripture weaves your story, your character, and your integrity, that I'm so proud of as your dad, into this episode on doing what you say you're going to do:

Proverbs 12:14

"From the fruit of their lips people are filled with good things, and the work of their hands brings them reward."

Steve Coplon: Andrew, it's been my wonderful honor and pleasure to have you, my son, on this episode with me and to be part of this series. Is there anything you'd like to say as we close, words of advice or something, you'd like to pass on to everyone?

Andrew Coplon: I think just to reiterate a lot of things we've already said to whoever is listening right now, that wherever you are in life right now is not necessarily where you're going to be tomorrow. If you stay positive, you stay passionate, and you work hard, you can get in a better place, whether it's starting your own business or just starting to work the baseball stadium, having fun selling snow cones. It doesn't necessarily matter what your position is, it's important to know that you enjoy it, you're in a positive atmosphere, and you're happy. I mean, that's the most important thing you can be. You want to position yourself in a place to be happy with yourself, and your family, and those around you.

Steve Coplon: Andrew, that was absolutely beautiful. I just want to tell you I love you, I'm proud of you.

Andrew Coplon: You too, Dad.

Steve Coplon: God Bless you in everything that you ever do. Thanks, Andrew.

Andrew Coplon: Thanks. Appreciate it.

Steve Coplon: Thanks for listening to *Right Thinking with Steve Coplon*. I look forward to being with you again next week. Remember: ***Don't Quit, Plan Ahead, It Will Get Better.*** God Bless you and have a great week!

To listen to the original interview, scan this QR Code with your camera, or visit:
https://rightthinkingeducation.com/FromtheLiptotheHip/Chapter-12/

CHAPTER THIRTEEN
Managing Expectations And Initiatives with guest Jim Stovall
Right Thinkings With Steve Coplon - Episode 171

Steve Coplon: Good morning. Welcome to *Right Thinking with Steve Coplon.* I'm your host, Steve Coplon. Thank you for tuning in. Let's have a great day!

Steve Coplon: Good morning everybody. Glad to be with you. Well, you've heard me say it over and over, week after week, but today it might go down in history as one of my very most special moments on *Right Thinking with Steve Coplon.* Episode 171, *Right Thinking with Steve Coplon* is very pleased to announce that this week's show is called *"Managing Expectations and Initiatives,"* with guest Jim Stovall. Tune in and hear Steve and Jim talk about how we control keeping our word, by being more careful when we give our word. Bestselling author, internationally renowned storyteller, Jim's wisdom has changed the lives of millions, and it will change your life too. I'm going to get right into it because I don't want to waste a single moment of this opportunity that we all have, to have Jim be my guest again.

Steve Coplon: He was on Episode 109, *"A Message from Jim Stovall"*. To get more of Jim's background, you can go back to that episode after listening to this show. I'm not going to give his phenomenal credentials, I'm not going to give them at all. Instead, I hope to have a conversation today that's from one man to another, who's here for one purpose and one purpose only. It's to try to help each one of us, and all of you listening, to come closer to the Lord and have a better life. And that's why we're here. Jim, thanks for being my guest today.

Jim Stovall: It is always great to be with you, and your viewers around the world. I appreciate it.

Steve Coplon: Well, Jim, I have a special hello that I'm supposed to give you. Dwayne Malave, he wished me well today, and said to say hi to you, and to thank you for introducing him to me. So, hello from Dwayne.

Jim Stovall: Well, I'm glad the two of you got connected.

Steve Coplon: You did me a real blessing when you connected me with him, he's just a beautiful person. So, we won't even talk about the background on that. We'll just get right into why you're my guest today. Episode 159 is called *"From the Lip to the Hip is a Pretty Far Distance."* And when I recorded that show, I realized that I wanted to get a lot of people who I respect because of what they've done with their lives, and their wisdom needs to be shared. And so, Jim, you are the final episode in this series. I'm saving the best for last.

Steve Coplon:	The series is about character building and integrity. The whole idea of Episode 159 is about doing what you say you're going to do. I use Napoleon Hill's famous *"Fifty-Seven Famous Alibis by Old Man IF."* I asked you to listen to it in preparation for this interview. Being the man of your word that I know you are, I'm sure you listened to it.
Jim Stovall:	I did. And I really enjoyed the quote from your mother. I had heard Hill's 57, what I call excuses, before. But the admonition and the wisdom from your mom, was really great.
Steve Coplon:	Yeah, I was blessed with a wonderful mom, as were you. So, was there anything in that show that you relate to, that I said correctly perhaps, that you agree?
Jim Stovall:	Well, I think overall, the importance of keeping your word is, an overly simplistic concept. But in the world today, it's much more complicated than it used to be, because we have all these variables in our lives and oftentimes, we avoid the discomfort of being totally honest, totally transparent, totally frank with people. And so, we tell people, "Maybe I'll call you back," or, "I'll try to be there," or whatever.
Jim Stovall:	And, one of my favorite scriptures is, "Let your yay be yay, and your nay be nay." Just tell people what you're going to do. And it makes life much simpler, and it makes you become a person that is known to be an individual of integrity.
Steve Coplon:	Jim, I'm going to do this early in the show. I was thinking I might wait until later, but I'll do it now. I want to give just a little teeny bit of backstory. Three years ago, give or take, Don Green, sent me approximately 56 copies of the book *"One Season of Hope."* I was teaching at a high school for the "at risk", called An Achievable Dream. I gave every student in that financial literacy class, a copy of the book. I read the book, and when I finished reading it, I called your office and your assistant answered the phone, I think her name was Beth.
Steve Coplon:	And I said, "Beth, my name is Steve Coplon, I have a foundation called Right Thinking Foundation and I would like," first I asked, could I speak to you, and she said you were tied up at the moment. I said, "I would like you to give him this message. Would you please tell him, that I just finished *reading "One Season of Hope,"* and the last 30 pages I was unable to see the words clearly because the tears were just streaming from my face. And I would like to just tell you that, would you please pass that message on to Jim?" And she said, "I will."
Steve Coplon:	You called me back 30 minutes later, and that's how I first met you, Jim. You have done more for me, than you can ever realize, and you've helped me so much. I've talked on show after show about how the main point I've gleaned from you is, you've helped me get rid of distractions and stay very, very focused. That's a whole theme that you've helped me through. Then after that, you talked to me probably three times within the next week or two, for a total of over two hours. You gave your time to me, and I wanted to come visit you, on my way to prison in Oregon.
Steve Coplon:	We're talking about people who do what they say they're going to do. You told me I could visit, but a couple of days later when I called to schedule it, you had retracted that. And let your yes be yes, and your no, be no. And I said, "Why?" And you said, "Well Steve, I think that you're looking for something from me that I'm not able to give you." And I said, "All I want to do is meet you, and shake your hand." And I gave you a whole story of why I wanted that. I gave you two stories of people who I had met in my life.

Steve Coplon:	One of them was Fred Pryor a motivational speaker who I had a chance to have a conversation with. He changed my life. And the day that I met him, he had recited *Robert Frost*, **"The Road Not Taken,"** just so unbelievable. I'll never forget it.
Steve Coplon:	And then I met Eugene Cernan, who was at VCU while I was there, in Richmond. He had just come back from a journey to the moon, and he gave a lecture, a talk, discussing the religious experience he had or the spiritual experience he had, standing on the moon looking back at the earth. So, I said to you, "I think that I'm in for an experience like that if I get a chance to meet you." And you continued to say, "All right, if you really want to come, and all you really want to do is meet me, then I'll let you come for 15 minutes."
Steve Coplon:	Well, I accepted that, and I want you to know that over 20 of my close friends and family said, "Hey Steve, you don't get it, man. He doesn't want you to come. He's trying to blow you off." And Don Green was the only one that got it. He said, "Steve, I've known you for five years now, and in all that time of knowing you, that's the very best thing that you've done. So just, make sure, you don't go a second over 15 minutes."
Jim Stovall:	Right.
Steve Coplon:	And so, I came, and I told you when I got there that this journey for me, I drove 900 miles out of my way just to come shake your hand. And I brought you some sea salt dark chocolate caramel ice cream sauce.
Jim Stovall:	I remember that.
Steve Coplon:	I figured that was the. Yeah. It was good, wasn't it?
Jim Stovall:	Absolutely.
Steve Coplon:	And I told you that this was like going to the mountain and asking the Oracle of Delphi a question. And the question that I asked you was, "Jim, will you do one thing for me?" And I had already agreed not to ask anything of you, but you said yes. And I said, "I'm going to prison in Oregon, Baker City, Oregon. To Powder River Correctional." And I asked, "Would you share something with me that I can say to those men, so they'll know that I'm bringing you along in spirit, and I'm not just there by myself." Do you remember? I'd rather you repeat it if you remember. I'll help you if you don't, but I know you do. Do you remember what you said to me?
Jim Stovall:	Well, I remember some of what we talked about, and taking the message that your past doesn't equal your future. You change your life when you change your mind. And, something to redirect the thinking, beyond yesterday and today into tomorrow.
Steve Coplon:	Yeah, it was that. And now your message is in my curriculum, being marketed into prisons all over the country. When you change your thinking, you change your life, and so forth. The reason this is so absolutely beautiful is without a moment of hesitation you said, "Steve, you tell those men, that if you were the only person on this earth, that God would have done the exact same thing with his son on that cross for you, because he loves you that much." And then you went on to say, "And you let them know, that in every adversity, failure and hardship there's a seed of benefit that's equal or greater."
Steve Coplon:	And when I got there and delivered that message, those men listened to every word I had to impart. And I gave them my library, I gave them a couple of your books, and so forth.

So, Jim, that was kind of the beginning, and now we're maybe three years later. And you introduced me to Dwayne Malave, that I've mentored for three years now.

Steve Coplon: Here's what I want to tell you next. I hope you can sort of take over for a while and just share your thoughts. I'm not giving them any of your background right now. They don't need that. When you speak, they'll know who you are. I related quite incredibly when I read your book, *"One Season of Hope."* Everybody knows my story about my terminal illness, I share it freely. Well, *"One Season of Hope"* really got to me, because it's about a high school boy who's got cancer and a very short time to live.

Steve Coplon: And in preparing for this conversation that you and I are having, I read that book last night and this morning. It's 170 pages of Harry Truman's wisdom woven into your personal story. And Jim, your personal story is throughout this book, in ways that I didn't even catch on to the first time I read it. Your story is about a football player by the name of Latrelle Johnston, and it's your story, too. Latrelle went on to the pros, he's the guy that you could have been. I mean, he's the guy that you were, but it stopped somewhere along the way.

Steve Coplon: The first time I read this book I left you a message with Beth. You promptly returned my call. I told her that the last 30 pages of the book, I couldn't see the words, because tears were dropping. I've matured a lot, since that day three years ago. I got to the last 25 pages today. And I could not, I just couldn't stop crying. The tears were streaming down my face. So, I just want everybody to listen. I'm going to turn it over to Jim for a little while, because I also want to hear more from him, because he's done so much for me already, and I want him to do so much for you.

Steve Coplon: We can have a conversation, and I know Jim wants that too. I have read so many of your books including your newest, *"Will to Win"*. My wife is immersed in it right now, and it's a beautiful book. Also, everything you do is beautiful. But, *"One Season of Hope"*, is especially beautiful, take my word everyone, read this book. It is absolutely amazing. It's about character. It's about life, it's about moving forward. It's about love.

Steve Coplon: Jim, this series that I'm doing, I think is going to end up being my legacy. It incorporates what I've always cared about, which is honoring your good name, character, and integrity. Opposite the last page of your book, where it describes the author, the last line reads: Jim Stovall can be reached at, your number and jimstovall.com, and that's why I called you. Because you offered an invitation. It was an ultra-call for me, and I accepted it. Last paragraph of the book says:

Harry Truman

"Fame is a vapor. Popularity is an accident. Riches take wings. Those who cheer you today may curse you tomorrow, and only one thing endures. Character."

Steve Coplon: That's a quote from Harry Truman. Jim God Bless you. Thank you.

Jim Stovall: Well, thank you. And the way I had the privilege of meeting you, is the way I get to meet a lot of people. I have written 47 books I think now, eight of them have been turned into movies. And in all of my books, there are 10 million of them in print, I have my contact information listed. And I've had publishers and other authors tell me for years, "You can't do that." Well, I beg to differ. I've been doing it for 25 years, and I return all my calls, and I'm available to people.

Jim Stovall: But you have to manage expectations and intentions. You have to have your yes, be yes and your no, be no. Because when you have 10 million people, all of whom you've given a free invitation to call you, and they've done nothing more than read one of your books. You have to be prepared to become your word. Because no matter what message I give in one of my books or in my movies, if I tell people you can call me, and they find out you can't, well then everything else I said before that in the book or the movie doesn't really matter.

Jim Stovall: And, as a blind person myself, the most debilitating thing about being blind is not the fact that you can't see. It's that no one has any expectations of you. If I did nothing with my life and sat in a room by myself and played the radio, people would say, "Well, that's good. At least he can play the radio. And he does that." They don't expect me to start a television network, and write a syndicated column, and 40 some odd books and eight movies and give arena speeches, and become a multimillionaire, and do all the things that have happened to me. You have to be internally motivated.

Jim Stovall: And as a very young man, I had the blessing of having a mentor, named Lee Braxton. He was quite elderly at the time, and he had a third grade education, and had become a multimillionaire during the Great Depression. And, I wanted him to just give me the shortcut, the simple way, "How do you get rich?" And he made me read "**Think and Grow Rich,**" and made me read it three times. That connection is how you and I met because I didn't know that at the time. But Lee Braxton was Napoleon Hill's best friend. He gave the eulogy at Hill's funeral, and they were friends for 30 plus years.

Jim Stovall: The things he taught me, were not get rich quick schemes like, buying some penny stock, or getting into some business or some little trick, or some secret. He said, "Well, if you really want to know how to get rich, get out a pencil and paper. Here's the thing. Number one," and it was number one, "Always do what you say." And then we went on into, "Deliver more than you promise." We went into, "Create value in the lives of other people." We went into, "Avoid excuses," and all those things. But number one was, you do what you say you're going to do. Otherwise, no one will ever do business with you. I mean, you do what you say you're going to do.

Jim Stovall: And that does a couple of things for you, Steve. Number one, it makes you become known as a person of honor. Number two, it makes you very careful what you tell people you're going to do. And we, in our society, avoid telling people, no. "No, I'm not going to do that." And we always want to come up with some excuse, why we can't do what they want us to do. And so, we kind of have these halfway commitments, to too many things. And, I do one speech for free, for everyone I get paid for. And when I do an arena speech, I make more money than the average family of four that lives in my state does, in a whole year. I make that for an hour, on stage.

Jim Stovall: When I'm willing to go out for charity, and do them for free, and we do have a lot of a demand for those, we have to come up with a system that works. Well, I was reticent for years to tell people, "No." So, I'd say, "Well, I'm not free on that date," or whatever. And, ironically, people would move their whole convention to fit my schedule.

Jim Stovall: Then Oprah said something, I'll never forget. She said, "You don't owe people an explanation. You owe them the truth." So, when people would ask Oprah, "Can you come and make this appearance, on the 18th?" She would either say yes, or she would say, "No, that's not going to work for me." And you don't owe them anything else. But what you do owe them is your yes is yes, and your no is no. And that, more than any single thing will change your world because people would commit to far fewer things if they knew beyond a shadow of a doubt, that they were going to have to do all these things.

Jim Stovall: Now, right now, and as you and I are having this conversation, I know this show will be evergreen, because people will watch it or hear it for many years. As you and I are speaking, it's Holy Week and we're in the middle of the corona-virus crisis, right now. Because of this pandemic a lot of people are not able to keep their word. But the minute you're not able to keep your word, you owe the people you have given your word to, an explanation and some way to work it out. There are people who, through no fault of their own, are not able to make their mortgage payment. They're not able to make their rent payment. They're not able to be places and do things they promised they would be and do. Those things happen. I wish I could control everything, but I can't. And those things happen.

Jim Stovall: The minute you know you're not going to be able to keep your word, you've got to protect your word, and you go out to those people. Number one, you admit, "I gave you my word, and because of these conditions beyond my control, I'm not going to be able to do that. So, let's come up with something I can do, to create value for you, and for me to fulfill the obligation I gave to you." And those are very, very important things to do, particularly during difficult times. We forget that quite often, but we owe those people those things.

Jim Stovall: I just would encourage people to be very cautious, when you give your word, because you're going to keep it. And you've got to write those down. I have been in meetings, Steve, and I know you have too, where I have seen guys promise to be two or three places, all at the same time on the same day. And, they give their word easily and they break their promises just as easily. Well, anything I promise to anyone, whether it's you or millions of my readers or anything else, it goes into a book in writing.

Jim Stovall: And because my word is important to me, more than it's probably important to the people around me... Because you know, most of the lies we tell Steve, are lies we tell ourselves. We tell ourselves lies and then, we accept that untruth and share it with the world. But if you know you're going to do everything you say you're going to do; it changes that. And the same thing happens, whether you make a goal or a new year's resolution, or anything else. When you promise yourself something, you've got to keep your word to yourself. "Hey, I said I would do this, and I need to get out there and do that."

Jim Stovall: And probably the most important thing, anybody who has children or if you interact with kids in any way, your word has got to be gold. It has got to be gold, good and bad. If you tell them, "You do this good thing, and I'm going to do something good for you," or, "You break this rule, and you're going to have to deal with the consequences." In both cases, your word has got to become reality for those young people.

Jim Stovall: So, I think that is probably the most important thing we could ever do to, to build success, and then to keep success. You've got to be your word.

Steve Coplon: Jim, I thank you for that message. I want to come back to something that I want to make sure I point out to you. When we talked and I invited you to do this interview, we talked about the baseball season not going on this year. We actually talked on Opening Day. You had recommended a book to me, and that's when I found out about your love for baseball. I was aware about your love for football, but I didn't know about your love for baseball. And so, you wrote another book on baseball. Actually, I apologize for the way I said that.

Steve Coplon:	Your most recent book, **"Will to Win"** in your *Homecoming Historical Series,* is about baseball. And oh, it's a wonderful book. So, I called you on Opening Day of this season, with the baseball season being canceled, indefinitely. And we started talking about it, and you said to me right away, "Have you read *'The Twelfth Angel'*, Og Mandino's book?" I said, "No," but I went ahead and ordered the e-book right away, due to the fact that the physical copy had a two-month delay for shipping.
Jim Stovall:	Right.
Steve Coplon:	Come to find out, I did have that book. I read that book when it first came out. In the year 2000, I was coaching "little league coach pitch." I coached a lot of little league baseball, and so forth. And Jim, 2000, was a good year for you. That's the year that you received the International Humanitarian of the Year Award if I'm correct. Well, on my desk right here is a little marble stand with a baseball glove, and it says, *"The Athletics, 2000, thanks, Coach Steve, for a great season."* In the stand is a baseball. It's been on my desk since 2000. I see it every day when I sit at my desk. It gives me such inspiration, but I want to tell you how things work.
Steve Coplon:	The book that got me started with you is **"One Season of Hope."** It's the story of Bradley Hope, which is all about hope. Harry Truman has all kinds of quotes in there. Harry Truman is phenomenal. The baseball in the stand has the signature of every kid that was on that team. All those little, six, seven-year old kids playing coach pitch. On the team was this one little girl who couldn't swing a bat. Even with coach pitch, you couldn't get her to even hit a ball. I sacrificed my life with this young girl. I got within four feet of her, almost to where, I could take the ball and extend it and just flip it four or five inches into her bat. Everyone was so fearful for me and would say, "Steve, she's going to hit it one day, and it's going to kill you."
Steve Coplon:	Well, her name was Hope. That's all I can tell you about that story. You know Jim, there's an expression that I picked up early out. "What goes around, comes around," and things of that nature. I've had a lot of time to reflect on my life, and you and I share a lot. You told a little bit just now about how nobody expected too much of you because of your blindness, but yet, you have just done phenomenal things.
Steve Coplon:	So, I'm going to talk in that area, just for a minute here. On page 160 of, **"One Season of Hope,"** when the team is getting ready to play in the state championship game, (which is kind of dedicated to Bradley Hope), the coach says, "You've exceeded everyone's expectations, but mine. You can win this game." And then he went on to make this profound statement. The character, "Coach Glen Fullerton", says:

"One Season of Hope"

"For the rest of this game, and for the rest of your life, always give it your all and leave your best out there on the field. You never want to be one of those sad souls, who goes through life wondering, what if? Now go out there, give it your best because your best is always good enough. And I'll always be proud of every one of you."

| Steve Coplon: | This series that we're just finishing up right now started with Don Green giving me permission to use *Napoleon Hill's,* **"Fifty-Seven Famous Alibis by Old Man IF."** You know, "if", is an amazing word. And we all use "if" at times, but we want to minimize that. And so, |

I'd like to give you an opportunity to add anything else, and then I can close out the show with just a couple more thoughts.

Steve Coplon: Jim, I guess what I'm saying is, because of my illnesses and my restrictions, it's very, very hard during this coronavirus. I'm in a very, very high-risk category, because of my immune system cancer, Multiple Myeloma, I have lots of other diagnoses that are at the top of the risk list. Chronic bronchitis, a respiratory disease, asthma, C.O.P.D. I can give you a good long list, but I'm not asking anybody to feel sorry for me, at all. I gave my life to the Lord a long, long time ago and just thank him for every day, to have the opportunity to serve him. Like Don Green says, he wakes up every single day and the first thing he does, he says, "Dear Lord, who can I help today?"

Steve Coplon: I'm surrounded with an incredible group of people, who I love and respect. What I'm basically saying is, that I've had all this time to reflect, and I really sometimes don't know how it's going to end up and where I'm trying to go. But I know one thing, I know it's going to happen because that's the faith that I have.

Steve Coplon: Again, I just want to thank you for being in my life. Jim, you're a great man and I love you. And anything you'd like to say right now to close out the show. This show's a lot shorter than most of my shows, because it doesn't need to be long. It just needs to be, to the point. I don't want to ask any specific questions about how you get people to get up out of their chair who are depressed and just won't listen. They just won't go forward. That' my biggest question that I live, in life. So maybe I will ask you, just for a thought on that. Everybody says, "You got to love them. You can't enable them. You have to let them know you're there. You never give up on them." There's a lot of people in my life, as well as in most people's lives who are depressed with their life and they just can't break the cycle.

Steve Coplon: Reading your books will pop people out if they would read. But the people who I'm talking to generally don't read. You can give them a book, you can take them to the page, but still some won't read. I think the biggest burden that I carry in my life and what the Lord has called me to do, is to help those who are falling through the cracks, and those who are at their lowest point. I love on them and empathize with them and try to give them a hug, and say, "Hey, I've been there too."

Steve Coplon: I have been there. I haven't shared a good portion of my life from the really, really dark years. When I was young, I sort of kept it inside, so to speak, however, I did come out of it. Everybody says the same thing. You can't do it for them. It's their choice. They have to make the choice. I'll ask you this in closing. Beyond the basics of loving them, letting them know that you're there, caring for them, and never giving up, what is a good way to help them? Prayer is the only answer that I've come up with. Just give it up to God. I'd like to throw that one to you.

Jim Stovall: Well, you cannot change other people and, prayer is great. Rarely does God change things. God changes people. People change things. I can sit here all day and pray that my lawn gets mowed. There are a few miracles in the Bible where it shows something like that happened. But by and large, if I want my lawn mowed, I've got to get inspired, which means the energy of God within, is what inspired me. And I've got to get there and go out and do something. God changes people. People change things. And when we can't motivate people beyond where they are, hopefully, we can give them a vision of who they might be.

Jim Stovall: We don't, life isn't fair. I get that now. I get it. I mean, you're talking to a blind guy. I get the fact that life isn't fair, and we don't always get what we want or need or deserve or earned. But we will forevermore get what we expect. And everyone listening to us or watching us right now, if you'll be totally honest with yourself, no matter how far up or down the ladder you are, you're about where you expected to be. But the great thing about that is, you can change that today. Because you change your life when you change your mind, you're one quality decision away from anything you want.

Jim Stovall: It starts, now. You have the right to choose. Anytime you don't like any part of your life, just get up off of your blessed assurance, and go change the channel. It's all about you. You get to decide. But once you decide, make a commitment, and give yourself a promise, "This is what I'm going to do." And then, keep that word to yourself. Because Steve, if you lie to yourself, you'll lie to me. So, the first person you've got to be honest with is yourself.

Jim Stovall: Then, from that day forward, tomorrow will be anything you want it to be based upon the choices you make, right now. And everybody within the sound of my voice has the wherewithal in their life to make that decision. And I can only hope and pray they will. And just like you, I will tell anybody, "Anytime you don't believe this works, anytime you need encouragement, anytime you need some help, you can email or call me."

S-T-O-V-A-L-L
jim@jimstovall.com
(918) 627-1000

Jim Stovall: And I will return your call or respond to your email every time. Because, that's a commitment I made to me. And so, I've extended it to you. So, I hope everybody who's part of this presentation today, will make a change. Because learning the information and not applying it, is about as useless as you can be. It doesn't matter what you know, it matters what you do. And we all have the ability to make that change, right now. And if not now, when? And if not you, who? Today's the day.

Steve Coplon: Today's the day. I'm going to recommend your series of **"Wisdom for Winners"**. At the end of each page it says, "Today's the Day". I recommend this strongly. If you're not a reader, but you've listened to this show, start reading. It's a great series of books to read because they're all generally about three pages. You don't have to get deep into a novel, that you can't finish, and you'll learn something from it.

Steve Coplon: And so, Jim, you've quoted Harry Truman in **"One Season of Hope,"** and I love this quote. I started copying and pasting all these great lines from that book into my notes, and it was overwhelming. I think I have brought some of them forth.

"One Season of Hope"

"It's what you learn, after you know it all, that counts."

Steve Coplon: Yeah, I like that. That one's right to the point. I'd like to end it right now with basically saying that, we set out today to talk about managing expectations and initiatives. We didn't use the word initiative, but everything Jim and I have talked about the last couple of minutes here, is about taking the initiative. Getting up out of your chair and moving forward. Don't be hung up with semantics. It's the action.

Steve Coplon:	We started off the first show in this series, *"Faith Without Works is Dead"*. We're talking about actions, and doing things, not just saying things. I did a show, I don't know what episode it was, but the title of it was *"Initiative versus Inertia."* And so, I deal with a lot of the things we're talking about there. But with that said, everyone, we've been blessed today. We've been honored by you Jim. Again, I just want to tell everyone, that in life, sometimes it takes believing that if you make that phone call, someone is going to answer it. Jim you answered my call, and you've been there for me, and we've touched a few lives together.
Steve Coplon:	I just want to say thanks for participating in this conversation with me today. Thanks for being the person that you are. And may you and your loved ones be always healthy and safe. Thank you for what you do. God Bless you, Jim.
Jim Stovall:	Thank you, sir.
Steve Coplon:	Everyone, I hope you've enjoyed this. Go out and read some books, especially Jim Stovall books. And call me if you need me, www.rightthink.org, and have a wonderful week. God Bless everyone.
Steve Coplon:	Thanks for listening to *Right Thinking with Steve Coplon*. I look forward to being with you again next week. Remember: ***Don't Quit, Plan Ahead, It Will Get Better.*** God Bless you and have a great week!

To listen to the original interview, scan this QR Code with your camera, or visit:

https://rightthinkingeducation.com/FromtheLiptotheHip/Chapter-13/

APPENDIX

THE JOURNEY TO RIGHT THINKING

by Steve Coplon

> *"Every adversity, every failure, every heartache*
> *carries with it the seed of an equal or greater benefit."*
>
> —**Napoleon Hill**

DEFINITENESS OF PURPOSE

> *"There is one quality which one must possess to win,*
> *and that is definiteness of purpose, the knowledge*
> *of what one wants, and a burning desire to possess it."*
>
> —**Napoleon Hill**

I have always known my purpose. **God** put me on this earth to love other people and help them to have a better life. I've just had a lifetime of distractions and setbacks that have kept me from fully living it.

THE SEED WAS PLANTED AT A VERY EARLY AGE

"Stevie, you're the man of the house now." I was seven years old. My mother called me into the living room. She and my sister were sitting on the couch, holding each other, and crying. There were several suitcases by the door. As my father walked into the room toward the door, my mother said, "Stevie, *your father is leaving us."* That night at dinner, mom said to me *"Stevie, you're the man of the house now."*

"Stevie, all that closeness that they say that is in Jewish families, I've never seen in my life. These Christian neighbors, they've got it right. They know how to love. We ought to be Christian." I was nine years old. We went to a Billy Graham Crusade that night and got saved. When we got home, my older sister called my father and told him what mom and I had done. He immediately called my mother, cursed her up and down and threatened that if she ever spoke another word of this to *"his"* son, he would take her back to court, have custody taken away from her, move me out of state and she would never see me again. Living outwardly as a Christian was suppressed for years, but it was in my heart.

I am so blessed to have the mother that **God** gave me. My mom's name was Rose. Nineteen years ago, when I gave the eulogy at her funeral, I said that everyone who knew my mom knows that Rose is a synonym for Love. She taught me Love. My mom was the original ***never met a stranger***, ***give you the shirt off your back*** person. She passed that on to me.

APPLIED FAITH

The 4th Principle of Napoleon Hill's Keys to Success

- 17 Principles of Personal Achievement

*"Faith is the element, the "chemical" which, when
mixed with prayer, gives one direct
communication with Infinite Intelligence."*

—Napoleon Hill

My mom had more faith than anyone that I've ever known. When her second husband would not give her any extra money to buy the ingredients for the baking that she wanted to do for family occasions, she told him that it cost two dollars a week to get the sheets done at the laundry and that she refused to do them herself. She did do the sheets, though, and that's how she got the money to take care of all of the baking that she needed to do. I will never forget when she would say to me *"Stevie, I don't know how it happened. I can't explain it but I know the exact amount of money that I put in that drawer, the two dollars every week that I've been saving, and when I went to count it today, there was five times as much in that drawer as what I put in there. The* **Lord** *did that Stevie."* I serve the same **God** as my mother.

THE ONLY ACCOUNTANT IN THE SECOND GRADE

My mother's brother, my Uncle Hy, took me to my first baseball game at Frank D. Lawrence Stadium in Portsmouth to see the Portsmouth Tides, when I was in the second grade. He was the head partner of the largest CPA firm in Norfolk. As he taught me how to keep the box score, he said *"Stevie, you'll make a great accountant one day."* *"What's an accountant?"* I asked. He said, *"A businessman that helps people with their money."* I asked, *"Why do you say that?"* He responded, *"Because you have a gift with numbers."* From that day forth, I knew that I was going to be an accountant. I was the only accountant in my second grade class on career day. Uncle Hy was the man that I admired most in my life. He was there for my mom, sister, and me when we were in need. When the wash machine broke down and my father wouldn't send any extra money because he said that he had sent enough and that my mother didn't budget it properly, Uncle Hy was there. I became an expert in budgeting.

During my senior year in high school, my accelerated English teacher, Mrs. Griffin took me out in the hallway after she read a paper that I had written comparing myself to Holden Caulfield in J.D. Salinger's classic, **Catcher in the Rye**. What I remember most from the book is that Holden could not stand phonies. Neither can I. She asked me, *"Steve, is everything in this paper true?"* I said, *"Every word of it."* She continued, *"What are you going to do with your life, Steve?"* I said, *"I'm going to be an accountant."* I knew that since I was in the second grade. *"May I say something to you that I've never said to anyone before?"* *"Please do,"* I responded. *"Steve, I've never met anyone like you. You have a gift, and I think that you should go out and live life to its fullest. Take every experience that comes your way and, when you turn forty, write about it."* From that moment on that was what I knew I wanted to do with my life. I'm about 25 years late doing it. But, at this stage in my life everyone that knows me is very pleased for me because I have my own talk radio show and because I'm writing. I am being published in national publications.

PERSISTENCE

*"Victory is always possible for the person
who refuses to stop fighting."*

—Napoleon Hill

I was a latch-key kid my entire childhood and developed great people skills. I had a paper route for three years and saved money to buy my first car. I wore hand-me-down clothes given to me from a cousin a year older and worked for all of my extras. I worked many jobs: doing yard work, in restaurants and at a fishing pier. I made extra money at the fishing pier by cleaning the toilets, a job that the owner would not ask any of the employees to do. So, I offered and increased my pay by nearly twenty-five percent. My mother did the best that she could working as a salesgirl at Lerner's Department Store in downtown Norfolk. She set every sales record and won every contest that the store had. She taught me that the secret to sales was to make friends with every customer and have them develop a trust in you. She sincerely cared about everyone. She knew that I had the gift that she had and cautioned me to use it only to help other people.

INTERRUPTED EDUCATION AND KARATE BECAME MY PASSION

The year was 1969. I went to college to study accounting, a no-brainer since that was my decision since second grade. I worked hard while in college and by the time I completed my sophomore year, I was becoming very disillusioned that I was preparing for a career that was not what I truly wanted to do with my life. I wanted to do something with helping people other than with their money, so I changed my major to Elementary Education. In the fall of 1971, when my junior year was to start, I would begin classes in the fall with a new major.

It never happened. I ended up deciding to drop out of college for a semester and transfer to Virginia Commonwealth University in Richmond. Counselors helped me to decide that I would be far better off if I stayed in accounting, because it would provide me with tremendous career opportunities, especially since I was at the top of my class. I could always go to graduate school in Elementary Education if I so desired.

I did extremely well in school at VCU, worked several jobs doing accounting management and participated in several business ventures that went very well. I had great relationships with my professors and was pointed in the direction of private accounting and entrepreneurship.

When I first transferred to VCU in January 1972, I joined American Karate Academy. Having been trained in Judo as a kid and working at fishing piers, I was well suited for the rigorous training that ultimately lead to my becoming a Karate master. My first instructor was Reuben Campbell, a former Marine Corp drill sergeant. We rode Triumph Bonneville 650 motorcycles for a few years together. Reuben came to me one day after he was turned down by a bank for a car loan and asked me if I could help him get his finances straight so that he could buy the Mustang Mach 3 that he had to have. I taught him the secret of personal finance which *is knowing how much money that is in your pocket is really yours and knowing how much is already obligated to someone else*. This teaching became the core of my **Personal Finance and Small Business Ownership** program that I have been teaching to thousands of people ever since. We got Reuben's finances in order and he got the loan for the car and trained me up through Brown Belt for free for helping him.

I only had one semester left to finish college, but in January 1974 I decided to drop out again to work full time with a company that was in serious financial trouble. They needed my services to help keep them alive. We successfully turned the company around. I enrolled to finish my last semester in the fall of 1974. The day before I was to start, my best friend, Jack, asked me if I wanted to go cross country with him to Colorado to visit his brother. I deferred finishing my last semester and went with Jack. My mother said that out of all of her four children, I was the only one that gave her any of her gray hairs. Jack and I had some incredible adventures on the road on the way to Colorado. I used a Texaco *"See America on Us"* credit card for all of my expenses on the trip, up until I worked as a waiter for fifteen days at Herb Wong's New China Café in Denver. I made $715, sent money home to my mom to pay on my bills, left Jack in Denver and hitch hiked to California. My adventure was cut short when I was crossing a ten lane Los Angeles freeway and passed out as I stepped from the street onto the curb. I went to the emergency room and was told that I needed surgery. I used a TWA *"Get Away"* credit card and flew back home to Norfolk.

I had quit a job as an accounting manager in Richmond and my Blue Cross/Blue Shield health insurance had lapsed for three months. I called the insurance agent and they agreed to make an exception to restore my coverage so that I could have the surgery if I would pay the three months of back premiums. Their normal policy was that after two months lapsed it could not be restored. This was the beginning of learning that truthful communication is the very best way to work through difficulties. The people that we share our situations with are real people, just like you and me, and when you treat them as such, they most often will try to help you through your situation. I often say to people when communicating difficulties, "*It's a rough economy out there.*" The expression that we used to say was "***We're all in the same boat***", but now that the world situation seems to be approaching biblical proportions, the expression I now say is "***We're all in the same Ark***"." Most everyone can relate to that.

Needing ninety-nine dollars to pay the three months back premiums, which back then were only thirty-three dollars per month, I hitch hiked to my Dad's in Maryland to ask to borrow the money so that I could have the surgery. He turned me down because, he said, that I had not paid back a small loan from a few years earlier and that his wife would not let him loan me the money. I told him that I got the message, and I thanked him for helping to teach me the need to take care of myself. I ended the conversation with telling him that I would never come into his house again. It was twenty years before I did. My dad is ninety-four years old now and we have long ago reconciled our relationship. I love him very much. He was right about much that he tried to teach me about savings and planning for a rainy day.

FEELING THE LOVE OF JESUS

I hitch hiked back to Norfolk from my Dad's. I had called my mom and shared with her the news that my Dad had turned me down for the $100 that I needed to restore the medical insurance so that I could have the surgery. A few minutes after I got home at my mom's, Catherine and Robert Sawyer, neighbors who lived five houses up the block, came over. They said that my mom had told them about my father turning me down for the loan and that they were very sorry that he had not wanted to help me. What happened next changed the course of my life. They said "*Stevie, we love you*" and asked to pray with me. We all sat down on the couch and held each other's hands, my mom, Catherine, Robert, and me. Catherine prayed, "**Lord**, *we love Stevie so much. We ask that you restore him to full health. Thank you for letting us be here for him through this difficult time.*" We all said, "*Amen*". Catherine then said, "*Stevie, we want you to take this money and pay your insurance premium so that you can have your surgery,*" as she put a $100 bill in my hand. She then said as she placed another $100 bill in my hand, "*Stevie, we want you to take this money and use it to help get yourself caught up. We never want you to pay us back. We just want you to always do for others.*" I cried as I hugged and thanked them and knew then that I would always put others before myself. I had experienced the ***Love of Jesus*** through Catherine and Robert.

PROVERBS 3:5-6

[5] *Trust in the **LORD** with all your heart
and lean not on your own understanding;*

[6] *In all your ways acknowledge him,
and he will make your paths straight.*

THE BIGGEST PARTY YOU'VE EVER HAD, SON

Now that the surgery was scheduled, my mom asked me to go back to school and finish that last semester and get that accounting degree. She said you're not going to be doing anything else for the next few months while recuperating so it would be a good time to go back to school. I didn't want to go back to school so she offered me a deal. She said, "*Stevie, if you'll do it, I'll throw you the biggest party that we've ever had*." That caught my attention. "*Will you bake all of the sweets*?" She was serious. She said, "*Yes, all of them*." "*The seven layers, the yum-yums, the buckeyes, the lemon bars, the carrot cake, all of them*?" "*Yes, all of them*." We shook hands. I had the surgery, went back to school, graduated in May 1975, we had the party. And she baked fifty-seven of her desserts for the party!

BACK TO KARATE, A MESSAGE THAT CHANGED MY LIFE

It was March 1975 before I got released by the doctor to go back to Karate workouts. After only training for a week, I pulled my right hamstring muscle. A week after that, I entered a Karate tournament in Fredericksburg, Virginia, not being able to use my right leg to kick with. The tournament was hosted by Master Roberts, a Seventh Degree Black Belt, who had a real Karate family: a wife and five kids that were all Black Belts. As was my custom, I sought out the host of the tournament, introduced myself and thanked him for letting me participate. I asked him if he could show me a stretch for my leg, as I knew that Karate was a self-healing art, and that I wanted to be able to use my right leg side kick which, was my best weapon. What he said to me, as he pointed his finger into my face, taught me something that changed my life forever.

"You must modify your technique,
in order to compensate for your injury.
Otherwise, the others, they will leave you behind".

—**Master James Roberts**

"The majority of men meet with failure of their
lack of persistence in creating new plans
to take the place of those which fail."

—**Napoleon Hill**

In April of that year, I went on to fight in the **Battle of Atlanta**, a Mecca of Karate. It and **Ed Parker's Internationals** in Los Angeles are the two biggest tournaments in the country. I competed in the Lightweight White Belt division. There were one hundred twenty competitors in the division. As I prepared to bow in for my sixth fight of the day, the championship fight, I turned to adjust my gi and tighten my belt. I closed my eyes and meditated on seeing myself just four months before, lying in a hospital bed after my surgery, when I had a vision of winning the **Battle of Atlanta**. My eyes filled with tears as **I thanked God** for bringing me to this moment. Nothing could stop me from winning this fight. I felt bad for the opponent who I was about to fight even though he had also won five fights to get to the championship fight. They could have put Mohammed Ali against me. I could not be defeated. I had been here before. I had seen the victory. I turned and bowed. I defeated my opponent in the tournament's fastest fight of the day. I scored the three points to win in just fourteen seconds.

"Whatever your mind can conceive and believe,
it can achieve."

—**Napoleon Hill**

BILL, THE PLANT MAN, INTRODUCES ME TO THINK AND GROW RICH

I was blessed that over 40 years ago, I met a man that I call **Bill, the Plant Man**. Shortly after graduating college and leaving Richmond, I had hung my shingle and opened my accounting practice. One day, I went to the Thomas Corner Exxon gas station to buy some house plants for a new apartment that I had recently moved into. The man selling the plants had driven up from Florida in an 18-wheeler and rented space in the parking lot of the station. We hit it off right away. He said that he wanted to give me a book. We met that evening at a Chinese restaurant, and he presented me with Napoleon Hill's **Think and Grow Rich**. He said, "*Steve, I'm giving you this book because it will validate everything that you've said to me about how you think about life.*" Ever since that day, I've never stopped sharing Napoleon Hill's **Philosophy of Personal Achievement** with everyone that I meet.

The three books that have influenced me the most in my life are **the Bible, Think and Grow Rich,** and **Outwitting the Devil**, also by Napoleon Hill. Napoleon Hill best stated the secret to success as "**Know Your Desire and Never Quit.**"

A LIFE OF THANKFULNESS AND SERVICE DESPITE TREMENDOUS ADVERSITIES

At a family reunion the other day, a cousin asked, "*So how are you doing, Steve?*" I said, "*I'm doing great. My foundation's moving forward beautifully, it's growing. It's gone national now.*" He asked, "*But how are you feeling?*" I said, "*I feel great, but I'm tired all the time, I battle fatigue. The multiple myeloma is a fatigue cancer, prostate removal and radiation cause a lot of fatigue. Thyroid issues and chronic kidney disease also cause fatigue. But I stay active. I play racquetball about four days a week and swim in the ocean four or five days a week. I still teach karate once a week.*"

That conversation with my cousin, pretty much sums up my life of perseverance. Seventeen years ago, I was diagnosed with multiple myeloma, incurable bone cancer. At the time of the diagnosis, the average life expectancy was five and a half years. I had major neck surgery twenty-five years ago and was told that I would have to give up all strenuous physical activities. How wrong the doctors were! I have experienced a total of fifteen surgeries to date including prostate cancer surgery.

Despite a lifetime of adversities, I thank the **Lord** every single day for using me and giving me another day to serve Him. I will never quit or give up.

I HAVE DEDICATED MY LIFE TO RIGHT THINKING FOUNDATION

The **Lord** has called me to work with economically, disadvantaged hardship populations, especially those that are incarcerated. The **Lord** has blessed me by giving me an assignment that combines my love of people, my financial expertise, my incredible energy level, and my passion to glorify **Him**. I founded **Right Thinking Foundation**, a 501 (c)(3) non-profit organization to accomplish this mission.

The problem of **Recidivism** is a national disgrace. The statistics are of epidemic proportion:

- **1** in **99** Americans are either incarcerated or will be.

- **1** in **32** Latino Americans are either incarcerated or will be.

- **1** in **15** African Americans are either incarcerated or will be.

- There are **2.1 million** people living in America that are incarcerated.

- **96%** of those incarcerated will re-emerge back into their communities at some point.

- The corrections budget in America was **80 billion dollars** last year.

- The worst statistic is that **85% of children** of incarcerated parents will probably be incarcerated sometime in their life. We must as a nation do more to solve this problem.

Through **Right Thinking Foundation,** I have been able to teach and deliver a message in prisons all over the country of **Love, Encouragement and Hope, and provide tools** that will help returning citizens to have a better chance of success upon release. RTF teaches returning citizens to **Think and Plan Ahead.** It's slogan is "**Don't Quit, Plan Ahead, It Will Get Better**".

I wish to thank each of you for taking the time to read this chapter of my story. Each one of us is a unique child of **God** with our own unique story. Our stories are a work in progress. I care about you and I am there for you. I want to know your story. To contact me and learn more about my story, please listen to **Right Thinking with Steve Coplon** and go to the **Right Thinking Foundation** website by going to the addresses found in my Biography

GOD BLESS YOU!

GUEST BIOGRAPHIES

ANDREW COPLON

Andrew started working at the age of 16, selling snow cones at minor league baseball games. He quickly learned the value of hard work and building relationships. While he graduated from Old Dominion University, he credits the majority of his knowledge to hands on experiences and the wisdom of others.

He has dedicated nearly 20 years to helping the foodservice oversee large events at sports and entertainment venues across the country. In doing so, he learned that it's about more than just a baseball game or concert. It's about creating an overall exceptional customer experience. He took this belief and combined it with his love for craft beer. Andrew and his wife, Stacie, co-founded Secret Hopper, a mystery shopping company for craft breweries. They are passionate about helping breweries create memorable experiences. Together, they help breweries monitor their tasting rooms, increase their in-house revenues, and learn to differentiate as the craft beer industry soars past 8000 breweries.

Whether baseball or breweries, Andrew is passionate about helping others succeed while providing them with the means to better themselves as well as their businesses. Success is defined by the strength of the community you build around yourself and he tries to apply this to all aspects of his life.

He lives in Norfolk, Virginia with his wife, and business partner, Stacie, his son, Max, and their three dogs, Roxy, Zoey, and Diamond. They enjoy seeing the world, warm bottles before bed, and dog treats.

DAVID RICHARDS

David has worked with companies ranging from his own pure startups to executive roles within mature enterprises. He's been CEO of several divisions within Landmark Communications, a large, privately-owned enterprise, and venture capital backed entities like Physician's Online, EDIT and his current company, Open Health Innovations.

David spends considerable time on non-profit boards and with social causes including the University of Virginia Children's Hospital, Right Thinking Foundation, Gold Star Mothers of America, and the Better Business Bureau of Central North Carolina.

David received his BA from Williams College and his MBA from the Colgate Darden Graduate School of Business Administration at the University of Virginia. He is married, has two sons, and lives in Charlottesville, Virginia.

DON PRICE

Don Price was born in Richmond, Virginia in 1950, and moved to Norfolk in 1955. He graduated from Norfolk Catholic High School and Old Dominion University, served in the Air Force, and worked as a banker (commercial loan officer) for 40 years in the Hampton Roads area, with a substantial portion of those years in the capacity of senior loan officer. In addition to his banking duties, he began contributing to the community in 1978 with volunteer activities, and has been involved with many worthwhile organizations since that time, among them United Way, Chamber of Commerce, Holy Trinity Church, Holy Trinity School, Right Thinking Foundation, Bishop Sullivan Catholic High School, St. Mary's Home for Disabled Children, the Barry Robinson Center and St. Patrick Catholic School, of which he was a founding board member.

He has been married to his wife, Barbara for 47 years and has two children and one grandchild. Retired for two years and still residing in Norfolk, he is fortunate to be able to play golf frequently and continues to enjoy serving on several boards of the aforementioned Hampton Roads organizations.

DONNA COPLON

Donna was born and raised in Norfolk, Va. Growing up, she loved being involved in church activities (which she lived right across the street from) and playing outside. If she wasn't at church, she was playing croquet, badminton, roll-a-bat, pickle, jump rope, or riding her bike. On cold and rainy days, she enjoyed listening to 45's on her record player, that cost 50 cents apiece that she paid for with her babysitting money. Around 12 years old, an uncle formed a softball team and a basketball team for the girls in the community. She loved softball and continued playing for years. Her love for the outdoors stayed with her forever. Along with her husband Steve, she has traveled to many beautiful places across the country, places she had never seen before. The love for the outdoors gives her a connection to God like nothing else she does.

Donna's desire is to help people understand their relationship with God will bring peace to their lives that the world cannot give. Waking up with a cup of coffee, meditation and prayer is how she starts her day. And of course, a daily walk is a must. Her heart and compassion is to the young mother who is trying to raise her children, be a good wife, be a volunteer and a good neighbor in the community while maintaining a healthy balance. She believes the role of a woman is crucial in God's eyes. She recognizes the gifts that God puts in all women, whether they are out-spoken or soft-spoken. It is really all about the heart. Donna serves the community through local churches in food pantries and dedicates herself to family. She is ever present with her elderly aunt's needs and her parents, helping them manage daily struggles of living with Alzheimer's. Her love and joy is spending time along with her husband with their eight grandchildren.

JIM STOVALL

In spite of blindness, Jim Stovall has been a National Olympic weightlifting champion, a successful investment broker, the President of the Emmy Award-winning Narrative Television Network, and a highly sought-after author and platform speaker. He is the author of 40 books, including the bestseller, *The Ultimate Gift,* which is now a major motion picture from 20th Century Fox starring James Garner and Abigail Breslin. Five of his other novels have also been made into movies with two more in production.

Steve Forbes, president and CEO of *Forbes* magazine, says, "Jim Stovall is one of the most extraordinary men of our era."

For his work in making television accessible to our nation's 13 million blind and visually impaired people, The President's Committee on Equal Opportunity selected Jim Stovall as the Entrepreneur of the Year. Jim Stovall has been featured in *The Wall Street Journal, Forbes* magazine, *USA Today,* and has been seen on *Good Morning America, CNN,* and *CBS Evening News.* He was also chosen as the International Humanitarian of the Year, joining Jimmy Carter, Nancy Reagan, and Mother Teresa as recipients of this honor.

JOHNNIE LLOYD

Johnnie Lloyd, Chief Visionary Officer for Johnnie Lloyd and Associates, financial guru - business2business consultant and coach that guides and trains. She specifically partners with females, CEOs, executives, entrepreneurs unleashing their superpowers. Preparing people and organizations for greater levels of productivity and profitability strategically. The problem she concentrates on strategically is resources – profitability and leadership that influences from anywhere in the organization. She makes hard things understandable and relatable. Dynamic high energy speaker, author, coach, and facilitator. Virtual inspirational keynotes and breakout sessions, empowering audience development, growth, and development.

Delivering strategic tricks and tips for profitable growth of people, money, and communication. Powerful backstory from homelessness to success as a senior-level executive in profit, non-profit, corporate, and government agencies. She deals with life transitions providing insight and hope. She is now retired from federal service where she traveled and spoke internationally. Her definite major purpose is to connect your passion to your purpose while you build your legacy and the brand called "Excellence". Her mantra "You are Fire When You are Focused" ®. Known as the "Pusher" proving guidance and motivation to start where you are, do what you can using what you have.

If you were to say what is her DNA you would get she puts God first, then family, and her love and compassion for people; she desires to impact lives in such a way that it transforms where a person is to unleash their potential. She knows from the beginning people were created to dominate, pursue, and know their purpose so that they answer the key questions of: Why am I here and Do I matter? Truth is part of her shield firmly standing on the Word of God with integrity and character. Her desire for each of you is to not just gather knowledge but move forward in understanding that greatness is within you.

LEFFORD FATE

Professionally I've lead mentored and served thousands of military members and their families during my thirty years in the United States Air Force.

Since retiring from the military, I have been the program director for a geriatric outpatient mental health program, deputy Director of Health Services, SC Department of Corrections, and now the Director Support Services, City of Sumter.

I am a husband, father, and grandfather, so I know it is not always easy to juggle our list of daily responsibilities. This makes it even more important to have a structured practical plan in place to avoid becoming overwhelmed. I hold a Master's Degree in Human Relations and a Bachelor's Degree in Social Psychology. Modeling the core values of Integrity first, Service before self and Excellence in all I do.

I believe there is a "why" for everyone; that each of us was created with the potential to achieve greatness, to make a difference in the world, to add value to others, and as a result, experience a full and rewarding life. For over 30 years, my purpose was to defend our nation, and now that purpose is helping people discover their life's purpose and grow to their full potential.

Learn More://www.leffordfate.com

RANDEY FAULKNER

While writing computer programs for a large corporation in 1969, he was introduced to *Think and Grow Rich*. Within one year of devouring this book, he paid cash for a brand-new Jaguar XKE and a Nova Super Sport. One day while walking out to the cars, he became awestruck by the fact that he owned 2 new vehicles, whereas 1 year earlier, he had a car parked there that he could hardly afford to put tires on. To him, this seemed like magic. That is when he started his small business called, "*Do You Believe In Magic?*" He made a flip chart with photos of these two cars, and for a short time became a motivational speaker explaining how he acquired them, by applying Napoleon Hill's principles in *Think and Grow Rich*. His closing line was, "If I can do it, so can you!" For the past 50 years he has been sharing these same principles, as well as *Think and Grow Rich*, with any and all.

He has applied Napoleon Hill's principles in every aspect of his life, including his Goodyear/Michelin Tire Businesses, Real Estate and Music Productions.

After retiring in Hawaii, he decided to move back to Southern California, so that he could fulfill his life's passion in completing an idea that came to him in the early 1980's. He started actual work on his project in the 1990's. His passion was to write a book to help anyone, especially younger folks, who aspire to become a professional in the field of art & music.

His desire was to emulate Napoleon Hill's method by performing research and interviews with those who have gained success in the art & music industry. He initially turned to Chet Atkins as a source of introductions to successful musicians and artists. When Chet slipped away from us in 2001, he turned to Mr. Les Paul, for the same source of introductions. Here he spent 4 plus years, off and on, under Les' direction. From there he performed research and continued to interview successful artists and musicians to complete his life's dream of publishing '*Think and Grow Through Art & Music*'.

REGINALD PONTON

Reginald Ponton was born in Roanoke Rapids, NC in 1971, He graduated from Northampton County High School West, Elizabeth City State University, Central Michigan University, and serve in North Carolina Army National Guard. He worked 14 years with Virginia Department of Corrections as a (Counselor, Offender Workforce Development Specialist, Cognitive Counselor, Institutional Program Manager, Unit Manager, and Chief of Housing and Programs. He had the opportunity to work with returning citizens educating them how to transform their lives to become productive citizens. He played an important role implementing the Transition Women's Work Release Program, planning and collaborating with community agencies to host Resource Fairs.

He was member of the Virginia Reentry Program Team, Culpeper Reentry Council Team, and Culpeper Freedom Folks while with corrections. Currently, he's a Financial Services Professional, member of Petersburg Chamber of Commerce, Freeman Community Empowerment Day Committee, Soaring Heights Business and Network Group, Trustee for New Hope RZUA Church Freeman, VA, and Volunteer for Communities in Schools of Petersburg. He has been married for 7 years and has a son.

RICHARD KAY

Richard Kay has had a diverse career history in the financial service industry. After studying business at the University of Nebraska and the University of Maryland, he served in the United States Marine Corps during the Vietnam War. Upon being honorably discharged, he began working in various sectors of business.

Being raised as a Jew, he accepted the Messiah through a course of events that led to a Billy Graham Crusade in 1969. He was called into "marketplace ministry" before many understood how believers can be used of God perhaps even more in business than in the pulpit. Richard served as an officer in the Full Gospel Businessmen's Fellowship International Organization and an is active Gideon. His dedication and devotion to help others is noted in all aspects of his personal and business life.

He is an ordained minister and has served the church for the past 50 years. He is on the Board of Directors and is the Treasurer of two non-profit, ministries in the USA and India. Richard is the international spokesman of Reflections On The Word, a daily ministry radio broadcast and the author of several books including "What it Means To Be A Jew"; "War and Victory, The Christian Fight of Faith" and the latest eBook "A Centurion's View Of Calvary".

He and his wife, Ellie, have been members of New Life Church in Virginia since 1991. They live in Chesapeake where they enjoy ministry, traveling and the ability to give back to the community.

SOFIA GIANNASCOLI

Sofia Giannascoli was born in Montgomery County Pennsylvania and was raised on the coast of New Jersey. She attended St. Benedict Catholic School, and later St. John Vianney High School. Very often Sofia would travel to visit family around the country, and she spent every summer visiting her father in Virginia Beach. Since she was a child her need to learn, explore, and create have driven her through her life. Sofia began working at the age of 14 in various volunteer positions in her hometown where her family was deeply involved in community outreach. She has had a lifelong passion for the arts and enjoys many different aspects of them. As a teenager she participated in acting classes at both The Barrow Group, and Stella Adler Studio of Acting, in New York City.

She currently attends Montclair State University, where she is pursuing a degree in Journalism. After completing her apprentice DJ training at MSU, Sofia now hosts a weekly radio show, for WMSC Upper Montclair. As a young woman, Sofia has developed passions for writing, photography, filmmaking, and storytelling. Her dreams include writing and producing independent films when she is not acting in them.

At the age of 19, Sofia walked away from habits and a lifestyle that no longer served her higher purpose and she turned to spirituality. Through this awakening Sofia discovered just how important the Divine was in her life. Through sharing her various life experiences and stories, she hopes to help people gain self-awareness as she did.

AUTHOR BIOGRAPHY

Steve holding the original manuscript of Napoleon Hill's "Outwitting the Devil" during a visit to the Napoleon Hill Foundation in Wise, Virginia

STEVE COPLON

Steve Coplon is the Founder/Executive Director of Right Thinking Foundation, a 501 (c)(3) non-profit organization whose mission is dedicated to fighting and reducing Recidivism, a problem of epidemic proportions. A highly successful lifetime entrepreneur personally involved in over hundreds of millions of dollars of economic development, he has developed a program that is based on biblical principles and proven business practices necessary for success. Following in the footsteps of Napoleon Hill, who he was first introduced to over 45 years ago, RTF's financial education program teaches responsibility and making good choices. He has a remarkable ability to connect with people using Napoleon Hill's principle of the Master Mind to work toward making the world a better place in which to live.

Persevering through severe health and financial difficulties, Steve stays focused on his lifetime purpose of helping other people, which he inherited from his mother. Steve has dedicated his life to serving the underserved. He has gone "behind the walls" in prisons hundreds of times as a Statewide Volunteer with the Virginia Department of Corrections and has presented his Personal Finance and Small Business Ownership seminar in numerous prisons nationally, helping returning citizens to better prepare to become productive contributing members of society upon release. His curriculum on Personal Finance and Small Business Ownership is available to prisons and jails throughout the country.

Steve believes that the very best way to fight Recidivism is to get to the youth and teach them to make good choices, before they go too far out into the world, making bad choices that can ultimately cost them their freedom. He has taught financial literacy at An Achievable Dream Academy, a charter school for the at-risk in the public school system in Newport News, VA where he brought real life experiences to high school students.

Steve is the host of *Right Thinking with Steve Coplon*, a radio show that is dedicated to helping anyone who is experiencing hardship and those that want to be there for them. Steve is embarking on an unusual goal. He is traveling to prisons in all 50 states delivering his message of **Love, Encouragement and Hope**.

Steve and his wife, Donna, are blessed with five children and eight beautiful grandchildren. They live in Norfolk, Virginia.

To learn more, visit: www.RightThink.org

To listen to *Right Thinking with Steve Coplon*, go to: www.talknetworkradio.com/right-thinking.html

Steve at his office at the beach

CPSIA information can be obtained
at www.ICGtesting.com
Printed in the USA
LVHW061340281220
674968LV00017BA/1231